R. Stutzman

D1595869

Monograph 49
THE AMERICAN ETHNOLOGICAL SOCIETY
Robert F. Spencer, *Editor*

WILLIAM A. DOUGLASS is a member of the
Department of Anthropology and coordinator of
the Basque Studies Program of the Desert Research Institute at the University of Nevada.

American Ethnological Society Monograph 49

145256

GT
3262
.D67

DEATH IN MURELAGA

Funerary Ritual in a Spanish Basque Village

BY

WILLIAM A. DOUGLASS

UNIVERSITY OF WASHINGTON PRESS

Seattle and London

GOSHEN COLLEGE LIBRARY
GOSHEN, INDIANA

Copyright © 1969 by the University of Washington Press
Library of Congress Catalog Card Number 70–93025
SBN 295-95002-1
Printed in the United States of America

To Patricia

Preface

$\mathcal{T}$HE data employed in this study were collected in the village of Murélaga in the Spanish Basque province of Vizcaya. I spent eight months in the village between January and August of 1965 and returned in the summer of 1966 for an additional stay of two months. I wish to thank the National Institute of Mental Health for supporting my field work and subsequent graduate training.

A shorter version of this study was presented to the department of anthropology of the University of Chicago in March of 1966 in partial fulfillment of the requirements for the degree of Master of Arts.

I would like to take this opportunity to thank the residents of Murélaga. They not only tolerated my presence as an investigator but also made my stay in the village a deeply satisfying personal experience. To my good friend Don Emilio, the local parish priest, I am particularly indebted. To the many scholars in the Basque country who assisted me with advice I extend my thanks. Don Julio Caro Baroja, Don Luis Michelena, and Don Fausto Arocena were particularly generous with their time and suggestions. I wish to thank Davydd Greenwood, Warren D'Azevedo, and Joy Leland for their comments on preliminary drafts of the manuscript. I am, of course, responsible for all shortcomings in the present version. Finally, to Dr. Julian Pitt-Rivers of the University of Chicago I wish to express my sincerest appreciation for providing me with more direction and encouragement than I deserved.

W.D.

Reno, Nevada
July, 1969

Contents

Introduction

THE Basques of southern France and northern Spain have long had the reputation of being the "mystery" people of Europe. This stems from the fact that they are demonstrably unique within the broader panorama of European cultures and ethnic groups—a conclusion based upon the findings of physical anthropologists and linguists.

The physical anthropologists rest their case on the evidence of blood typology. They find that the Basques have a lower incidence of blood type B and a higher incidence of blood type O than any other European group. Furthermore, the Basques are found to have the highest incidence of the Rh-negative blood factor of any ethnic group in the world.

For several generations professional and amateur linguists have attempted to demonstrate an affinity between Basque and other languages. At one time or another they have postulated similarities between Basque and such disparate languages as Ancient Egyptian, Berber, Japanese, and Iroquois. Less inhibited theorists have suggested that Basque was the original human language spoken in the Garden of Eden or that it was the vernacular on the lost continent of Atlantis. Currently, linguistic research is focused upon the possibility that Basque is related to languages in the Caucasus Mountains of Russia or that it is a direct descendant of Iberian (a language spoken on the Iberian peninsula before it was subjected to Roman influence).

The majority of outside investigators have directed their attentions to the biological and linguistic uniqueness of the Basques, and the related problem of their origins. However, these efforts are but a small part of a lengthy tradition of scholarship in Basque studies. Over the past two centuries there has been an enormous amount of investigation into Basque culture—sponsored by academic institutions located in the Basque country or carried out independently by individual Basque scholars. These studies have been less concerned with the origins problem and more directed toward investigating facets of Basque culture, history, literature, and folklore. During the past ten years there have been a number of sociological and social anthropological investigations conducted in the Basque country. However, to date there have been no published descriptions, employing methodology and theory current in the social sciences, of the social structure of a rural Basque community.[1] It is one purpose of this study to provide such an account.

Any attempt to describe the social structure of a community en-

---

[1] I do not mean to imply that there have been no previous investigations into the nature of rural Basque society. The present study differs from a number of former ones in perspective and methodology, not in subject matter. The statement by Bonifacio de Echegaray on the structure of the rural neighborhood remains extremely useful to this day (Echegaray 1933). Julio Caro Baroja in his monograph on life in Vera de Bidasoa (Caro Baroja 1944) and in his book *Los Vascos* (Caro Baroja 1958) provides penetrating insight into the workings of the rural society. Philippe Veyrin's work *Les Basques* (Veyrin 1955) contains similar insight into the nature of rural French Basque society. José Miguel de Barandiarán applied an extensive ethnographic questionnaire in several rural communities which later served as the basis for short published accounts of the rural way of life (for example, see Barandiarán 1948). Finally, the many articles on ethnographic materials which have appeared over the years in the journals *Eusko-Folklore* and the *Revista Internacional de Estudios Vascos* are particularly useful to the student of rural Basque society. However, none of the above accounts employs a community study approach (as the term is commonly understood in social anthropology).

tails a great deal of selectivity on the part of the investigator. He formulates his model by observing the behavior of individual actors and groups of actors in different social contexts. His final description necessarily highlights consistencies or patterning in social behavior rather than the less consistent or fortuitous. Furthermore, his description of the social structure is not meant to be entirely congruent with the ways in which the individual actor views his community. The actor, as participant, necessarily has an egocentric view of the village society which is highly colored by his position within it. As such the actor's view of the whole is biased and is a part-perception. Although the investigator takes a broader view of the totality, this is not to say that his description is a greater approximation of social reality. If the actor's perspective is limited by his egocentricity, the investigator's view is likely to become overly eclectic. His description of the society is necessarily of an ideal typical sort. Models of social structures, whether stated mechanically or statistically, exist in the minds of social scientists, not in nature.

The social interaction of the actors manifests a degree of consistency or patterning insofar as there is some adherence to a common system of values. It is only with reference to the value system that ego is able to predict the responses of alter. It is this predictability which allows them to enter into meaningful social interaction. Similarly, it is only through an examination of the value system that the investigator is able to appreciate the significance of patterned interaction. A particular value system is characterized by certain emphases or themes which distinguish it from any other. It is through a thorough examination of these themes that the investigator is able to test his theories within a cultural context ripe with sociological significance and detail. E. E. Evans-Pritchard demonstrates this approach by exploring the bovine theme in Nuer culture. He states, "Most of their [the Nuers'] social activities concern cattle and *cherchez la vache* is the best advice that can be given to those who desire to understand Nuer behavior" (Evans-Pritchard 1940:16). Clifford Geertz takes a similar approach in his study of Javanese religion when he explores the significance of the *slametan* ritual. He states, "At the center of the whole Javanese religious system lies a simple, formal, undramatic, almost furtive little ritual; the *slametan*" (Geertz 1960:11). Furthermore, "the *slametan* forms a kind of social universal joint, fitting the various aspects of social life and individual experience together in a way which minimizes uncertainty, tension, or conflict—or at least is supposed to do so" (*ibid.*).

It is my contention that in Basque society the individual and collective responses to the crisis occasioned by a death in the membership are of such a complex nature and occupy such a prominent place in the world view of the actors that we can distinguish a *death theme* in the value system. Just as knowledge of the bovine theme is crucial to an understanding of Nuer behavior and knowledge of the significance of the *slametan* ritual is basic to an understanding of Javanese religion, in rural Basque society the death theme is of such importance to the actors themselves as to make it a convenient vehicle with which to approach the study of the social structure of the local community.

A final note concerns the use of Basque terms in the text. I have employed -*zh*-, for example, in the term *familizhe,* in order to cover a dialectical peculiarity of the speech of Murélaga. This feature would not be covered by the current Basque orthographc rendering of the term—*familie.* The letter *j* is pronounced like the Spanish *j,* which is somewhat similar to the English *h.* The letter *z* is pronounced like the English *s.* Finally, whenever a term is used in plural form, I follow Basque usage by employing the pluralizing -*k* suffix. Thus *auzoa* (neighborhood) becomes *auzoak* (neighborhoods).

Death in Murélaga
Funerary Ritual in a Spanish Basque Village

It is a fact that a man's dying is more the survivors' affair than his own.

THOMAS MANN

1

The Setting

$\mathcal{M}$ URÉLAGA is a small agricultural village in the Basque country of northern Spain. It is located in the province of Vizcaya, close to the border of the neighboring Basque province of Guipúzcoa. The spoken Basque of the village is the Vizcayan dialect, although local speech reflects a Guipúzcoan influence. Murélaga is representative of the more traditional rural Basque village in that agriculture continues to occupy a prominent position in the local economy.

Forty difficult kilometers separate Murélaga from Bilbao, the provincial capital and a burgeoning industrial center. Distance and poor transportation facilities combine to make contacts between the village and Bilbao infrequent. Nineteen kilometers separate Murélaga and Guernica. Guernica is the most important regional market town and a center of recreational and political significance. There is a public bus service daily between Murélaga and Guernica. However, most villagers visit Guernica only to attend an occasional market, to consult a medical specialist, or perhaps to view a *jai alai* match. The twelve kilometers separating Murélaga from the coastal town of Lequeitio are sufficient to prevent villagers from participating in the maritime activities of that port. Unlike other villages close to the sea, Murélaga sends few of her sons to join the ranks of the globe-trotting Basque fishermen and sailors. The distance between Murélaga and the large industrial town of Eibar (Guipúzcoa) is twenty-one kilometers. A number of persons have left the village and now reside in Eibar where they hold factory jobs. However, the fact that there is no direct line of public transportation between the village and Eibar minimizes the day-to-day influence of the larger town upon village life.

The physical isolation of the village is neither absolute nor insurmountable. It has been partially nullified by improved means of transportation and communication in both the public and private sectors. There is daily public bus service to Bilbao, Guernica, and Lequeitio; and asphalt roadways permit individuals to travel by motor bike to Eibar and Marquina (a smaller but nearer industrial town). Contact with the total surrounding area is much greater than was the case even a few years ago.

These contacts are not unidirectional. Fish vendors from Lequeitio and bread vendors from Marquina visit Murélaga daily to test the local market. Frequently trucks supply the village stores, coming from as far away as Bilbao.

Intrusions upon local autonomy are not restricted to transitory contacts. There have been some lasting modifications of the local scene. A fish cannery, based in Lequeitio, recently established a branch processing plant in Murélaga and provided part-time employment on a seasonal basis (during the tuna and anchovy runs) for a number of women in the village. The local religious authorities persuaded a large shotgun manufacturing concern based in Eibar to erect a small assembly plant in Murélaga; it employs about fifteen men.

A number of men work full time in the nearby (eight kilometers) town of Marquina, where small factories and marble quarries have attracted much of the excess male labor force of the surrounding smaller villages. There are several marble quarries, both within the municipality of Murélaga and in bordering areas, which provide full- and part-time employment for the males of several domestic groups. Approximately thirty-five men from the village work in quarries. There are three local sawmills, each of which employs four to eight men. Finally, there are a few household industries in the village. Three domestic groups process raw wool into yarn which is either sold or processed into wool stockings. Two domestic groups manufacture wicker baskets which are sold both to villagers and to commercial representatives who market them in other areas. Two domestic groups manufacture chocolate, marketing it locally and regionally. In all instances, employment in the household industry is a part-time activity.

In sum, although Murélaga occupies a position at the margin of the fishing and heavy industry complexes which are reshaping the Vizcayan economy, it does not remain unaffected by them. Physical isolation is increasingly less effective as insulation against these major external influences but is still sufficient to keep the village at the periphery of the movement. To date the village is only indirectly caught up in the process of modernization.

A strong indication of the indirectness of village participation in the present-day processes of social change is seen in an analysis of the ethnic make-up of the local population. Throughout this century Vizcaya has received large numbers of immigrants from other areas of Spain. Workers from poorer regions flocked to the growing factory complex of the North. As industries began to penetrate the countryside, appearing in formerly agricultural communities, large numbers of non-Basques took up residence in many small Basque villages. Wherever this occurs, the consequences for the local Basque population are the same: a rapid breakdown in Basque culture and in the use of the language.

This aspect of change has not affected Murélaga as yet. Its relative lack of local industry and its physical isolation from industrial centers make Murélaga unattractive for potential immigrants. The make-up of the local population is therefore almost homogeneously

Basque, and Basque is still the principal language in the village.[1]

Agriculture dominates the local economy. The total population of the village in 1960 was 1,133 inhabitants, and of this total 787 resided on rural farms (*baserriak*).[2] The remainder lived in the village nucleus, which is located roughly in the center of the 2,436 hectares that comprise the municipality.

The *baserria* or rural farmstead consists of a dwelling, household furnishings, agricultural implements, landholdings, and a household site on the floor of the village church (*sepulturie*). The *baserria* is regarded as being immutable through time. That is, each *baserria* is felt to contain sufficient resources to maintain a single domestic group engaged in agriculture. In the actors' view it is reprehensible on both moral and economic grounds to dismember a *baserria* either through land sales or divisive inheritance practices (for example, naming two or more heirs to the patrimony in a given generation). The strong emphasis upon the immutability of the farmsteads means that most of the *baserriak* of Murélaga have historical roots reaching back several centuries into the past.

The durable *baserria* is not anonymous; every farmstead has a name which is equally resistant to change. The name distinguishes it in the minds of the villagers from other *baserriak*. There is a strong identification of the domestic group with its farmstead of residence. Within village parlance persons take their social identity from the name of their *baserria*. Pedro Armaolea, who resides on the *baserria* Zuberogoitia, is referred to as "Zuberogoitiko Pedro"[3] or "Pedro Zuberogoiti." Thus, the identification between dwelling, landholdings, and the domestic group is complete. The identification

---

[1] The non-Basques living in the village are the doctor and his family, the two schoolteachers, the village secretary, the wine seller, and two families of migrant workers who live in the village nucleus and commute to the quarries in Marquina.

[2] I choose to employ the Basque term *baserria* throughout the present work. However, most of the cited sources are printed in Spanish and employ the Spanish term *caserío* for farmstead.

[3] The suffix *-ko* of the term *Zuberogoitiko* signifies possession.

derives from the permanent elements in the triad, namely, the *baserria* dwelling and the landholdings.[4] That is, the symbolization is not contingent upon a series of consanguineally related domestic groups occupying the *baserria* through time. A *baserria* may have sheltered several unrelated domestic groups at different points in its history.

Ideally, only one domestic group resides on each *baserria*. Normally this group includes an active man (*echekojaun*), his spouse (*echekoandria*), their children, and the parents and/or unmarried siblings of the spouse who is residing in his (or her) natal household. There is also the possibility that a male or female agricultural hand or servant will be present as well.

The domestic group membership engages primarily in agricultural activities. There are some exceptions in that one or two male members of a given farm may be employed gainfully in the marble quarries or the timber industry. However, even they are part-time agriculturalists after their normal working hours and on week ends. We might say, then, that the agriculturalist household, the *baserria,* is the basic unit of the rural society and economy.

The *baserria* dwelling is an imposing three-story stone structure. It is a self-contained agricultural and domestic plant. The bottom floor consists of a stable, a poultry run, and a tool-storage area. The second floor is the domestic group's living quarters. The third floor is a storage area for the winter hay supply, corn and wheat crops, and orchard produce.

The broken nature of the countryside and the extremely poor soil conditions produce great diversity in the nature of the landholdings pertaining to any one *baserria*. Degree of slope, depth and condition of the soil, exposure to the sun and wind currents, and distance of a field from the dwelling all determine the value of the plot. The

---

[4] This is the reverse of the Irish situation described by Conrad Arensberg. In Ireland, where there is a similar bond between the farmstead and domestic group, the farm takes its name from the family (Callahan's place) (Arensberg 1938:43).

landholdings of an individual *baserria* are likely to be divided up into as many as thirty to fifty parcels varying in size from a few square meters up to one or two hectares. The average size of a *baserria* is approximately ten hectares. Some of the larger *baserriak* contain as many as twenty or more hectares and the smaller ones about four. The majority fall between seven and thirteen hectares in size.

Of the ten hectares comprising an average *baserria,* about seven constitute forest and wasteland. Presently these forest lands are put to pine and provide a long-term cash income. Approximately two of the remaining three hectares comprise the meadowlands, which provide the green forage and dried hay to sustain the livestock. The remaining hectare is the household's arable land, where all of the other crops are cultivated. Ideally, the arable hectare is divided into two sections, each of which supports a different type of grain crop each year. One section is put to corn and the other to wheat. The following year the distribution is reversed. In addition to the grain crops, the same plots yield a winter root crop which is used for animal fodder, and clover which is cut in the early spring for the same purpose.

Agriculture is intensive on the limited arable land pertaining to each *baserria.* The fields are never fallowed, bearing crops even during the winter months. This intensive exploitation is possible only through the liberal use of both organic and chemical fertilizers. The climate lends itself to intensive agriculture. The Basque country is characterized by a maritime climate of mild winters and cool summers. Rainfall is dependable; most heavily concentrated in the late autumn, winter, and early spring months, it is adequate throughout the year. It is unnecessary to practice irrigation agriculture. Frost danger exists only from December through March. Snow is rare.

In addition to the major crops of wheat and corn, a very small portion of the arable land serves as a household garden. Here the domestic group grows a wide variety of garden produce to supplement its diet. The preferred vegetables include tomatoes, lettuce, beans, carrots, leeks, peppers, onions, and garlic. Every domestic group reserves another small plot for a potato patch. With respect to potatoes (an important staple in the diet), the majority of domestic groups are self-sufficient. Households also raise fruit trees (cherry, apple, peach, and pear) and nut trees (chestnut and walnut). Of these, apples are by far the most important. Most households have extensive apple orchards planted on the meadowlands. The fruit may be made into clear cider (which is used as a table beverage), eaten raw or preserved, or taken to market in Bilbao.

The emphasis in agriculture is both upon meeting the domestic group's own demands for certain products (for example, garden produce, fruits and nuts, cider, and wheat flour to make bread) and upon commercial livestock production. Vegetable products are rarely a direct source of cash income, although apples may be sold occasionally. Cash income is generally derived from the sale of animals and their by-products.

Presently (1967), livestock production in Murélaga means milk cow production. Each household maintains one to ten milk cows, depending on its resource base, size and condition of its labor force, and the degree to which the domestic group is still committed to an agricultural way of life. The milk is sometimes sold directly, at other times it is used to raise calves. Indeed, calf raising takes precedence over milk production. Normally, the farmer has about twice as many calves as milk cows, augmenting the yearly production of the herd by purchasing calves in nearby market towns. The calves are fattened on milk and green fodder for a period of twelve to eighteen months and are then sold for meat.

The cows produce other benefits in addition to their milk: they provide the quantities of fertilizer essential to the intensive agriculture; they are used as draught animals for plowing and to haul heavy loads; when they are old, they are sold for meat, and the money is used to purchase replacements.

Other farm animals play relatively less important roles in the domestic economy. Chicken production is often geared both to the

needs of the domestic group and to the market. The chickens themselves provide a protein in the diet, eggs being a main staple. A few
households raise pigs, but not commercially. The domestic group
simply buys one small piglet each year at a local market and fattens
it for home consumption. Sheep raising was formerly important in
the local economy. Most of the households had small flocks of fifteen
to perhaps fifty animals, which were pastured on communally held
lands. Presently, only a handful of households raise sheep. Finally,
most households have a small donkey, which is used for lighter agricultural tasks and for transporting supplies from the village nucleus.

The over-all picture is one of intensive agricultural production
practiced by a single domestic group on a small and ill-suited land
unit. Through highly specialized and diversified cropping the domestic group is able to meet much of its demand for foodstuffs without making many purchases in the market place. Dependence upon
purchased foodstuffs is generally limited to such staple items as coffee, sugar, rice, dried codfish, garbanzo beans, and lentil peas. In
addition, the domestic group occasionally purchases luxury items
such as canned preserves, pastries, and fresh fish and meat. However,
the emphasis upon household self-sufficiency leaves the domestic
group with few sources (agricultural) of cash income. In the agricultural sector of the economy, cash income derives from the sale
of milk and milk calves, poultry, eggs, and apples. However, the domestic group's income is supplemented in many cases by some wage
labor and by the infrequent sales of tracts of pine trees.

This sketchy description of the farm economy in Murélaga is not
meant to be exhaustive. It is particularly deficient in that it conveys
an impression of stability which in fact is not characteristic of the
present-day situation. Throughout the twentieth century there has
been a trend toward greater involvement in commercial agriculture
at the expense of subsistence farming. There have been major technological innovations and modifications in cropping technique
which have significantly altered the rural economy. Finally, there is

an over-all trend away from active involvement in agriculture as former cereal lands and meadows are put to pine plantations.

The farms or *baserriak* are arranged into different neighborhood units (*auzoak*), located at varying distances from the village nucleus. While the neighborhoods are dispersed with respect to the village nucleus, the dwellings within the individual *auzoa* tend to be nucleated. Each neighborhood therefore constitutes a discrete hamlet. A typical neighborhood unit consists of eight to twelve dwellings located roughly in the center of their combined landholdings. This unit is connected to the village nucleus by a road system maintained by the neighborhood. The neighborhood also maintains an internal road system which provides access to all of the landholdings of its constitutent households. The neighborhood unit may further act as a corporate body with respect to providing a domestic water supply and electric power line for all of its households.

Neighborhoods have separate identities. That is, each has a name (for example, Zubero, Malax, Narea). The neighborhoods also have a religious identity in that each has a chapel and a patron saint. The feast day of the patron saint is an excuse for an *auzoa* fiesta.

In addition to the physical isolation, social identity, and religious identity which set each *auzoa* off from the others, the neighborhood has an internal political structure. Each neighborhood has a *mayordomo,* who serves as the caretaker of the chapel and as the nominal authority figure in secular matters.

Beyond the neighborhood level of social organization, the political structure is atrophied. Part of the reason for this is the intrinsic lack of interest on the part of the neighborhood membership in affairs beyond the neighborhood sphere. But it is also due to recent Spanish political history. There is a village council and mayor, who theoretically represent the village in the provincial and national polities. There are presently no formal lines of communication between the neighborhood structure and the village council. Council members and a mayor are elected by the villagers to a six-year term of office. The mayor and council must be acceptable to the central government, and because Murélaga was actively Basque separatist during the Spanish Civil War, it is difficult to fill these positions with local personnel. Under the circumstances, persons who serve in these offices are highly suspect and cannot command the respect and trust of a majority of the villagers.

A further explanation for the ineffectiveness of local government is that the officials in Murélaga have tended to be illiterate or semi-literate, a situation which has left the real political authority in the hands of the village secretary. This person is invariably a career man (usually non-Basque) and thoroughly loyal to the central government. He is in a position to make most of the administrative decisions. The complaint is that he fails to defend the village's interests before Madrid, but rather represents Madrid's interests in local affairs.

The *baserriak* are dependent upon the village nucleus for a wide variety of goods and services. The nucleus is the seat of local religious and administrative authority. Both the church and the town hall are located there. Specialists residing in the nucleus include a doctor, a veterinarian, two schoolteachers, masons, livestock buyers, carpenters, a seamstress, a blacksmith, two mechanics, a beautician, two barbers, and a banker. There is also a post office and a central telephone switchboard. Taxi service is available. There are eight general stores, each dealing in everything from dry goods and food-stuffs to hardware and livestock feed. The five taverns in the nucleus are the major focus of recreational activities, particularly, but not exclusively, for the male population. There is a *frontón* (ball court) where the young men gather to play handball and *jai alai*. Occasionally matches of village-wide interest are held. Thus, the nucleus is the religious, civil, educational, economic, and recreational center for the outlying *auzoak*.

Despite its economic heterogeneity, the nucleus does not escape the pervading agricultural stamp which characterizes the village as a whole. The majority of domestic groups in the nucleus maintain a life style differing but little from that on the rural farms. Their memberships own and farm land in the relatively rich and flat bottom lands that surround the nucleus. Even those domestic groups which engage in commercial activities are often, to a greater or lesser degree, agriculturalist.

In Murélaga, social class is a difficult feature to define. There is a rather explicit cultural norm of egalitarianism. However, one major distinction is made—that between the Basques and the non-Basques in the village. The Basques in Murélaga make up the total farming population while the non-Basques tend to be professional people (for example, the doctor, the village secretary, and so forth). It is difficult to view this as a social class distinction because it is debatable whether the non-Basques even enter into the Basque frame of reference. Villagers usually disparage these outsiders in every way. They are deemed to be racially inferior, are excluded from normal social intercourse linguistically, are often despised because of their political identification with the present government, and are set apart by virtue of their occupations (which are felt to be parasitical and certainly less honorable than working the land). More significantly, the non-Basques are believed to be a transient population with no local loyalties or roots. No one expects the non-Basque to remain in the village for a very long period of time. The arrival of a new non-Basque does not create much interest in the village.

The non-Basques reverse the definition and consider themselves a class apart from the villagers and superior to them. They emphasize their identification with the existing polity, their role as bearers of the great traditional Spanish language and culture, and their occupational freedom from manual labor. It is this last point which forcefully demonstrates the cultural difference between the Basques and the non-Basques. For the former the only "honorable" life involves hard work and careful management of the farm resources. For the latter, hard physical labor is a demeaning experience and a means of losing, rather than gaining, prestige.

One occupational difference within the Basque population that could conceivably serve as the basis for class distinctions is that be-

tween the farmers and the tradesmen. This is partially nullified by
the fact that the tradesmen are usually part-time agriculturalists. In
most cases they were born and reared on *baserriak*. Nevertheless,
there is potentially some friction between the two groups. Farmers
boast, "If it weren't for the farmers who produce the real wealth of
the village, they (the tradesmen) would have to close up their
shops." Farmers ask, "What will become of the landless shopkeeper
if we fall upon hard times?" The shopkeeper does not have the land
as security against hunger.[5]

More recently economic differences have distinguished the farmer
from the villager who continues to live in Murélaga but works in
one of the quarries, sawmills, or small industries. The decision to
become a wage laborer is not made easily. It invariably produces a
certain amount of criticism from family and neighbors. "A man
has an obligation to the land." "It is undignified to subject oneself
to another's authority." In defense of his decision he can point out
that the land in the Basque country is poor and hilly. It guarantees
nothing and often leaves one prey to misfortune. Wage labor, on
the other hand, is steady; and one's income is assured. The distinction between farmer and wage laborer is seldom absolute. The
farmer may himself engage in some wage labor during the course
of the year. Generally the wage laborer will remain a part-time agriculturalist. If the *echekojaun* becomes a full-time wage laborer,
his domestic group will usually adjust by curtailing, but not aban-
doning, its involvement in agriculture.

Other persons who are differentiated from the majority of villagers are the *Amerikanuek* and the *pelotariak*. The former are men
who have spent some time herding sheep in the American Far West.
The latter are professional *jai alai* players who often travel on
player contracts to North and South America. In either case economic success has been achieved outside of the village. When they
return, they often assume airs which set them apart from their fel-

---

[5] The farmer feels a similar superiority toward the people who live in urban
areas and are dependent upon factory work.

low villagers. They spend a great deal of money, standing rounds of drinks in the local taverns and squiring young ladies. Usually they buy automobiles and travel from town to town on a gay fiesta circuit. This behavior often impresses the young men who aspire to similar success, but it invokes censure from the adult members of the society. The presumptuous person, rather than gaining the prestige he desires, usually loses respect because of his "frivolous" behavior. He is given the pejorative label *buru ariña* (lightheaded), which is a serious affront in a community where sobriety and dedication to hard work are deemed virtues.

Throughout the last century it was quite common for domestic groups to rent their *baserriak*. Land then, as today, was scarce and there were fewer outlets for excess population (that is, fewer factories, less emigration, and the like). A wealthy industrialist or aristocrat often owned a number of *baserriak*. In the last century the majority of farming domestic groups rented their *baserria* of residence from an absentee landlord.

During the twentieth century there has been a growing trend in the opposite direction, and many former renters have purchased their *baserria*. This is true in spite of the fact that the value of land (particularly when put to pine trees) has risen constantly. However, two factors have encouraged the reversal. First, under Spanish law it is very difficult for the owners to raise rents without the consent of the renting domestic group. Rents have remained fairly stable throughout the century while the Spanish economy has inflated catastrophically. The imbalance between rents and economic reality is in many cases so extreme that the rent fails to cover even the property taxes. Second, there was a flood of emigration to the New World during the present century. Many renters left, were successful, and returned to live in Murélaga. In some cases these individuals assumed full jural status in their natal domestic groups and even became heirs. Since they had a large cash surplus, they were in a position to pay good prices for the *baserria*. In the last century approximately three-fourths of the domestic groups residing

on *baserriak* were renters. Today, only 51 of the 141 farming domestic groups are renters. A facet of Basque common law which
guarantees the owner all rights over the standing timber pertaining
to the *baserria* explains why more absentee landlords have not sold
to their renters. Since pine plantations have been very profitable
throughout this century, many owners have preferred to put the
mountain holdings of the *baserria* to pine and not worry about the
rest. The renter, in this circumstance, retains the rights to the
dwelling and fields at a rock-bottom rental.

Access to mountain lands is the only salient economic difference
between owner and renter domestic groups. While the renter domestic group must pay a rent on its holdings, rent varies little from
the amount of land taxes paid by an owner domestic group. Then,
too, the renter has no building maintenance costs. The renter's right
to continued residence is secured because Spanish law makes evic-
tion very difficult. Furthermore, he may confer this right to his
appointed heir. Therefore, the renter *echekojaun* is as much an
echekojaun as the one who owns his farm.[6] There is no difference
in the respect accorded to each within the society. For example, in
the formation of common activity groups, the renters normally participate to the same degree and on the same basis as owners.[7]

However, the economic difference between owner and renter domestic groups, resulting from the owner group's control over forest
reserves, is often significant. In pine production the owner domestic
group has a major, long-term source of income. Owners may realize
as much as several thousand dollars from their pine production
(from seed to harvestable tree takes roughly twenty-five to thirty
years). One context in which the difference is apparent is that of

---

[6] The term *echekojaun* means literally "lord of the house." *Jauna* means
"lord" or *"señor"* (elevated status). The Basque term for God is *Jaungoikoa*
("Lord on high").

[7] One exception to this is found in the *auzoa* Ibarrola. In Ibarrola renters
do not serve as *mayordomo* for the chapel.

dowry payments. A person marrying into a renter domestic group will necessarily receive a smaller dowry from her domestic group than one marrying into an owner domestic group.[8]

In summary, the major class distinction perceived by the farming population—that between owners and renters—is not a significant one and rarely leads to behavioral differences.

Before describing funerary ritual in Murélaga, it is necessary to make a distinction between three closely related concepts in the Basque world view: (1) *familizhe* (family), (2) *echea* (household), and (3) *echekoak* ("those of the household" or domestic group). These concepts will be examined in greater detail in Chapter 3. For present purposes, however, they may be defined thus:

> *Familizhe.* An ego-specific category of kinsmen which includes ego's spouse, offspring, siblings, and parents whether living or dead, whether or not they are residing with ego, and whether (in the case of siblings and offspring) married or unmarried.
>
> *Echea.* The dwelling, household furnishings, agricultural implements, landholdings, and the household site on the church floor (*sepulturie*) viewed as a unit which is ideally immutable over time.
>
> *Echekoak.* The persons who maintain common residence in the household or who, while absent, retain the right to return and take up residence. Ideally the core of the *echekoak* includes an active married couple (*echekojaun* and *echekoandria*), a retired married couple who are the parents of either the *echekojaun* or the *echekoandria,* and the unmarried offspring of both couples. However, the *echekoak* membership may also include adopted members and servants.

---

[8] Henceforth, the inmarrying spouse will be referred to as the "affine," as opposed to the spouse who is "heir" to the household.

The rural household or *baserria* is the basic unit of the rural sector of the social structure in Murélaga. The farm and domestic group have a linked social identity within the society. The *baserria* is fixed in space and durable as an identifiable unit through time.

The *baserriak* units are arranged into neighborhoods or *auzoak* which are discrete territorial entities, having a social identity within the wider society. The *auzoa* has a rudimentary authority structure (the *mayordomo*), and a few communally held assets (roadways, water and electrical systems, and the chapel).

The *auzoa* is linked to the village nucleus, physically by a system of roadways, and socially and economically by its membership's dependence upon the nucleus for a wide variety of goods and services. Similarly, the nucleus is dependent upon the *baserriak* and *auzoak* for its clientele. This reciprocity is coterminous with the widest range of social organization at the local level—the village.

2

Death and Funerary Rites in Murelaga[1]

𝒟 EATH is not always fortuitous or unpredictable. Various signs may presage an imminent death. If in the stillness of the night the rooster awakens and begins to crow, someone is going to die. The howling of a dog in the darkness is another warning that death is near (see appendix). During Sunday High Mass when, at the consecration of the Blessed Sacrament, the altar boy rings the bell to inform the faithful and, at the same time, the clock in the church tower begins to chime the hour, a feeling of uneasiness passes over the congregation. Surely death is imminent for one of them (see

[1] The appendix has been compiled from the literature dealing with funerary ritual in Basque society. The purpose of the appendix is to show that the funerary practices of Murélaga are but one variant on a theme which holds throughout the entire Basque country. The present description of eschatalogical beliefs and funerary ritual is not restricted to events surrounding a particular death (although these events are covered by the account). In this treatment I take into account the changes which have taken place in funerary practices during the past two or three decades. Thus I combine information derived from personal observations during my stay in the village and data from interviews with middle-aged and elderly informants. Whenever reference is made to a practice that no longer obtains, this fact is noted in the text. The important point is that this description is *not* to be taken as an exercise in salvage ethnography. In Murélaga today the death theme is as elaborate and as important a feature of the village way of life as at any time in the past.

appendix). Death's warnings are not always impersonal. A widow who fails to hear the call of the returning cuckoo bird before the first day of May (the day of the Virgin Mary) may be assured that she is entering the last year of her life.

Death may come from unnatural causes. Some people have the power to kill with their evil eye (*begizkue*). Unbaptized children are particularly susceptible:

> One of Iciar's four children was particularly large and beautiful at birth. The doctor was quite pleased with the infant and wished to weigh her. Iciar's mother-in-law cautioned her not to permit this since someone possessing the power of *begizkue* might hear of the child's beauty and try to harm her. Iciar refused to let the doctor weigh the child.

The harm which an adult may cause to an infant is neutralized by an open declaration of good intent. Thus, when the infant is presented to an adult for the first time, the adult is expected to declare, "God bless this child, let not my eyes bring it harm."

Both children and adults may be killed by curses (*maldiciones*) (see appendix). The power to inflict death with a curse is possessed by few persons, but recently such a person lived in Murélaga:

> She rented a *baserria* in *auzoa* X, and all of her neighbors were frightened by her. Once in a rage she cursed a young woman in the *auzoa,* and within six months the girl died of cancer. On another occasion she cursed her own son, and he died shortly thereafter. The death of another young girl, who suffered from tuberculosis, was attributed to this woman. Her most awesome accomplishment came as a result of an argument which she had with her landlord. He refused to make the repairs that she had demanded, so she cursed her own dwelling. Within a short time the front of the house crashed to the ground.

Often death does not come suddenly or unexpectedly, and the marked person enters a long period of decline. His final agony signals the preliminary preparations. By this time he is confined to his bed, and members of the domestic group advise his relatives of his condition. Those who reside in the village, or reasonably near, come to visit him. Persons residing on other farmsteads of the *auzoa* are also likely to pay a visit. Not all of the visitors to the dying man have a kinship or common residence tie with him. Friends and persons with whom he maintained strong economic ties (for example, the storekeeper with whom he regularly traded) are certain to come. The visitors are treated to refreshments by the *echekoandria* and, in their turn, leave a small gift of a chicken, a bottle of wine, or money.

The obligation of relatives not residing on the farm varies. It is felt that all who can come to visit the dying person should do so. In some instances the perceived obligation may be quite extreme:

J.'s mother was dying. Relatives in Guernica and Bilbao were advised and came to pay their respects. One morning a stranger appeared. She stated that she was from the village of Ea (some distance away and difficult to reach by public transportation). She had come to visit the dying woman. It seems that both J. and the visitor had daughters attending the same girls' school in Guernica. J.'s daughter mentioned to her school mates that her grandmother was dying. The girl from Ea returned home and told this to her family. When she stated the dying woman's name, her mother recalled that her parents used to have relatives in Murélaga with that last name. She resolved to make the trip. To this day neither J. nor the visitor are certain that they are related. Neither was successful in reconstructing a genealogical tie, and the dying woman was too ill to help them.

While the role of the relatives is normally that of "guest," in unusual circumstances a relative may actually live in to assist the domestic group until the death:

F. was dying of cancer. She lived with her aged sister and the sister's son. She required daily injections, but the farm was isolated, making it impossible for the village doctor or male nurse to make a daily visit. Therefore, F.'s first cousin, a woman skilled at giving injections, resided on the farm for a period of several weeks before F.'s death.

The duration of the visiting period varies with the amount of time that elapses between the first recognition that the individual is dying and his death. If he lingers for a long period of time, the visits may be repeated on more than one occasion. But at some point the domestic group decides that death is finally near and calls the parish priest to administer the Last Sacrament of the Church to the dying person. The domestic group may send one of its own members to the village nucleus or call upon the neighboring household with which it has a special relationship to send one of its members. This neighboring household is referred to as the *auzurriḳourrena,* or literally "the nearest of the neighborhood."

While waiting for the priest, the *echeḳoandria* busies herself with the preparations for his visit. She cleans the sickroom, washes the patient, and changes his bedding and dressing gown. She then places a blessed candle and container of holy water on the bedstand for the priest's use.[2] The priest usually arrives on foot, accompanied by an altar boy (sometimes the sacristan performs this service). He enters the room and anoints the body by applying both holy water and holy oils in accordance with the Catholic Sacrament of Extreme Unction. Usually one of the domestic group members exposes the extremities of the dying person's body so that the priest may anoint them.[3] If at all possible, the priest hears the confession of the dying man and gives him the Sacrament of Holy Eucharist. When the priest is finished, he goes with the altar boy to the kitchen to partake of refreshments prepared by the *echeḳoandria.* At this time she gives the altar boy a small sum of money for his trouble. The priest may repeat his visit on a regular basis if the failing person does not die within a short time after the initial application of the Last Sacraments.[4]

Attitudes toward death may be divided into (1) the reaction of

[2] Water and candles are each blessed once annually in the village church. The candles are blessed on the Day of the Candles (February 3), and the water is blessed during the Holy Week services which precede Easter Sunday. Villagers who attend these affairs take a candle and container of holy water home with them to be used in event of a death.

[3] In some parts of the Basque country the *echeḳoandria* from the *auzurriḳourrena* performs this service.

[4] If death comes with considerable pain and torment, this may be a sign that the deceased will be condemned in the afterlife. It is a much better omen if he slips away quietly with a smile on his face (see appendix).

an individual to his own death, and (2) the individual's reaction to the death of another. As a rule, individuals are calm in the face of death. Persons who have suffered long illness normally welcome death and are frank about it. The parish priest recounts one extreme case where a woman withering away with cancer would hold up her emaciated arm and announce with a laugh, "The worms will have little work with me." Not everyone has the same degree of resignation, but the over-all impression is that the Basque it not unnerved by the prospect of dying.

This same attitude of resignation characterizes the reaction of an individual to the death of another person (even a close relative). Overt grief is carefully controlled. Immediate female kinsmen may weep, but males are denied this outlet for their grief, and are expected to remain stoic. The death is discussed openly and frankly. No attempt is made to hide the facts of death from children. The parish priest provided the following account:

> Whenever there is a death in the village nucleus the children know that I will go at dusk to the house of the deceased to lead the first Rosary of the vigil (*gauela*). They wait for me at the entrance to the church and beg for permission to attend. As many as thirty children follow me to the house and enter the room of the deceased. They pray the Rosary along with the rest and then crowd around the corpse for a closer look.

This frank disclosure of death to children is reflected further in the custom of selecting the *anderuek* or pallbearers for a child's burial from among the children of his own *auzoa*.

The first reaction after a death is for the domestic group to inform the membership of the nearest neighboring household, the *auzurrikourrena*. The *auzurrikourrena* domestic group then assumes the responsibility of making the necessary preparations. The *echekoandria* of the *auzurrikourrena* goes to the household of the deceased and assumes the domestic duties such as cooking and cleaning. Some member of the *auzurrikourrena* immediately informs the other domestic groups in the *auzoa*, and within a short period of time the dwelling of the deceased is filled with neighbors meeting their obligation to assist and offering their condolences to the members of the deprived domestic group.

A member of the *auzurrikourrena* goes to the village nucleus to inform the priests, the civil authorities, and the sacristan. Formerly, a carpenter was also informed so that a coffin might be prepared. The priest sets the hour of the burial service, and the messenger returns to advise the *auzoa* membership of the time. The *auzurri-kourrena* representative consults with the members of the domestic group to ascertain where their relatives are residing. Relatives who live in Murélaga are informed of the death by a member of the *auzurrikourrena,* who visits each personally. He telephones those living outside of the area. When this is not possible, he makes a trip to the nearby towns (see appendix).

A female member of the domestic group who is capable of the task will prepare the corpse for burial. If there is no one who can do this, a neighbor may offer her assistance.[5] She washes the deceased with holy water and combs his hair. She then dresses him in his best clothes or in special clothing made by an order of nuns in Marquina for the express purpose of burials. The eyes are closed with dabs of candle wax, and the mouth is tied closed with a cloth (see appendix). The hands, brought together at chest level and tied in a prayerful attitude, hold a crucifix made of wood or two crossed candles. A lighted blessed candle is placed by the head of the deceased. A shallow dish of holy water which has a sprig of laurel leaf dipped into it is placed on the bedstand. The deceased is now ready to receive the mourners.

Since the 1930s, there have been several changes in the manner in which the corpse is presented to the mourners. Formerly it was placed on a table in the center of the room. However, in the words of one informant, "this caused too great an impression because the

---

[5] In some parts of the Basque country there are persons in the neighborhood or village who perform this service in all the households. In other areas, this obligation falls upon the *auzurrikourrena.*

setting was stark." It then became customary to leave the prepared body in the deathbed. This had the advantage of presenting the deceased as if he were reposing. Finally, around 1958, it became fashionable to place the corpse directly into the coffin. This was facilitated by a new custom of purchasing ready-made, factory-manufactured coffins. These coffins are available within a few hours after a death and have the advantage of a clear glass top. The corpse can be placed in the coffin and the coffin sealed without preventing the mourners from viewing the body. Later, just before the body is taken from the house for the procession to the village nucleus, a wooden lid is secured over the glass cover.

In former times, when coffins were manufactured by the local carpenter, their construction reflected the relative economic status of the bereaved domestic group. Renters purchased rough-hewn coffins and used ordinary cloth for the lining. Owner domestic groups were expected to purchase finer coffins and line them with black velvet. Deviance from expected behavior was noted and, in some instances, is remembered to this day:

The owners of the *baserria* E. are remembered for the fact that they would order the cheapest coffin and lining, dress the corpse in ordinary clothing, and then order the most expensive burial service (compare pages 36–37 for a typology of burial services).

The wooden lid to the coffin comes equipped with a fine crucifix. This crucifix remains on the coffin throughout the vigil, the procession, and the burial service. However, the bereaved domestic group removes the crucifix when the coffin is handed over to the grave-diggers. This crucifix becomes a permanent fixture on one of the walls of the dwelling and is a memento of the deceased for the survivors.

If death occurs during the night, the deceased will spend the entire next day and night in his dwelling, and the burial will be held the following day. If the death occurs during the daytime, the burial is usually the following afternoon. Sometime between dawn and dusk on the day after the death, the sacristan rings the church bells in order to announce the event to the entire village. If the deceased is male, the large church bell is rung three times, followed by ten seconds of continuous pealing; if female, the large bell is rung twice (see appendix). The *mayordomo* rings the *auzoa* chapel bell on three occasions. He rings it at dawn, at midday, and at dusk. He makes no sexual distinction. In both cases the ringing of the bells is redundant because the news had circulated to a majority of the villagers by word of mouth within a few hours after the death.

THE "GAUELA"

The night before the burial, the *gauela*[6] or night vigil is held (see appendix). Throughout the hours of the night someone is always present, keeping watch over the body. The main actors in the *gauela* are the adult men and women of the dead man's *auzoa*. In addition to the *auzoa* membership, several relatives of the deceased may also be present. Kindred representatives are normally limited to those who reside in the village. Relatives who live in more distant places will not have had time to arrive. Other participants are the same persons who came during the agony because they had a personal tie with the deceased.

The *gauela* begins at sundown and ends at dawn. At dusk those who wish to attend begin to arrive. They go through the ritual of sprinkling the corpse with holy water while reciting an "Our Father."[7] People come and go throughout the night, and at any one time there may be only five or six persons in the room. They sit and talk in lowered voices. Others gather in the kitchen where the conversation is lighter. At midnight the *echekoandria* serves refreshments which are eaten in the room of the deceased. As the night wanes, usually only those who feel a special obligation to the deceased remain. The last to leave, at the first light of day, is often

---

[6] The term *gauela* comes from the words *gaba* (night) and *bela* (vigil).

[7] If the death occurs in the village nucleus, the priest puts in an appearance at the beginning of the *gauela* to lead those present in the Rosary. This custom was initiated in the late 1950s.

the *echekojaun* or *echekoandria* of the *auzurrikourrena* of the deceased (see appendix).

The activities and the tone of the discourse during the *gauela* illustrate further the participants' matter-of-fact attitude toward death. Both grief and solemnity are minimized. From time to time a woman spontaneously initiates the recitation of the Rosary (generally, but not necessarily, recited in Basque). The mourners recite five of the fifteen mysteries of the Rosary. Once they have finished, the person leading the Rosary makes a comment upon the character of the deceased:

When A. finished reciting the Rosary she announced, "You will note that I mixed sorrowful mysteries with glorious mysteries. This was not confusion on my part. I did it because Panchica lived in misery and sorrow in this world, but she is now in her glory."

The participants then turn to any subject of conversation. They complain about the current price of milk or about labor conditions in the factories of Eibar. Someone recounts the latest news from his son who is herding sheep in Idaho. Another speaks of his brother who is working as a sugar-cane cutter in Australia. A third adds comments about his son who owns a tavern in Caracas. It may be that two or three of the persons in attendance are relatives who have come from other areas. They are eager to swap family news with their local relations. So the conversation is light, and gentle joking and laughter are not deemed out of place. After about half an hour another woman entones the first prayer of a new Rosary. This is the signal for all to return to prayer. In this manner the participants pass the evening. Some leave; from time to time there are new arrivals.

In the course of the conversation the subject of death is broached openly. Reference to this specific death is common and expected. Each new arrival is treated to a vivid account:

Poor uncle was seated in his chair eating his dinner. The attack seized him. He dropped his cup of coffee, soiling his clothing. He keeled sidewise out of his chair and dropped to his knees. He groaned and began to thrash about on the floor. Then God took him.

The details are repeated over and over, and no attempt is made to avoid the subject in the presence of immediate family members or domestic group members of the deceased.

In the course of the evening, there is frequent reference to the personality of the deceased. This topic of conversation is stylized and consequently varies but little from one *gauela* to another. The rule is that only favorable remarks should be made. No matter how badly the deceased was regarded while alive, or how many enemies he had, those at the *gauela* repeat the fact that, "There was never anyone like him; his death is a great loss for everyone." One female informant recounts an incident from a *gauela* held for a local industrialist:

I was dizzy so I left the room to get some air. While outside I met M. who remarked, "To listen to them inside you would think he was a saint. If you really want to know what he was like ask his workers." I was shocked by this and excused myself.

The implication is clear. It is during the course of the *gauela* that the social personality of the deceased is "laundered." The *gauela* is attended primarily by the dead man's neighbors, the persons who knew him well and are likely to bear him a grudge. In the *auzoa* context face-to-face interaction is constant, and gossip is most effective as a sanctioning device. It is in the *auzoa* that competition between domestic groups is greatest, and the likelihood of quarrels is ever present. The chickens from one household may enter the garden of another and cause damage; one man may feel that his neighbor has trespassed on his land. If the neighborhood is to function as a unit in the face of crisis, and if the bereaved domestic group is to receive the moral support it needs, then it is first necessary that those who knew the deceased best "let bygones be bygones"—even if this entails fictionalizing a man's reputation.

THE FUNERARY PROCESSION

The day after the *gauela* is the day of the burial. The custom is for a burial to take place in the late afternoon (this allows relatives from distant places to arrive in time). Throughout the morning relatives begin to gather. They pay their respects and repeat the ritual of sprinkling holy water on the corpse. (Formerly, about noon, the carpenter delivered the coffin. He placed the body in the coffin himself. The coffin was not closed until the procession to the village nucleus began.)

About an hour before the funeral procession, the neighbors and several relatives begin to gather in front of the house. A few may enter to pay their last respects. Relatives are dressed in black.

At the appointed hour the priest arrives with the sacristan. The latter bears a large metal crucifix. They are flanked by two altar boys, who carry large, torch-like candles. The priest goes into the house and enters the room of the deceased. He begins to recite a Psalm for the dead. The pallbearers lift the coffin and carry it outside. The priest then chants the Miserere Psalm of David ("You will wash me; You will make me cleaner than snow; You will cleanse me of sin").

The bereaved domestic group selects four men to serve as pall-bearers or *anderuek*.[8] The choice is usually made from among the men in the neighborhood. In some instances, however, relatives are chosen, in which case the pallbearers all stand in the same kinship relationship to the deceased (for example, all are nephews of the deceased).

The structuring of the funeral procession is as follows: the sacristan, bearing the crucifix, flanked by the two altar boys; next the priest, then the coffin, supported by the four *anderuek;* then come the male members of the bereaved domestic group, led by the *echekojaun,* followed by male members of the *familizhe* (for ex-

---

[8] *Anderuek* probably comes from the Spanish *andas,* meaning "litter" (Caro Baroja 1958:327).

ample, a married brother of the deceased); then the male members of the kindred of the deceased, followed by the male members of his *auzoa;* then all other male participants; then the female members of the domestic group, led by the *echekoandria;* female *familizhe* members, the female kindred members and female members of the *auzoa* in that order; and last, all other attending females. It is likely that persons from nearby neighborhoods, particularly those which are on the same road network that links the *auzoa* of the deceased with the nucleus, will join the procession. In this case the males will enter at the rear of the male section and the females behind their section (see appendix).

During the procession to the nucleus the priest will occasionally chant another verse of the Miserere. He attempts to measure out the verses so that he will finish the Psalm at about the time the procession reaches the village nucleus. Formerly, in between verses of the Psalm, the participants chatted as they walked along. The parish priest during the early 1960s felt that this was disrespectful, and he introduced the custom of reciting the Rosary for the soul of the deceased.

The procession follows the main roadway that links the neighborhood to the nucleus. The name of the roadways reflects the nature of the occasion, since they are referred to as *andabideak* or "coffin roads." Whenever the procession reaches a crossroad, it stops and the priest recites an "Our Father" (see appendix). At the crossroads the ranks of the procession may be swelled with people from other neighborhoods.

When the procession reaches the edge of the nucleus, the participants recite an "Our Father." At this point the church bells ring out, and two or more priests come from the church.[9] One or more of the priests is brought in from another town for the occasion. By this

---

[9] In the years since 1958 this has been simplified. Presently, only two priests attend the entire burial service. One remains in the village nucleus and receives the procession in the portal of the church.

time, the procession swells noticeably as people from the nucleus
and other distant rural reighborhoods join in. Each new arrival
takes his proper place in the procession.

The membership of the deceased in a voluntary religious association may also be reflected in the structuring of the procession.
In the village there are associations for married persons, unmarried
women, and unmarried men. The association to which the deceased
belonged is represented by its head, who enters the procession immediately behind the priests as the procession enters the nucleus. He
(or she) carries the banner of the association. If the deceased were
a member of either the Luises (the unmarried men's association) or
the Hijas de María (the unmarried women's association), its entire
membership enters the procession directly behind the coffin, taking
precedence over the bereaved domestic group, relatives, and neighbors. This means that if the deceased is an unmarried woman, the
formal structuring of the procession along sexual lines is altered,
for members of her association go before all males. The participants
of the association wear their identifying scapular medals.

THE BURIAL SERVICE

The procession makes its way to the church and enters. The men
file to the front of the church and take their places on the benches
which flank both sides of the center aisle. The women follow and
occupy the middle and rear sections of the church. In the women's
section the church floor is marked with a series of contiguous rec-
tangles.[10] Each rectangle corresponds to one of the *baserriak* or to
one of the households in the village nucleus. This identification between a floor site and a given household is felt to be immutable and
in most cases can be traced back in time for several centuries. The
floor site is called the *sepulturie* (sepulture). It is the spot where
the women of the domestic group sit whenever they attend a re-

---

[10] For a diagram of the church floor see Figure 2 on page 51.

ligious service. On each *sepulturie* there is a low wicker chair which serves as both a seat and a kneeler.[11]

The coffin is placed upon a linen-covered table in the center aisle, midway between the men's and women's sections of the church, with the feet of the corpse in the direction of the altar. The sacristan and his wife prepare the table prior to the service. The coffin is flanked by a large number of candles, which are employed later in several ritual contexts. It is therefore necessary to examine the arrangement in detail.

Figure 1 is a diagrammatic overview of the coffin, table, and candles (the small circles represent candles). In the figure we have both the present arrangement and that which obtained in the past. In both diagrams the letter D indicates the coffin (which is resting on the table). The letter E designates wooden candle racks. The candles identified by the letter A are referred to as *kandelak*. They are approximately two feet tall and are made of beeswax; they are provided by the household of the deceased. The *kandelak*, located at the four corners of the table, are the candles which are physically closest to the corpse throughout the services. They later play an important role in the year-long cycle of mourning since they are to be used on the household *sepulturie*. That is, during the year of mourning, a female representative of the bereaved domestic group has the obligation of activating the *sepulturie* on religious holy days and during the Sunday High Mass. Part of her obligation is to light the *kandelak* and keep them burning for the duration of the service (see the section on mourning practices). The candles designated by

---

[11] In this description the *sepulturie* complex is described as it was until 1958. At that time the parish priest decided to replace the *sepulturiek* with benches in order to increase the seating capacity of the church. However, to this day women who are in mourning continue to carry out the rituals associated with the *sepulturie*. They set up a substitute *sepulturie* along the side aisle (on that side of the center aisle where their household formerly had its *sepulturie*). They are careful to place the simulated *sepulturie* as close as possible to the former site. A more detailed description is provided in the sections on mourning practices.

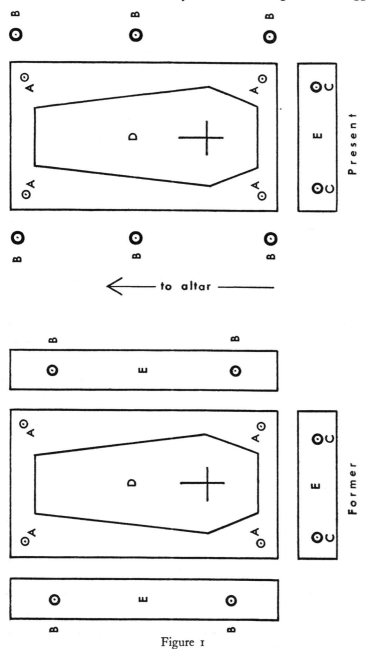

Figure 1

the letter B are called *achak*. They are about four feet tall. They belong to the church and are used for every funeral. Formerly, when there was a particularly sacred religious holy day (for example, Easter, Pentecost Sunday, Saint John's Day, Christmas, Corpus Christi), these *achak* were placed on the altar in lieu of the smaller, everyday candles. The two candles in each diagram designated by the letter C are also called *achak*. They are about three feet tall, are church property, and are used for more than one burial.

A Catholic Mass of the dead is the major church event. Before the Mass begins, the officiant priest approaches the coffin and sings the same Psalm for the dead which initiated the procession at the home of the deceased. The choir then sings a hymn beseeching the angels to come and lead the departed soul into heaven. The proceedings are in Latin, although one priest is stationed in the pulpit to explain (in Basque) the significance of the hymns. The apocryphal *Dies Irae* is interjected between the Epistle and Gospel of the Mass. At the Offertory there is an intrusion of local custom. Two representatives of the *auzoa* of the deceased go forward to meet the priests in front of the coffin. They are the *ogidune* (see appendix), the breadbearer, and the *estipendiyue,* the stipend bearer.[12] The *ogidune,* a woman, gives the priest a basket filled with a large loaf of bread, which is removed by the sacristan's wife. The role of *estipendiyue* is filled by a man. He gives the priest a small sum of money (1.50 *pesetas*) wrapped in paper. The *ogidune* returns to her place in the congregation, but the *estipendiyue* goes to the choir loft and makes a similar offering to the organist. Both *estipendiyue* offerings are payments for services rendered. The amount is fixed by tradition. In recent years the payment has become symbolic since the amount involved is insignificant.[13] The selection of *ogidune* and

[12] *Ogidune* comes from the Basque term *ogia* (bread) and the suffix *-dune* (bearer of). *Estipendiyue* is a contraction of the term *estipendie* (stipend) and the *-dune* suffix, that is, from *estipendidune.*

[13] The Spanish *peseta* has been devalued repeatedly in the twentieth century. The present exchange rate (1967) is approximately sixty *pesetas* to the dollar. That the *estipendiyue*'s payment is presently insignificant in terms of

estipendiyue is made by the bereaved domestic group. The only restriction is that the selected persons have the same marital status as the deceased.

Payment for services must be made to other participants in the burial. The bereaved domestic group pays a fixed sum to the religious authorities. The amount is determined by the class of service that is held (see page 36 for typology of burial services). Out of this fixed sum the priests pay the chanter or singer, the organist, and the sacristan. Formerly the chanter received one hundred *pesetas* per service, but as of 1965 he receives six thousand *pesetas* annually. His fixed duties include providing music each Sunday during the High Mass. The organist comes from the nearby village of Arbacegui. She used to receive one hundred *pesetas* plus carfare per service. Now she receives two thousand *pesetas* annually, regardless of the number of burials. The sacristan receives an annual salary of twelve thousand *pesetas*. His duties are complex and time-consuming. They entail general upkeep of the church and the preparations for any religious service. In addition to his fixed salary, he receives a percentage of the *artu-emon* Mass donations, which are occasioned by a death (see pages 37–40).

After the Mass the priest approaches the coffin and chants a hymn *Liberame,* imploring God to spare the soul of the deceased from the eternal fires. The priest then circles the coffin while he anoints it with holy water and incense. He then sings the *Benedictus* of Zachariah, which is a hymn praising the Lord.

Once the services in the church have ended, the procession reforms and conducts the coffin to the cemetery, located at the edge of the nucleus. The men enter along with the priests; the women remain outside the cemetery gates.[14] If the deceased is an unmarried

---

the local economy is clear if we consider that an average daily wage is between 250 and 300 *pesetas.*

[14] While in some areas of the Basque country (Echalar, Navarra, for example), the women do enter the cemetery, both Caro Baroja (Caro Baroja 1958:323) and Veyrin (Veyrin 1955:270) concur that in most villages the women remain outside.

woman, the unmarried women's association enters the cemetery, each member carrying a lighted candle.

There is a small chapel in the cemetery, and the priests enter to recite the last prayers for the deceased. They mention him specifically and ask God for mercy on his soul. The officiating priest then leads the congregation in the recitation of an "Our Father," offered on behalf of the souls of all the persons ever buried in the cemetery.

Formerly, there was no post-church-service procession to the cemetery.[15] The "Our Father" for all the deceased of the village was recited after the burial service in the plaza in front of the church. Presently, when the "Our Father" is finished the procession disperses, and the deceased is remanded to the care of the gravediggers.

The burial services, including the functions in the church, are largely dictated by Catholic practice. However, until quite recently [16] the domestic group could choose one of four classes of services (see appendix):

1. *Primerísima* (ultra-first class). This was the most luxurious type of burial. All of the lights in the church were lit, and the altar was covered with candles. During a *primerísima* burial service, the *achak,* designated by the letter B in Figure 1, were placed on the altar, while smaller *achak* were substituted around the coffin. Both an officiant priest and a predicator were brought in from another area. An organist and a choir were provided. This type of service was short-lived. It was initiated about 1940 and abolished about

[15] Until recent years the corpse was conducted to the cemetery *before* the procession entered the church for the burial service. During the church service a block of wood was substituted for the actual coffin. It is only since 1958 that the corpse enters the church.

[16] The class difference between types of burial services existed until about 1958. At that time the parish priest insisted that a single, uniform type of burial be given for everyone. In 1965 the same priest abolished all charges for performing a burial service.

1955. Informants relate that while it was in existence it was the most frequently commissioned service. It was more expensive than the other services. The cost was at least two thousand *pesetas,* but varied according to the elaborations.

2. *Primera* (first class). This service differed from the above in degree only. The first-class funeral had less light in the church and on the altar. Perhaps there would be no special predicator. One characteristic of both *primerísima* and *primera* was that all proprietors were expected to have one or the other. That is, all of those domestic groups that owned their *baserria* of residence were expected to ask for *primerísima* or *primera* when one of their members died. For practical purposes there is little distinction between them, and in later discussion both are subsumed under the category *primera.* The cost of this service was nine hundred *pesetas.*

3. *Segunda* (second class). This service was much less elaborate than the two described above. There were far fewer lights in the church and on the altar. In a second-class service there were only two *kandelak* on the coffin table. These were placed near the head of the corpse. Neither a predicator nor an officiant priest was brought in from another village to assist the local priests during the Mass. This was the prescribed type of service for the renter families. The cost was seven hundred *pesetas.*

4. *Tercera* (third class). This service was reserved for the poor and mendicant. It lacked all luxury and was usually a charity function. Since this type of service was seldom held, informants are unable to provide many details. However, the present sacristan believes that during third-class services there were no *kandelak* on the coffin table. If not a charity function, the cost was 450 *pesetas.*

THE "ARTU-EMON" RELATIONSHIP

Both before and after the burial service the sacristan places a small table at the entrance to the church. He then occupies this post as a representative of the bereaved domestic group. One individual, usually the *echekoandria,* from each of the domestic groups with members attending the burial leaves a donation. This money is used to pay for Masses on behalf of the deceased. The sacristan writes the name of the donor's household in a book. After the name he records the sum of the donation. The Basque term for this gift is *artu-emon,* which means "to take and to give." The terminology implies a reciprocity that exists in the relationship. The reciprocity is played out at a later date. The bereaved domestic group receives the completed notebook from the sacristan. With this book they will be able to identify those domestic groups with which they have an *artu-emon* obligation. They consult their books whenever there is a death in the village (see appendix).

The sacristan keeps a portion of the *artu-emon* donations for his services throughout the burial ceremony. He turns the remainder over to the priests. The total sum is then divided by the thirty-five *pesetas* that are required for a Mass, and the resulting number of Masses will be offered for the soul of the deceased.

Presently, minimal *artu-emon* donations are collected on two occasions. At the burial service it is customary to give ten *pesetas* as the minimal gift. This is referred to as a gift of "two Masses," a usage which dates from a period when the cost of a Mass was five *pesetas.* The second *artu-emon* donation is at the *ogistie* ceremony (see pages 59–60), which signals the end of the year-long mourning cycle. In 1968 the minimal donation per domestic group was five *pesetas* or one Mass.

Although in 1967 the minimal *artu-emon* donation at a burial was ten *pesetas,* this was not always the case. Formerly the sum was less. Also there were three occasions on which *artu-emon* was collected. A standard offering followed the burial service and the *ogistie* cere-mony. However, following the *onrak* service (see page 46) the donor could choose between a donation of 1.25 *pesetas* for a *misa rezada* (a prayed Mass) and 1.65 *pesetas* for a *misa cantada* (a sung Mass). The difference was significant in that it determined the extent of the donor's right of participation in the funerary banquet.

There is a more elaborate form of *artu-emon* donation, which is

referred to as *arimen onrak* ("honors for the soul"). This gift is
made by those who perceive a special relationship existing between
themselves and the deceased (for example, a close relative or neighbor). The *arimen onrak* are collected by the sacristan along with
the minimal *artu-emon* donations. These donations are recorded in
the book along with the others. The majority of *arimen onrak* donations are made at the burial service (or shortly thereafter). However, a few offerings are collected at the *ogistie* ceremony as well.
Persons desirous of making such donations are free to do so at any
time until the Sunday after the death, that is, the day on which
the *argia* ceremony is held (see pages 43–46). As a part of the *argia*
ceremony the priest reads the list of *arimen onrak* donors to the
congregation.

The *arimen onrak* donation is forty *pesetas*. Of this total thirty-
five *pesetas* are applied toward the cost of a Mass on behalf of the
departed soul. The local religious authorities usually contract out
these Masses to religious orders located elsewhere in Spain. The
remaining five *pesetas* are used to pay for a *nocturno* (nocturn).
The *nocturno* must be said on the *sepulturie* of the deceased. Each
nocturno consists of three Psalms and one "Our Father." Normally,
the priests say the *nocturnos* at their own leisure after weekday
morning Masses. The *echekoandria* of the bereaved domestic group
may or may not be present. The sacristan sees to it that one *kandela*
(Figure 1, letter A) and one *acha* (Figure 1, letter C) are lit and
placed on the *sepulturie*. A given death may occasion as many as
forty *arimen onrak* donations, with the corresponding forty *nocturnos*. The priest says as many as four *nocturnos* on a particular
day. He repeats this on consecutive mornings until the list of
donations is exhausted.

Informants agree that in the last twenty-five years there has been
a tremendous proliferation of *arimen onrak* donations. Formerly,
only the domestic group and *familizhe* members (for example, the
married siblings and offspring who are residing elsewhere), godparents or godchildren of the deceased and his *auzurrikourrena*

gave *arimen onrak*. In all, it was unusual to collect more than ten *arimen onrak* at a given death. Now it is customary for all persons who come from outside the village to attend the burial, whether friend or relative, to make an *arimen onrak* donation. A partial explanation is that such persons normally attend the banquet and therefore feel obligated to make more than the minimal *artu-emon* donation. However, even within the context of the village the custom has tended to proliferate. Today neighbors and distant relatives are more likely to make the elaborate offering than was formerly the case. The contrast between the present and past is illustrated by an example:

On one farm the *echekojaun* died in 1940. A total of five *arimen onrak* donations were made (all from immediate family). In 1960 his widow died and received twenty-four *arimen onrak* donations (including one from the fiancée of her grandson).

In summary, *artu-emon* reciprocity (that is, both minimal *artu-emon* and the *arimen onrak*) covers a wide range of relationships between the donors and the domestic group of the bereaved household. At the widest and minimal level, all domestic groups with members attending the burial make a donation. At this level reciprocity may link two domestic groups which are otherwise unrelated through kinship ties or bonds of common *auzoa* residence. Although there is no demonstrable tie between the two domestic groups at the time the donation is made, it will be shown (see pages 197–201) that minimal *artu-emon* reciprocity is often the residuum of a former kinship tie or common residence tie. If a kinship tie or bond of common *auzoa* residence is in effect, then the *artu-emon* is likely to be more intensive. At this point the *arimen onrak* donation is made.

THE BURIAL SERVICE BANQUET

Once the burial procession disbands, certain persons go either to the dwelling of the deceased or to a local tavern for a banquet hosted by the bereaved domestic group. Participation in these banquets has declined since the 1930s. Presently, attendance is restricted to relatives of the deceased who have come from outside the village, a few close relatives from the village, and the four men from the *auzoa* who serve as *anderuek*. Formerly the *ogidune* and *estipendiyue* also attended the banquet (see appendix).

POST-BURIAL CEREMONIAL CYCLE

The Bederatziurrune *Cycle*

On the days immediately following the burial service, the bereaved domestic group initiates a novena of Masses for the soul of the deceased. A female representative of the household must attend and activate the *sepulturie;* male members also attend. The sacristan's wife prepares the *sepulturie* by placing a black cloth (symbol of mourning) under the white linen cloth that normally adorns the site. She places two lighted *achak* on the *sepulturie*. The *echekoandria* of the bereaved domestic group places the four lighted *kandelak* on the site. Every domestic group in the village has a number of brass candlestick holders which are employed for this purpose. The *echekoandriak* of the *auzoa* of the deceased each place a single *kandela* on his *sepulturie*. Close relatives of the deceased are also expected to provide a *kandela*. These *kandelak* remain on the *sepulturie* until they are consumed. The *echekoandria* lights them whenever she is activating the *sepulturie* during her year of mourning. The result is that during the *bederatziurrune* functions the *sepulturie* is adorned with about two dozen *kandelak*.

The *bederatziurrune* cycle consists of nine Masses. The Basque term derives from the word *bederatzi* (nine) and *urrena* (a word which means both proximity and consecution). The terminology implies a state of transition. The completion of the nine Masses represents a widening of the gulf—through the intrusion of passing time and ritual—between the living and the deceased.

The nine *bederatziurrune* Masses must be completed before the **argia** ceremony, which ideally takes place on the first Sunday after the death. However, if the death occurs near the end of the week, the *argia* is held over until the following Sunday. Until the 1930s there were as many as five priests residing in Murélaga. Then it was a simple matter to complete the nine Masses in a short period of time (Church regulations restrict each priest to one Mass each day). Now (1967) there are only two priests in the village, so it is more difficult to fit in the nine Masses. For this reason the burial service is counted as one of the *bederatziurrune* Masses. Then on three consecutive days both priests offer their daily Mass as part of the cycle. Later in the week one of the priests offers a single Mass for the deceased. The *argia* Mass is regarded as the ninth and final *bederatziurrune* Mass.

The three consecutive days of two Masses which immediately follow the burial are of prime importance for those who have *bederatziurrune* obligations. On each of these mornings a female representative of the bereaved domestic group activates the *sepulturie*. A male representative must also attend. Close female kinsmen residing in Murélaga accompany the household representatives. While attending the service they kneel on the *sepulturie* site (or immediately behind it). Male members of the bereaved domestic group sit in the first row of the male section (*luto bankue*) on that side of the center aisle where their household *sepulturie* is located. Close male kinsmen are in the rows immediately behind the household representatives. Each *auzoa* household is expected to send both a male and female representative. The females sit on their respective *sepulturie* sites while the males occupy the benches behind the male kinsmen. Finally, close friends of the deceased, those who visited him during the agony, are seated behind the kinsmen and neighbors. The total number of persons in attendance is not great (rarely exceeding fifty) since only those residing in Murélaga are expected to come.

The assemblage attends the first Mass of the morning. The female representative of the bereaved household and close female kinsmen are likely to be the only persons in attendance at the second service, and even they may be absent. However, the *kandelak* and *achak* burn throughout both services, and the rituals are identical in both cases.

The actual service consists of an ordinary Low Mass. Once the Mass is terminated, the officiant priest leaves the altar and goes to the *sepulturie* for the ceremony called the *responsuek* (responses). He is accompanied by an altar boy who carries a vessel filled with holy water. The priest stations himself at the head of the *sepulturie* and sprinkles the burning candles with holy water. He recites a prayer ("You who resurrected Lazarus resurrect this soul"), then an "Our Father." Finally, there is a prayer asking God to forgive the sins of the deceased. The priest then leaves the church, and the congregation follows. He stops in the plaza in front of the church and turns to face it. The male representative of the bereaved domestic group stands on the priest's right side. Then come the immediate male *familizhe* members and the more distant male kinsmen (*familizhekue*), followed by the neighbors, and, finally, the friends of the deceased. The arrangement is repeated by the women on the left side of the priest, with the *echekoandria* of the bereaved domestic group standing next to him. The priest then repeats the same *responsuek* recited on the *sepulturie*. With this the service is terminated.

Custom dictates that the male representative of the bereaved domestic group (normally the *echekojaun*) invite those who attended the *responsuek* to a snack in one of the local taverns. This might consist simply of sweet wine and cookies; however, it may be more elaborate—for example, a prepared hot dish of codfish and tomato sauce, bread, and wine. Informants note that the elaborate snack was more common in the past than at present.

Those who attend the *bederatziurrune* service on the first day are expected to attend all three days. Both the church services and the snack are repeated on each of the three mornings.

The Argia Ceremony

On the first Sunday after a death, the church holds a ceremony for the deceased called *argia*. *Argia* means "light" and refers to the

fact that all who give even minimal *artu-emon* at the burial service
are expected to place a *kandela* on the *sepulturie* of the deceased for
the duration of the service. Consequently, during the *argia* ceremony the *sepulturie* is covered with dozens of lighted candles.[17]

The *argia* ceremony initiates a year of formal mourning for the
members of the bereaved domestic group. The tremendous show of
kandelak during *argia* initiates a year-long obligation for the *echekoandria*. She is expected to burn *kandelak* on the *sepulturie* during
the High Mass on Sundays and holy days. Until the 1940s, during
the *argia* ceremony, the *echekoandria* placed a bread offering on the
sepulturie. This initiated a series of bread offerings made at all
High Masses during the year of mourning (for details see pages
54–55).

The practice of making a bread offering during the *argia* ceremony was not restricted exclusively to the bereaved domestic group.
All domestic groups in an *artu-emon* relationship with the bereaved
domestic group (that is, those providing *kandelak*) were expected
to make a bread offering consisting of a one-kilo loaf. The sacristan collected the offerings, which were used to defray partially
the salaries of the priests, sacristan, and *difunterie* (a female religious specialist in charge of caring for the *sepulturiek*).

The *argia* ceremony consists of a High Mass which is offered for
the soul of the deceased. Theoretically, all who attended the burial
service have an obligation to attend the *argia* ceremony. Once the
Mass is terminated, the officiant priest leaves the altar and goes to
the *sepulturie* of the deceased to sing *responsuek*. He approaches the
echekoandria, and she gives him a sum of money.[18] He then begins

[17] Formerly there was an *argia* ceremony on Sunday followed by *onrak* or
a funeral service on Monday. However, since 1950 the two have been combined into a single Sunday service. Informants note that the modern tempo of
living makes it impossible for persons to leave their work on weekdays to
attend.

[18] Until about 1952 the money offerings for *responsuek* were placed upon a
white sheet of cloth or *isharra* placed at the head of the *sepulturie*. For this
reason many people used to refer to the ceremony as *"isharra."* But the *isharra*
is no longer employed.

to intone *responsuek* for the soul of the deceased, the number being determined by the amount of the *echekoandria*'s offering. The format of the *responsuek* is the same as that described in the section on the *bederatziurrune* cycle, except that they are sung rather than recited. Presently (1967), just one *responsue* is sung regardless of the size of the offering. The priest then leaves the church, followed by the congregation. In the plaza he turns to face the church. The males gather on his right and the females to the left. The internal structuring of the groups is such that domestic group (*echekoak*) and family (*familizhe*) members are closest to the priest, then distant kinsmen, neighbors, and acquaintances. The priest then chants another *responsue,* and the congregation disbands. The members of the bereaved domestic group invite the participants to a snack in one of the local taverns.

That afternoon the weekly Rosary and Vespers ceremonies are offered for the deceased. Those who attended the morning's services are expected to attend as part of their *argia* obligation (although there are invariably fewer persons at the afternoon service). Before the Rosary begins, the priest says four *responsuek* on the *sepulturie* of the deceased. The *echekoandria* and close female kinsmen of the deceased activate the *sepulturie* and light the *kandelak*. These *responsuek* are recited rather than sung. After the Rosary and Vespers the congregation follows the priest out into the plaza. There the morning's spatial ordering of the congregation is repeated. Four more *responsuek* are recited, and the congregation disbands. Once again the bereaved domestic group hosts snacks in a local tavern.

At this point the domestic groups with a simple or minimal *artuemon* tie claim the *kandela* which they placed upon the *sepulturie* of the deceased. Those having a more intensive tie (such as a bond of kinship or common residence—the same *auzoa*) with the deceased leave their candle on the *sepulturie* site. During the formal year of mourning the *echekoandria* will continue to light the remaining *kandelak* until they are consumed. At that time she returns the candlesticks to the donors. A domestic group with a particularly

GOSHEN COLLEGE LIBRARY
GOSHEN, INDIANA

close tie to the deceased (for example, a sibling or the *auzurrikour-rena*) will replenish the candle as it is consumed; they do not re-move their candlestick until the termination of the year of mourn-ing (see appendix).

The Onrak *Ceremony*

Formerly (until about 1950) the funeral or *onrak* ceremony was held the day after the *argia* service. Those who attended the *argia* were expected to come. The *onrak* ceremony consisted of two Masses (an ordinary Low Mass at nine o'clock in the morning and a sung High Mass at ten). Close relatives and neighbors of the deceased attended both services; the members of domestic groups with a minimal *artu-emon* obligation attended only the ten o'clock service. After the second Mass *responsuek* were recited, both at the *sepulturie* and in the plaza.

It was during the *onrak* ceremony that the second *artu-emon* of-fering was collected. Those attending the services made both a money (*artu-emon*) donation and a bread offering. The bread offerings were placed on the *sepulturie* of the household of the deceased. The nature of the bread offering differed according to the sum of the *artu-emon* donation. Those domestic groups which gave the minimal 1.25 *peseta misa rezada* gave an inferior loaf known as the *olata*.[19] The *olata* loaf is small, unleavened, disc-shaped, and prac-tically inedible. However, if the donor gave the 1.65 *peseta misa can-tada* he would also give an *opille,* a small loaf of edible leavened bread.

It was after the *onrak* service that the funerary banquet was served. Presently (1967), the *argia* and *onrak* services are both held on Sunday, and if there is a banquet, it takes place between the morning Masses and afternoon Vespers.

---

[19] The Basque term *olata* comes from the Latin *oblata,* meaning "offering" (Azkue 1959:203).

The Funeral Banquet

Presently there is a tendency to give only one banquet. It may be held either on the day of the burial service or on *argia* Sunday. Attendance at the banquet(s) is more restricted than was formerly the case. Today only relatives who have come from other areas, close relatives from Murélaga, and the *anderuek* are asked to participate. The banquet may be held in the home of the deceased or in a local tavern.

Before sitting down to the meal, the assembly prays in unison for the soul of the deceased. One of the relatives eulogizes the deceased by emphasizing the good qualities of his personality. When this obligation is completed, the affair takes on a different aspect. The mood is gay and may even become quite ribald. At a minimum, conversation is lively and there is joking and laughter. This may be the first family gathering in several years, and everyone is interested in catching up on family news.

The present-day version of the funerary banquet fails to reflect the wealth of sociological detail that formerly characterized the affair. Until the Spanish Civil War there were as many as three banquets occasioned by a single death. The first was held on the day of burial and was a simple affair for the immediate relatives, *anderuek,* and the *ogidune* and *estipendiyue*. On the day of the *argia* ceremony, visiting relatives attended a second banquet. The third or funerary banquet took place after the *onrak* ceremony, and it differed sharply from the first two.

This third banquet was more elaborate and included all those who had an *artu-emon* relationship with the deceased. To sponsor this meal represented a tremendous economic hardship. Informants readily remember how many domestic groups sold a large portion of their livestock or borrowed heavily in order to meet this obligation. This fact may be appreciated by examining the menu of an *onrak* banquet held in 1928 at the death of Martin Anitua. The account was taken from the books of the tavern owner who catered the dinner. The banquet was attended by seventy-four persons, and the following items were expended:

40 pounds of stew meat	45 liters of wine
13 pounds of veal chops	17 two-kilo loaves of bread
20 pounds of tripe	11 sausages
2 pounds of bacon	8 cans of peppers
4 pounds of garbanzo beans	1 box of cookies
6 pounds of navy beans	18 *pesetas* worth of coffee liquors

In addition, the sponsoring domestic group was charged for wood and coal, broken glassware, spices, and the salaries of the cook and table help. The total cost was 254.45 *pesetas*. This amount was considerably more than the domestic group spent in the stores during an entire year!!

The following account of a funerary banquet for all having *artu-emon* relations was given by an informant who once owned a tavern and prepared many funerary banquets:

Following the *onrak* Mass the *echekoak* of the deceased was faced with a decision. They had to decide whether or not to accept *artu-emon* Masses. This was a second *artu-emon* donation, apart from the first which normally took place on the day of the burial. If they accepted, they would instruct the sacristan to remain by the church door to collect offerings. Almost everyone accepted *artu-emon*. Failure to do so reflected upon the household's economic status. It was an admission that one couldn't or wouldn't afford the banquet. If the sacristan was not instructed to collect *artu-emon* Masses, the bereaved *echekoak* need only provide all who assisted at *onrak* with a *merienda* or snack in one of the taverns. The snack consisted of codfish, bread, and wine.

However, once the *echekoak* accepted the *artu-emon* Masses, as happened in a majority of cases, they had to provide a banquet. The banquet was held in one of the taverns. The tavern provided two separate rooms and cooked two different menus. All those who gave a less expensive *misa rezada* gathered in one dining room away from those who donated the expensive *misa cantada*. The latter were served a sumptuous meal consisting of soup, kidney beans, garbanzo beans, tripes, roasted meat, a steak, a cup of coffee, a glass of cognac, a cigar, and all the wine they could drink. The former received only soup, kidney beans, garbanzo beans, tripes, and roasted meat. They were not given steak, coffee, cognac, or a cigar. Furthermore, they were only given one bottle of wine among eight guests. They paid for any additional wine they might consume.

Such meals were often the ruination of the household. They cost a great deal more than a wedding banquet. They often had the further disadvantage of degenerating into drunken revelry. At such occasions many famous wagers were made and tests of strength and skill scheduled.

Some individuals were notorious opportunists with respect to *artu-emon*. They would give the relatively inexpensive donation so as to be able to participate in the meal. In this manner they would taste wine and eat meat, which were luxuries they seldom allowed themselves at home. They would go from table to table scraping up the bread crumbs and emptying the remains of the wine bottles. They would then send this to the kitchen with orders that a wine soup be prepared. In the early hours of the next morning, the tavern keeper would have to dispatch them from the premises. For this reason many *echekoak* began to refuse the second *artu-emon* offering, and it fell into disuse.

Today many informants approve of the progressive decline of the funerary banquet custom. Some point to the inordinate expense; others note that drunkenness and revelry are out of place at what should be a solemn occasion.

Lutue *or Mourning Cycle*

The *argia* ceremony initiates the mourning cycle. The mourning obligation is in effect for at least one year. Mourning restrictions apply only to members of the bereaved domestic group and do not normally include friends, neighbors, or relatives.[20]

Mourning practices may be divided into those which are ritualistic, performed in public, and publicly sanctioned, and those which are personal, affect only the mourners, and are performed largely

---

[20] However, it is possible for married siblings and offspring of the deceased to observe personal mourning practices as an expression of their personal loss of a *familizhe* member.

within the context of the domestic group. Examples of the former are those acts performed by members of the household in the church with respect to the *sepulturie* site and the *luto banķue* or mourning bench in the men's section of the church. Examples of the latter are such observances as dressing in black and refraining from participation in recreational activities.

Ritualistic Mourning Practices

Ritualistic mourning practices are centered upon the church and may only be understood in terms of the physical layout of the church floor (see Figure 2).[21] The church floor is divided by the center aisle into two broad divisions, each of which is further subdivided into a men's section and a women's section. The men's section is that closer to the altar. It contains several rows of benches where all of the men in the village sit when they are attending any religious service. The first row in the men's section is designated by the term *luto banķue* or "mourning bench." The women's section, located immediately behind the men's, occupies a much larger area of the church floor. It is made up of the previously mentioned *sepulturiek*, each of which corresponds to one of the households of the village [22] (see appendix).

The structuring of the men's and women's sections of the church does not correspond to the physical dispersion on the landscape of the *baserriak*. That is, there is no underlying structuring of the *sepulturiek* according to broad divisions such as neighborhoods or by class distinctions such as owners versus renters. The system seems to have grown up organically, with the important factor being inclusion within the total structure rather than within a substructure. With the exception of the *luto banķue,* the men's section is totally undiffer-

---

[21] This figure details the church floor as it was up to the year 1957. At that time the *sepulturiek* were removed and benches put in their place.

[22] Not all the households in the village possess a *sepulturie,* although the majority are represented. The exceptions will be treated at a later point in the description.

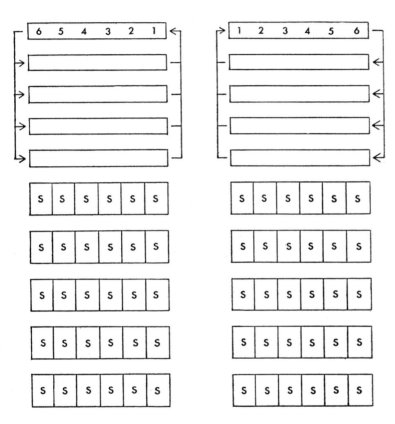

Figure 2

entiated. However, in terms of seating order there is a broad correlation between the men's and the women's sections, for the men
from a given domestic group sit on that side of the center aisle where
their household has its *sepulturie*.

We may now consider the *sepulturie* and *luto banƙue* in greater detail. The *sepulturie* is a symbolic burial plot on the church floor, but its burial role was not always symbolic. At least as early as the thirteenth century (Echegaray 1925:192) and until the end of the eighteenth century, the dead were buried directly beneath the church floor on their household's *sepulturie* site (Caro Baroja 1958:329). This former practice is not unknown to the people who presently activate the symbolic sepultures.

The identification of the *sepulturie* with a given household (*echea*) rather than with a particular *familizhe* or *echehoaƙ* is complete. The *sepulturie* is not the property of the owners or residents of the *baserria* at a particular time; rather it pertains to the territorial unit. If a *baserria* is sold or if a new domestic group, acting in the capacity of renter, replaces a former renter domestic group, the new resident group assumes full control over the *baserria sepulturie*. At the same time, the departing domestic group relinquishes all rights to the *sepulturie* that it formerly activated. The following example illustrates the degree to which the *baserria* dwelling, the landholdings, and the *sepulturie* are conceived as an immutable triad:

About ten years ago there was a dispute in the village over the ownership of a *sepulturie*. The problem arose when *baserria* X was left in the hands of a senile old man who lived alone. Since he was incapacitated, he rented the lands to *baserria* Y. He had the obligation to send a female representative to the household *sepulturie* because he was in mourning for his recently deceased wife. He had no relatives in the village, so he agreed to pay the *echeƙoandria* from *baserria* Y to activate his *sepulturie*. Shortly thereafter, he was forced to enter a home for the aged. He sold the lands to *baserria* Y. However, the domestic group in *baserria* Y did not wish to buy the dwelling as well. The dwelling was sold to *baserria* Z. This set the stage for a dispute between the domestic groups in Y and Z.

The *echeƙoandria* of Y decided that she liked the *sepulturie* of X better than her own. It seems that it had a better view of the altar. She pressured the old man to sell her the *sepulturie* on the grounds that she had purchased the lands and was also tending the site as his representative.

However, the *echekoandria* of Z pressed her claim to the *sepulturie* on the grounds that she had purchased the dwelling. The issue was of particular interest to her since she was a renter and had to share a single *sepulturie* with another domestic group which rented from the same landlord.

The issue became quite heated when both domestic groups threatened formal litigation. Public opinion was on the side of the woman from Z on the grounds that the *sepulturie* pertains more to a dwelling than to the lands. However, the issue was not clear, since the act of partitioning the lands and dwelling through separate sales rarely occurs and was itself morally reprehensible. Both women tried to enlist the parish priest on their side but he was determined to remain out of the conflict. The issue was up in the air for a couple of years and was resolved only by the unrelated decision of the priest to do away with all *sepulturiek* in favor of benches.

The *sepulturie* is the place where the women actually resident on the corresponding *baserria* are to sit while attending any religious service.[23] It is felt that every Sunday during the High Mass at least one female domestic group representative, preferably the *echeko-andria,* should activate the *sepulturie*. The representative(s) places a single lighted *kandela* on the site. Formerly, she made a standard weekly bread offering of one *olata* as well. Small girls collected the *olatak* during the Offertory of the Mass. The girls then went forward to meet the priest at the foot of the altar where they would leave the bread offerings in a basket and kiss the priest's stole. The *olatak* were worthless as food, so the following Sunday they were redistributed to the *sepulturiek* by the *difunterie*.

The *difunterie* was usually an elderly woman with little means of support. In addition to distributing the *olatak,* her duties included cleaning the *sepulturiek,* and preparing and placing on them the bread offerings and *kandelak* of domestic groups in mourning. For her services she received a yearly payment of twenty-five kilos of wheat from each of the households owning a *sepulturie*. Out of this

[23] Attendance is not restricted solely to the *echekoandria* and the adult female members, it includes junior female members of the domestic group as well.

she prepared the normal bread offerings, retaining the remainder as her compensation.[24]

In addition to a payment in wheat to the *difunterie,* the domestic group had a further economic obligation with respect to the sepulture in the form of a yearly tithe to the church, which was construed as rental for its spot on the church floor. This payment consisted of six kilos of wheat for domestic groups owning their *baserria* and three kilos of wheat for renter domestic groups.

The period of formal mourning for the bereaved domestic group lasts for one year. When a domestic group is in mourning, the duties of its female membership with respect to the *sepulturie* are prescribed and intensified by weight of tradition. We have seen that the domestic group of the deceased places four *kandelak* on the table supporting the coffin during the church burial service. These *kandelak* then revert to the household *sepulturie* to be utilized throughout the year of mourning. In addition, those domestic groups having a close tie, either by blood or by common residence (*auzoa*), are also likely to leave one *kandela* on the *sepulturie* of the deceased. During the year of formal mourning, the female members of the domestic group (preferably the *echekoandria*) have the obligation of attending Sunday High Mass and the High Masses on all religious holy days in order to activate the *sepulturie* by lighting the *kandelak.*

The practice of burning candles on the *sepulturie* (presently on a substitute site) continues to this day. Until the 1940s, the bereaved domestic group had an obligation to make bread offerings throughout the year of mourning (on the occasions when the *sepulturie* was

---

[24] Presently there are no bread offerings and no *sepulturiek* sites to be cleaned. The remaining duty of the *difunterie,* caring for the *kandelak,* is done by the sacristan's wife. The majority of domestic groups in the village leave their *kandelak* with the sacristan's wife and inform her when they wish her to place one of them on the substitute *sepulturie* site of a recently deceased person (in compliance with their *artu-emon* obligation). Most domestic groups give her a small sum of money for performing this service.

activated).[25] The *difunterie* arranged to have the loaves prepared in a local bakery, and she placed the bread offering in a basket on the *sepulturie*. The nature of the bereaved domestic group's obligation to make a bread offering varied according to the type of burial service offered for the deceased:

1. If the bereaved domestic group chose a burial service of *primera* or first class, they would make a weekly offering of five pounds of leavened bread.

2. If the bereaved domestic group chose a service of *segunda,* their bread obligation dropped to three pounds per week.

3. If the bereaved domestic group chose a service of *tercera,* they assumed no bread obligation beyond the one kilo offered during the burial ceremony (see appendix).

The bereaved domestic group also made bread offerings on religious festivals not falling on a Sunday. At this time, the standard offering was one *olata.*

The *sepulturie* is central to the formal mourning cycle. It is a stage upon which the relationship between the deceased and his domestic group is dramatized. The deceased occupies the stage during the first year after his death. But with the termination of the formal period of mourning, he enters the realm of all the dead who have ever been memorialized on the particular *sepulturie.* The single *kandela* and the token *olata* offerings, which are repeated down through time, remain as the last tenuous ties between the living members of the domestic group and the deceased members of the territorial unit (*baserria*) taken as a category. This relationship is activated, preserved, and symbolized by the *echekoandria* when she assists weekly at religious services. In this capacity, every *echekoandria* is the priestess of a household (*echea*) religious cult.

[25] The *artu-emon* bread donation (as well as the subsequent bread offerings throughout the year of mourning) terminated with the Spanish Civil War. According to informants, bread rationing during and after the Civil War has been instrumental in halting the practice. A further contributing factor is the declining emphasis locally on wheat production over the last twenty-five years.

The *luto banƙue* lacks the territorial expression of the *sepulturie*. It singles out a category of individuals (*echeƙojaunaƙ* from bereaved domestic groups) and segregates them from the larger body of males. The connection between the domestic group representative and the *luto banƙue* is temporary, and it ends with completion of the formal year of mourning.

The men enter the *luto banƙue* from the center aisle and leave it by the side aisles. That is, when an individual dies, a male representative from his domestic group occupies the position in the *luto banƙue* that is right next to the center aisle. As there are subsequent deaths and new representatives arrive to take their places, the former occupant of the aisle seat moves over to make room. In this manner, during the course of the year of mourning, the representative moves in stages from the center aisle to the side aisle (that is, from seat number 1 to seat number 6 in Figure 2). The *ogistie* ceremony (see pages 59–60) terminates the year of formal mourning, and the male representative leaves the *luto banƙue* to rejoin the congregation of men. A spatial relationship exists between the *luto banƙue* and the *sepulturieƙ*: the representative of the bereaved domestic group enters the *luto banƙue* which is on the same side of the center aisle as his domestic group's *sepulturie*.

The male representative takes his place in the *luto banƙue* only during Sunday High Mass or High Mass on religious holy days (that is, during the Masses at which a female member of his domestic group activates the sepulture). He first attends the *luto banƙue* during the *argia* ceremony, and he abandons it upon the completion of the *ogistie* ceremony. Formerly, all males attending the *luto banƙue* were draped from head to toe in a black funeral cape.[26]

The duties of the male representative to the *luto banƙue* are not restricted to simple attendance at religious services. On occasion they

[26] The acquisition of this cape was one of the first events in the life of a newly married man. The cape stressed that the male representative to the *luto banƙue* should be the *echeƙojaun*. Such funeral capes were also worn by all married males representing their domestic groups at a burial, *argia,* or *ogistie* ceremony. The use of the capes declined after the Spanish Civil War.

function as a group. Whenever the Blessed Sacrament is exposed (on the third Sunday of every month and on religious festivals such as Corpus Christi, the Immaculate Conception, the Ascension of Christ into Heaven), four representatives of the *luto banḵue* (the two closest to the center aisle on either side and, therefore, the representatives of the most recently deceased members of the community) leave their places and go forward to the foot of the altar. The sacristan gives each an *acha* or large candle. These men maintain a vigil until the Blessed Sacrament is retired. Each Sunday just before the High Mass there is a procession around the interior of the church. The priests lead the procession, and they are followed by the men from the *luto banḵue*. In addition, the members of the *luto banḵue* play a special role during the church processions in which the Blessed Sacrament is taken from the church and carried through the streets (for example, Immaculate Conception, Corpus Christi, and Holy Thursday). Regardless of the additional structuring of the procession, the representatives of the four most recently deceased villagers carry *achaḵ* and walk immediately before the canopy which protects the priest bearing the Blessed Sacrament, and the remaining members of the *luto banḵue* follow directly behind.

Thus, there are two immediate consequences of the structuring of the *luto banḵue*. It segregates the male representatives of the recently deceased from the wider male congregation, and it places them into close physical proximity to the sacred symbols of religion.

Personal Mourning Practices

Personal mourning practices include the wearing of black clothing and withdrawal from normal social activities. The use of black clothing as a personal sign of mourning is by no means restricted to the Basques.[27] Here, as in many other areas, black is the symbolic color of death. Personal mourning practices are normally observed only by members of the bereaved domestic group. The degree to

[27] Men now tend to substitute a black ribbon or button attached to their everyday clothing. Women still observe full dress restrictions.

which an individual observes dress restrictions and withdraws from social intercourse varies according to his position within the domestic group structure. It is also conditioned by the position that the deceased occupied in the domestic group structure. We shall return to this point in Chapter 3.

Withdrawal from social intercourse during mourning means that the mourner will not participate in activities that might be deemed recreational or frivolous. The *echekoandria* is seen in public as little as possible, the *echekojaun* decreases or abolishes his visits to the local taverns, and the junior members of the household refrain from attending fiestas and dances. The bereaved domestic group will not host a banquet on the feast day of their neighborhood's patron saint, nor will it normally sponsor a wedding. In the rare event that a wedding is held during the mourning period, the festivities are kept to a minimum.

The bereaved domestic group is also at liberty to convert its formal mourning practices in the church into a personal expression of grief. After the conclusion of the year of formal mourning, the *echekoandria* can continue to make the bread offering and to light three or four *kandelak* when activating the *sepulturie* during Sunday High Mass as an expression of personal grief. During the year of formal mourning these practices meet the social demands of her position, but after that time she is acting alone, or as a representative of the attitudes of the members of her domestic group. Her neighbors and relatives do not accompany her beyond the *ogistie*. Thus, the only *kandelak* are those which she herself provides. If she is mourning the death of her husband, her self-imposed expression of grief may last indefinitely.

Often if the *echekoandria* chooses to extend her activation of the *sepulturie,* she does so in an effort to make her mourning period in the church coincide with the usual duration of personal mourning. It is felt that members of the bereaved domestic group should observe a period of intense personal mourning, lasting about eighteen months, followed by a six month period of half mourning. For the initial mourning period, dress restrictions and social withdrawal are observed fully. The period of half mourning, when these restrictions are relaxed, constitutes a transitional state between bereavement and the resumption of normal social activities.

The Ogistie *Ceremony*

The formal period of mourning begins with a service—the *argia*—attended by representatives of all domestic groups that have *artu-emon* with the bereaved domestic group. It terminates with a similar ceremony. On the first anniversary of the *argia* service, the bereaved domestic group sponsors a second ceremony (the *ogistie*) which marks the termination of the formal mourning obligation. The parish priest announces an impending *ogistie* during his sermons on the Sunday preceding the affair. The domestic group advises relatives who are residing in other areas.

The Basque term *ogistie* means "giving up the bread" (from *ogia* "bread" and *uste* "to give up"). The terminology refers to the fact that the domestic group's obligation to make a weekly bread donation to the church (one facet of the formal mourning practices) is terminated (see appendix).

The *ogistie* ceremony is an exact replication of the *argia*. All who were present at the *argia* ceremony are expected to attend. The service consists of a High Mass offered for the soul of the deceased. This is followed by a series of *responsuek* on the *sepulturie*. Finally, the faithful go out into the plaza to form a semicircle and pray *responsuek* for the soul of the deceased. When the service is over, the bereaved domestic group may invite those in attendance to a round of refreshments in one of the local taverns.

The *artu-emon* relationship is activated at the *ogistie* with those attending making a donation (usually five *pesetas*) for Masses to be said on behalf of the deceased. Those having *artu-emon* will also place one of their *kandelak* on the *sepulturie* for the duration of the service. Formerly, they would also make the same one-kilo bread offering that characterized their participation in the *argia* ceremony.

Those who perceive a special tie with the deceased (for example, the *auzurrikourrena* or a sibling) make an *arimen onrak* donation. This means that for a number of days after the *ogistie* service the priests recite *nocturnos* on the site of the *sepulturie* of the deceased.

We can say, therefore, that the *argia* and *ogistie* ceremonies are identical, both in form and content. The only significant difference is that one signals the beginning of a mourning obligation while the other signals its termination. With the completion of the *ogistie* service the public expression of concern at a loss in the membership is concluded.

ANNIVERSARIES, NOVENAS, AND

MASSES FOR THE DEAD

There are several religious *cofradías* or voluntary associations in the village. We have already considered the roles of the Luises and the Hijas de María in the description of the burial procession. If the deceased were a member of either of these groups, or of one of the other religious *cofradías* (see Chapter 6), the membership sponsors a Mass on his (or her) behalf. The Mass normally takes place within a week or two after the *argia* ceremony. The service is attended by the bereaved domestic group, representatives from each of the domestic groups in the *auzoa* of the deceased, and close relatives who are residing locally. However, the membership of the sponsoring voluntary association must also attend. The affair is really an activity of the voluntary association and is not a part of the mourning cycle of the bereaved domestic group.

Once the formal year-long period of mourning is terminated, there are no prescribed practices occasioned by the death of an individual. However, it is quite common to celebrate memorial or anniversary Masses (*memorizhek*) for a number of years after a death. The decision to offer *memorizhek* originates in the bereaved domestic group. The priests are informed and a date is set; the impending celebration is announced from the pulpit beforehand. On the day of the service the *echekoandria* places her *kandelak* on the household *sepulturie.* In addition, close relatives (usually only those residing in the village) and a few neighbors who perceive a special obligation, such as the *auzurrikourrena,* will also place a *kandela* on the *sepulturie* of the deceased. Those domestic groups donating a *kandela* for the occasion send a member to attend the service. The Mass is preceded by a *nocturno* recited on the *sepulturie.* Once the Mass is over, the priest goes to the *sepulturie* to recite *responsuek* (the number varying according to the amount of money allotted by the *echekoandria* for this purpose).

In form, the *memorizhe* may be considered a less elaborate version of the *argia* and *ogistie* ceremonies. All are celebrated for a specific deceased individual. The *memorizhe* ceremony is reserved for individuals who were formerly *echekojaunak* or *echekoandriak* (either active or retired at the time of death). It is highly unlikely that deceased unmarried siblings or deceased children would be so honored.

The frequency with which *memorizhek* are offered varies with the individual domestic group. Anniversary Masses may be held annually for four or five years and then dropped. However, if one spouse dies at a relatively young age, the other may offer yearly *memorizhek* until his or her own death. In any event, with the passing years, participation on the part of relatives and neighbors tends to decline. Ultimately, it becomes solely a domestic group affair, and finally it may terminate altogether.

Another, less common, practice occasioned by the death of a particular individual is that of sponsoring a novena of Masses on behalf of the deceased. The local parish priest estimates that each year he receives approximately twenty-five such requests. The practice consists of sponsoring a Mass for the soul of the deceased on nine consecutive days. The *echekoandria* and other domestic group members attend the services and activate the *sepulturie,* usually only with their own *kandelak.* Some households sponsor a novena memorial once annually for several years. There is no obvious or prescribed point at which the practice is abandoned.

The novena costs 550 *pesetas,* and the Masses must be said in

Murélaga. Likely donors of novenas include the bereaved domestic group and *familizhe* members (particularly married siblings or off-spring) who are residing elsewhere. The following are examples:

The husband of M. was killed in an accident while working as a logger. This took place in 1959. Although the widow is relatively impoverished, she sponsors an annual novena for her deceased spouse. She times the novena offering to coincide with the anniversary date of her husband's death.

When J.'s mother died, J. informed her sister's daughter (who was residing in Switzerland). The latter sent a large donation in Swiss francs with the stipulation that it be used for Masses on behalf of the deceased. J. ordered a novena.

The family C. moved to Australia several years ago. Once annually, they send enough Australian pounds to the local priest to have a novena of Masses said for their "obligations."

There is a shortened version of the novena which consists of Masses said on three consecutive days for the intention of the donor. The term in Basque for this practice is *iru urrune*, from *iru*, meaning "three," and *urrune*, which is a transformation of the word *urrena*, meaning both "proximity" and "consecution." The most common reason for sponsoring a triad of Masses (at a cost of 150 *pesetas*) is to benefit a recently departed soul. The sponsor is usually the bereaved domestic group of a *familizhe* member. However, the *iru urrune* is also offered for departed souls in general. Such an offering is normally made when the donor is undergoing a crisis or is faced with a major decision. The avowed intention is to curry the favor of the deceased in heaven. This point will be re-examined in the section on eschatology.

Finally, there is a belief on the part of the villagers that thirty Masses said on successive days is a sure way of freeing a soul from purgatory. These Masses are referred to as *misas gregorianas*. The local priest assures me that the practice is known in other parts of the Catholic world. The *misas gregorianas* are very costly (fifteen hundred *pesetas* for the series). This seems to be the main reason that they are not offered at the majority of deaths.

Activation of the *sepulturie* is not solely with reference to the memory of a particular deceased individual. The domestic group may decide to have a Mass said for its "obligations." In such instances the *echekoandria* attends the service and activates the *sepulturie* by lighting *kandelak*. However, at this point she is participating in a memorial service for all of the deceased of a related series of domestic groups reckoned lineally (or conceivably ambilineally) from the present heir of the *baserria*.

Even if the specific intention is mundane, the *echekoandria* never forgets her obligations to the deceased who formerly inhabited her *baserria*. While she may offer a Mass for the safe passage of her son to the New World or for the recovery of a sick cow, she still activates the *sepulturie,* and the service terminates with *responsuek* on the site. They are said for all of the deceased who have ever occupied the *baserria*.

This last point is of particular importance. It indicates that on some occasions the *echekoandria* may be representing deceased members of the community who are not related through descent to either her spouse or herself. We may therefore distinguish three broad categories of Mass offerings—Masses given by individuals or domestic groups for the soul of a particular individual; Masses given by individuals and domestic groups for their "obligations" (that is, ancestors lineally or ambilineally related to the present household heir); and Masses given for all of the deceased who ever held jural rights in the *baserria* territorial unit.

The majority of Mass offerings require that the donor attend the service. The impending affair is announced from the pulpit beforehand, and the actual Mass must be said in Murélaga. Examples are those Masses given by individuals having intensive *artu-emon* relationships with a deceased individual, anniversary Masses offered by the bereaved domestic group, and novena Masses. Masses offered as minimal *artu-emon* donations do not fall under this rubric. It is common to collect thirty or forty Masses at each of the three occasions (the burial service, the *argia* ceremony, and the *ogistie* service) when minimal *artu-emon* is given, and it would be impossible for the priests to say them all in the village.

We have noted several fashions in which death and death-related activities are announced to interested parties. Immediately after the death a representative from the *auzurrikourrena* informs the village authorities and contacts kinsmen of the deceased. The sacristan rings the church bells to announce a death to the village, while the *mayordomo* follows suit by tolling the bell of the *auzoa* chapel. The impending *argia, onrak, ogistie* and *memorizhe* services are announced in advance by the priests at Sunday Mass. However, there are two other ways in which news of death and death-related activities is disseminated.

The first means is the *recordatorio*. A *recordatorio* (reminder) is a small printed card announcing the date and place of an individual's death. The *recordatorio* may also carry a photograph of the deceased, the names of his *familizhe* members, and a prayer. The bereaved domestic group orders the *recordatorios* from a commercial printer in Guernica or Bilbao. They normally receive between thirty and fifty copies, which they give to close friends, kinsmen and neighbors. Generally, the recipients place *recordatorios* in their missals where they are reminders to pray for the deceased individual during religious services.

Most *recordatorios* are selected from printers' catalogues and hence follow a set format. However, occasionally the bereaved request special messages. For example, one *recordatorio,* prepared for an individual from Murélaga who died in 1966, contains a verse by the Basque poet Orixe:

Jaio nintzan iltzeko
Aldi-oro noa iltzen
Ildakoan erabat
Asiko naiz bizitzen.

[I was born to die
Every moment I die a little
It is once I have died
that I will begin to live.] [28]

The second fashion of announcing a death is by means of public communications such as the radio and newspapers. Until 1965 there was a radio station (Radio Arrate) with programing in Basque. The station carried local news from many rural communities of Vizcaya, including Murélaga. Deaths in Murélaga were always announced over Radio Arrate.

Until 1965 the parish priest of Murélaga and a few nearby communities published a monthly newspaper which was sent to sons of the villagers who were working in the United States, Latin America, and Australia. The newspaper carried the announcement of all local deaths.

Finally, throughout the Basque country, city newspapers sell space for large, elaborate death notices. These are like *recordatorios,* but they usually give the time and place of an upcoming burial service or anniversary Mass as well. The number and elaboration of such notices is startling. For example, a page in the Bilbao newspaper *Gaceta del Norte* for July 24, 1968, contained seven burial service notices, two notices of thanks to those who attended funerary proceedings, two notices of anniversary Masses to commemorate the first anniversary of a death, and two notices of anniversary Masses commemorating the fourth anniversary of a death! While, in fact, this is mainly an urban custom, it should be mentioned, since from

[28] A revealing verse with respect to the matter-of-fact attitude toward death.

time to time a bereaved domestic group from Murélaga will insert such a notice in one of the Bilbao papers.

Up to this point we have considered funerary ritual which takes place with reference to the death of a specific person. The date of the death determines when the proceedings begin and end. However, there are several occasions during the year when all the deceased of the village are remembered by the living. These occasions are determined by the yearly calendar of religious events. A clear example is participation of the male representatives of the *luto bankue* in the processions held on major Catholic feast days, such as Corpus Christi and the Day of the Immaculate Conception. The *rogativas* or "petitions" ceremony held in the spring is another religious event in which the deceased of the village are remembered. This ceremony is widespread throughout the Catholic world, but in Murélaga it takes on a special significance.

The *rogativas* take place within a few weeks after Easter. They are held to petition God for a successful harvest and for protection against crop-destroying droughts and insect plagues. There is no set date for the ceremonies, since Easter Sunday varies from year to year. Also, the actual date of a particular *rogativas* ceremony is at the discretion of the parish priest. In general, the ceremonies are held near the end of April or the beginning of May. They should be held after the new crop has sprouted, but before it begins to develop. Since the *auzoak* are widely scattered, it is necessary to have a series of *rogativas* ceremonies. There is normally a few days' interlude between each.

On the day of a given *rogativas* the priest, the sacristan, two altar boys, a few very devout persons from the village, and *a representative from every domestic group in the village which has experienced a death since the previous year's rogativas* gather in the church and pray the Rosary. This takes place early in the morning. The assembled persons then leave the church in procession and start in the direction of the *auzoa* chosen for the day's ceremony. The membership recites the Rosary as it moves along the *andabidea* that connects the host *auzoa* with the nucleus.

When the procession reaches its destination, at least one representative of each *echekoak* in the host *auzoa* joins the group. Most domestic groups send several members, and most commonly both the *echekojaun* and *echekoandria* attend.

The *mayordomo*'s wife and several female volunteers from the *auzoa* have prepared the chapel on the previous day. The altar is arranged so that Mass may be celebrated. The priest's vestments and the altar linens are laundered and laid out. As the procession approaches the chapel, the *mayordomo* rings the bell to signal its arrival. All then enter the chapel to hear Mass.

During the Mass the priest blesses a large bowl of salt that has been placed on the altar by the *mayordomo*'s wife. This salt is distributed to everyone present during the Offertory of the Mass. The altar boy takes the salt to the foot of the altar, and the people come forward, each carrying a large piece of paper to receive his portion of several handfuls of salt. At the same time he deposits a small money offering into a sack carried by the other altar boy; these offerings revert to the treasury of the chapel. The faithful also bring to the service a number of simple wooden crucifixes, made by crossing two pieces of wood. These are blessed by the priest. Later the salt is mixed with holy water and sprinkled on each of the fields pertaining to the household, and one of the crosses is pushed into the ground at the edge of each field. Both the salt and crosses are felt to ensure a bountiful harvest.

Every domestic group experiencing a death in the course of the year must send a representative to all of the *rogativas*. At each *rogativas* the participants go forward with the members of the host *auzoa* to leave an offering and receive salt. Later the salt collected from all of the *rogativas* is mixed together and applied to the fields pertaining to the households of bereaved domestic groups. Once the

Mass is completed in the *auzoa* chapel, the priest reads a list of all those who have died in the village since the last *rogativas* ceremony.

Throughout the Basque country, Saint John's Day (June 24), or the day after, is another occasion when the living may honor the dead, although this is not the custom in Murélaga. Rather, on the second Saint John's Day (August 29), there is a procession to one of the chapels in the village (Murla) which has John as its patron saint. Anyone is free to join this procession, and attendance is generally good. In the chapel the priest offers a Mass of the dead for all of the persons who have ever lived and died in Murélaga.

The most important annual commemorative events for the deceased (as a category) of the village take place on All Saints' Day (November 1), All Souls' Day (November 2), and the following Sunday. All Saints' Day and All Souls' Day are celebrated throughout the Catholic world, but rarely with the intensity characteristic of the practices in Murélaga.

On the morning of All Saints' Day (Basque term *Domuru Santuru*) there is a High Mass. Every domestic group in the village activates its household *sepulturie* as if it were in mourning, placing a black mourning cloth and three or four *kandelak* on the site (formerly, each domestic group made a one-kilo bread offering). The riot of light from the hundreds of flickering candles is truly an impressive sight.

After the High Mass there is a seemingly interminable series of *responsuek* as the priests move from one *sepulturie* to another. In addition most domestic groups make offerings of *arimen onrak,* and regular Mass offerings (thirty-five *pesetas*) for their "obligations." [29]

---

[29] Informants differ in their interpretation of the "obligations" which are implied. Many state that the offerings are intended for the ancestors of the active spouse who is residing in his (or her) natal household (that is, for the lineally related ancestors of the present heir). Others take a wider view and state that the offerings are for all the dead who have ever held jural rights in the *sepulturie.* That is, for all those who retained at the time of their death the right to have their funerary rituals performed at the *sepulturie* in question. They cite the fact that the dead used to be buried beneath the church floor

Once the *responsuek* are finished, the congregation forms into a procession and goes to the cemetery. Until a few years ago the procession was led by a standard bearer, who carried the standard of the Cofradía de Animas (Confraternity of Souls), a white standard depicting Saint Michael crushing the head of a serpent. The standard bearer was flanked by two men carrying *achak*.[30] The congregation enters the cemetery and prays for the souls of all who were ever buried there. It then disbands, and members of recently bereaved domestic groups place chrysanthemums on the grave site.[31]

On the second day of November, All Souls' Day (Basque term *Arimen Egune*), there is again a High Mass. The *sepulturiek* are activated, *responsuek* said, and the proceedings in the cemetery repeated. However, there is one salient difference. On this occasion those spouses who are residing affinally take a *kandela* from their present household of residence and place it on the *sepulturie* of their natal household. They then make *arimen onrak*, or regular Mass offerings, and *responsuek* offerings for their ancestral "obligations."

On the Sunday after All Souls' Day the Cofradía de Animas holds a special *onrak* (High Mass) service for its deceased members. All of the living members of the *cofradía* are expected to attend. In the past the function was repeated on Monday. However, this second service was abandoned. In the words of one informant, it was just "too much of a burden."

The occasion of the *cofradía onrak* service is used by former vil-

---

on the very site where persons now activate *sepulturiek*. Under this interpretation "obligations" of the living may include persons who are not blood ancestors.

[30] Elderly informants recall that formerly the standard of the Cofradía de Animas figured into the burial procession as well. Furthermore, when a death took place in the village nucleus, the standard bearer accompanied the priests to the house of the deceased to receive the corpse.

[31] The use of flowers to adorn grave sites is quite recent in Murélaga. However, it has gained widespread acceptance. Most domestic groups in the village now reserve a small corner of the household garden for chrysanthemums. The only time they are employed is during the All Saints' Day and All Souls' Day proceedings.

lagers who are residing in the Basque country (usually in nearby villages but often as far away as Bilbao) to return to their natal *sepulturiek*. They activate the *sepulturie,* make *arimen onrak* or regular Mass offerings, and make *responsuek* offerings for their ancestral "obligations."

On All Saints' Day, All Souls' Day, and the following Sunday an afternoon Vespers service is offered in the church on behalf of all the deceased (recent and remote) of Murélaga.

The preceding practices occasion a veritable deluge of Mass offerings. The parish priest estimates that he collects over thirty-five thousand *pesetas* each year. Calculated at a rate of thirty-five *pesetas* per Mass, this means that the priests receive over one thousand Mass offerings. It would be impossible to say them in Murélaga, so all but the *arimen onrak* are contracted out to secular priests and religious orders elsewhere in the Basque country and Spain.

A final remembrance of the deceased takes place in each domestic group during its Christmas celebrations. When they are about to sit down to the Christmas meal, the *echekojaun* leads them in prayer for all of the deceased of the *baserria.*

THE "ANDABIDEAK" OR FUNERARY ROADS

We have already noted that when a death occurs on a *baserria* the corpse must be brought to the village nucleus over a fixed roadway called the *andabidea* or "coffin road." The salient characteristic of the *andabidea* is that ideally it is deemed to be immutable through time. This immutability is traditionally sanctioned, and the villagers are reluctant to alter one of these roads. Every *auzoa* is seen to be linked to the nucleus by an *andabidea,* maintained by the *auzoa* membership. While the roadway has many important economic functions, the reason given for its existence is sacred rather than profane. Informants state that the road must be maintained because corpses must be carried to the nucleus for burial.[32]

---

[32] A similar situation is found throughout the Basque country. In some areas the road is referred to as *difuntuen bidea* (road of the dead), in others

The route of the *andabidea* is well-known to the members of the *auzoa*. Whenever a new priest comes to the village and makes his first trip to the *auzoa* for a burial, the membership is quick to inform him of the traditional route. For example, the following incident took place in Murélaga several years ago:

A funeral procession left an *auzoa* for the village church. It progressed over the *andabidea* until it reached a spot where the road was impassable because it was overgrown with brambles. The priest suggested that the procession simply take a detour around the difficult spot. Indeed this would have been a simple matter because there was already a footpath making such a detour. The members of the procession refused. They sent a man to a nearby farm for a scythe. He returned and cut away the brambles. The procession then continued over the *andabidea*.

Similar examples are common from other Basque villages. The sacrosanct conception of the *andabidea* is forcefully demonstrated in an account from the village of Kortezubi, Vizcaya:

The *andabidea* of the *baserria* Gerio passed right through the house called Fradue. Thus a funerary procession entered by the main door and left by way of the stable area. It is said that this came about either because the house Fradue was constructed on the pre-existing *andabidea,* or that on one occasion the crucifix of a funerary procession had to pass through the *baserria* because of the bad condition of the *andabidea,* or had passed by accident. It should be known that if the cross, which always leads off on these occasions, passed over private property, from that moment the spot was considered to be like an *andabidea* for future occasions, without any right of complaint on the part of the owner [Barandiarán 1923c:39].

This second example shows clearly the connection between right-of-way and *andabidea*. The sacred conception of the road reinforces its existence. Thus it becomes impossible for a man owning the property on both sides of it to close the *andabidea*.

---

it is called **gurutz bidea** (crucifix road) or *eleiz bidea* (church road) (Echegaray 1933:42–43). But in all instances the road has sacred significance, and the connection is seen as one between a household and the *eliza* (church) rather than between a household and the *erria* (village nucleus) (see appendix).

While ideally the network of *andabidea* remains immutable, in fact it has undergone alteration. In recent years several of the *auzoak* have been linked to the village nucleus by asphalt roads. Some of these roads parallel traditional *andabideak,* although this has not always been the case. At first there remained rigid adherence to the old *andabideak,* but in some instances the traditional dependence began to erode. As the *auzoa* became increasingly dependent upon the new road system, no one used the *andabidea* except in the case of a death. Gradually it became more difficult to enlist the support of the *auzoa* membership to maintain the *audabidea.* The asphalt road was maintained in good condition by the provincial government. Furthermore, it had a guaranteed right-of-way. Through time, then, the traditional dependence upon the *andabidea* decreased, and a new *andabidea* emerged which incorporated part of the asphalt roadway and part of the traditional system. This new definition in some cases became permanent, or the transition may have continued and terminated in full dependence upon the asphalt roadway.

In this manner the route of some *andabideak* was altered. However, the content of the conceptualization remains the same. Every neighborhood is viewed as being linked to the village church over a defined road system. The church is the focal point toward which all the *andabideak* lead. The relationship between the village church and the disseminated neighborhoods is expressed and conceptualized in terms of the death theme.

THE "IL ERRIA" OR CEMETERY

The village cemetery is located at the edge of the nucleus. It consists of a walled area containing a small chapel, an ossuary, and the grave plots. The Basque term for cemetery, *il erria,* means literally "village of the dead."

In contrast to the emphasis placed upon the *sepulturiek* on the church floor, the *sepulturiek* (same term) or grave plots in the cemetery are seldom the focus of activity. The cemetery plots are not allocated according to households.[33] Whenever there is a death, the gravediggers exhume a previously buried corpse, deposit the bones in the ossuary, and then bury the newly deceased. Little attention is paid to where the individual is buried. In a few months the weeds claim the grave, and it is often impossible to distinguish the outlines of the grave plot. Some domestic groups place a headstone on the grave of a deceased member, but with the knowledge that a few years later the body will be exhumed, the headstone discarded, and a new corpse interred on the site.

The over-all appearance of the *il erria* is one of almost total neglect. Except on the day of a funeral or on All Souls' Day, no one visits it. The massive iron gates remain locked. There is no one who takes care of the cemetery. But this impression of neglect is illusory, for, in fact, the cemetery is held in great respect. Stories of witchcraft and apparitions of deceased individuals are often set in the cemetery. Furthermore, the cemetery is felt to be a place of religious importance rivaled only by the church itself. The journalist G. L. Steer provides an account from the Spanish Civil War which underlines this attitude. Steer refers to an event that took place in the last days of effective Basque resistance to the Nationalist forces. The *cinturón* or ring of defenses for the city of Bilbao had been breeched, and the Basque army was in retreat. German aviators bombed the retreating columns and, as a strategic move, attempted to hit an important road and rail junction in the town of Derio. They were off target and the bombs landed flush in the municipal cemetery—disinterring the corpses. Steer writes:

---

[33] This is not the case throughout the Basque country. In parts of the French Basque provinces little or no emphasis is placed upon the church floor, but the grave plots in the cemetery are emphasized. These plots have much the same properties as the church-floor sites in Murélaga. They are fixed in space and linked through time to a given *baserria*. The inverse relationship between the cemetery and the church floor is now apparent in Murélaga as well. Since the parish priest replaced the church floor *sepulturiek* with benches, there has been a greater tendency to emphasize the cemetery plots. There is now some agitation for the construction of a new cemetery with grave plots allotted by households and transmissible through time.

Their [the corpses'] grandchildren took the bombardment of the cemetery of Derio more seriously than the loss of the line before the *cinturón*.
It touched their religion deeply. It could not have happened in any other
country; but in Bilbao the President himself sat down to write a note to
over twenty nations protesting against this criminal assault upon the
sacred dead. My own, and I am sure the German tendency was to laugh,
but in the Presidencia one had to keep a straight face, for the faces of so
many were rigid with sorrow and rage [Steer 1938:304–5].

The "village of the dead" is not entirely unstructured with regard to its occupants. There is a very large section which corresponds to the *campo santo,* or blessed ground, in which the majority
of individuals are buried. One corner of the cemetery remains unblessed and set apart from the remainder by a small wall. This is
where the "non-Christians" are buried. Non-Christians might include anyone unknown to the villagers who happened to die in the
area and who could not clearly be identified as Christian (specifically Roman Catholic).[34] The death of an infant before his baptism
also presents a problem. In such cases the deceased may not be
buried with the others in holy ground, and the baby's body is con-
signed to the unblessed section of the cemetery.[35]

Similarly, there is the question of what to do with the individual
that is suspected of being a poor Catholic, that is, the "baptized
pagan." There is some reticence to bury the deceased in blessed

[34] This problem arose in another Basque village (Echalar, Navarra) studied
by this investigator. The body of a Portuguese laborer, who died while trying
to cross the border into France, was found in the mountains pertaining to the
village. He was brought to the village nucleus and prepared for burial. However, the priest was undecided as to whether the man could be interred in the
campo santo because he might not be a Catholic. It was finally decided to go
ahead and bury him in holy ground on the grounds that he was wearing a
scapular medal.

[35] Such a burial only takes place if the corpse is handed over to the religious authorities. Usually this is not done. An unbaptized person lacks a social
personality. His death is therefore not of societal concern. The usual procedure is to bury the corpse in the household garden without ceremony. This
practice has been recorded throughout the Basque country (Barandiarán
1948:175; Barandiarán 1961:91).

ground, but this is usually overcome by invoking the biblical parable of the eleventh-hour redemption. Suicide is not so ambiguous. Since self-destruction is a mortal sin, and unrepented mortal sin excludes one from heaven, the act of self-destruction is a clearcut cause for damnation. Furthermore, the very act removes the perpetrator's ability to repent. Until recently, suicides were also buried in the unblessed section of the cemetery.[36]

In summary, the cemetery is divided into two sections—that of the Christians (Catholics) and that of the non-Christians or damned. Admittance into the blessed or sacred area requires not that a man be demonstrably in a state of grace at his death (and therefore a sure candidate for heaven), but rather that there exists a reasonable doubt that he is not damned.

ESCHATOLOGICAL BELIEFS

Central to the villagers' attitude toward funerary ritual is a belief in the efficacy of ritual per se. This is apparent in the rigid adherence to traditionally defined practices and the resistance to change in form.[37]

To the Basque, ritual is order, and order is ritual. This is seen in the emphasis upon strict spatial ordering of the participants and religious symbols during a funerary service. Every individual knows just where he is to stand or sit with respect to the others. Deviation

[36] This has been altered somewhat during the last few years along with other modifications of Catholic practices initiated by the Church itself. The mental state of the deceased at the time of his suicide is taken into consideration, along with any other extenuating circumstances. The last case of a suicide in Murélaga was buried in the blessed section. The priest ruled that the deceased was mentally unbalanced and therefore unaccountable for his actions.

[37] Rapid change in all areas of life has been the rule in Spain since the Spanish Civil War. However, resistance to changes in funerary practices has been strong, and modifications in form have been imposed by an external force. The wheat shortages following the Civil War contributed to the cessation of the bread offerings. The loss of the *sepulturiek* on the church floor and abolishment of a typology of burial Masses were directly imposed by the religious authorities.

from accepted custom produces insecurity. Strict compliance to traditionally defined ritual is not solely an expression of solidarity in the face of death but also a way of ensuring the deceased individual's orderly entrance into the realm of the dead. Failure to comply with ritual form may have some disturbing effects:

> An old woman named Teresa died in the dead of winter in one of the most isolated neighborhoods of the village. There was a great deal of snow on the ground and the *baserria* of the deceased was over an hour's walk uphill, so the priest refused to ascend beyond a certain point. He sent word ahead that the *anderuek* should bring the corpse down to meet him. The incident touched off a great deal of comment in the village as all felt that the priest had no business departing from custom and should have gone all the way to the house of the deceased. One man from her *auzoa* summed up his feelings in the matter by stating, *"Teresan arima an dabil ondiño"* (Teresa's soul still walks up there).

A second case also centered upon "negligence" on the part of the religious authorities:

> Several years ago there were three or four domestic groups in the village that refused to pay their annual *culto y clero* tithe (a yearly assessment set by the religious authorities whereby each domestic group pays a fee to the church for the maintenance of the priests). The parish priest was very angry but had no way to enforce his assessments. Then a little girl in one of the delinquent domestic groups died. The priest saw an opportunity to retaliate. He refused to bury the corpse. The civil authorities in the village had to hold a civil burial and put the child in unblessed ground. Of course, this caused a great scandal in the village and a good deal of consternation to her parents. However, the matter was not closed. It seems that the parish priest owned some pine trees on a mountain behind the *baserria* belonging to the child's father. When the trees matured and it was time to harvest them, the priest was forced to ask this man for permission to cross his property. The man refused, saying that the priest must make a public statement from the pulpit repenting his actions, and the child's body must be exhumed and reburied properly in blessed ground. The priest complied. The body was exhumed. To everyone's excitement the body was found to be undecayed and lifelike. Informants observed that something like that could have been expected as the child had not been "properly buried."

The two cases mirror the potential tensions existing between the religious authorities and the villagers over the latter's belief in the efficacy of ritual form and the former's commitment to the meaning which the form symbolizes. The priests place little importance on ritual forms and, if permitted, freely substitute elements or omit them entirely. However, permission is not granted readily by the villagers. Elderly informants recount that every deviation (imposed by the priests) from traditional practice met initial adverse commentary, if not overt resistance.

What are the implications of this belief in the efficacy of ritual? First, there is a strong sense of obligation. The living must lend some sort of moral aid to the deceased as one of the necessary elements in his salvation. Second, certain aspects of ritual serve as prophylactics against the sinister properties of death.

The first of these distinctions is consistent with Catholic doctrine. The Catholic Communion of Saints is composed of both the living and the dead, and there is a relationship between them. According to Catholic belief, the living must activate this tie because the dead cannot. When the individual dies, his life is judged by God. God may condemn him to Hell, admit him to Heaven, or send him to Purgatory for a cleansing period. A soul in Hell is lost, and no amount of effort may alter the situation. If the soul is in Heaven, assistance from the living is not required. It is to those souls who are in Purgatory that the living must turn their attention. This relationship is central to an analysis of Basque funerary practices.

It must be assumed that the majority of deceased who have passed the age of reason are in Purgatory. It is very difficult for an individual to avoid at least some minor sins in the course of his life. While a true act of contrition just before death theoretically absolves the dying man from sin, one cannot really be sure that his repentance was valid. There is also a strong belief that everyone must pay for his sins in some manner. Evil does not go unpunished. Conversely, even the most wicked person may repent at the last moment. Thus from the viewpoint of the living, the salvation of most individuals who die after attaining the age of reason is in doubt. The full cycle of funerary ritual takes place only when the fate of the departed soul is in question.[38]

The fact that most of the deceased in the village may be classified as cases of uncertainty with regard to salvation poses a problem for the living. This problem derives in part from the Catholic position that the departed person who is suffering in Purgatory (and Purgatory is defined as a place of suffering not unlike Hell but of temporary rather than eternal duration) has no means at his disposal to alleviate his suffering or shorten his stay. He is a passive agent condemned to do penance until God permits him to enter Heaven. But the Church maintains that the living are able to mitigate this sentence by acts of sacrifice. Such acts may be made on behalf of a particular person or for all souls. Catholic indulgences, which may be purchased or earned through acts of prayer and sacrifice, relate to the problem of souls in Purgatory. While not indulgences, the Masses offered for the deceased and the rituals themselves become very important for the Basque as a means of helping a suffering soul.

The fact that the living are somehow intercessors for the deceased is apparent throughout Basque funerary practices. From the moment the person dies until he is placed in the ground, the corpse is never left alone. Throughout the burial services representatives from each social context in which the deceased participated while living (for example, domestic group, *familizhe, auzoa,* kindred, voluntary associations, and village ties as expressed through the

[38] The blessed ground in the cemetery is reserved for the doubtful cases, that is, the majority. The only exception is the baptized child who dies before reaching the age of reason. It is believed that this child is in Heaven, but since the ultimate goal is to assure the entrance into Heaven of all those buried in the blessed ground, the child is buried there too. When a baptized child dies, the *misa de gloria* (the Mass of glory) is celebrated rather than the Mass of the dead. *Artu-emon* is not offered. Neither is it proper for the domestic group to initiate formal or informal mourning.

artu-emon) are present. *Artu-emon* Mass donations are collected on several occasions. These Masses are all offered as a means of assisting the departed soul if he is in Purgatory. Throughout *lutue* the bereaved domestic group preserves his memory, makes offerings on his behalf, and sponsors *responsuek* for him. Also, occasions are singled out when the living remember all the suffering souls who have ever lived in the village. The funerary Mass on Saint John's Day and the services on All Souls' Day and All Saints' Day are examples.

The conviction that the recently deceased pass through a transitional state before entering the next world gives rise to many customs throughout the Basque country. The soul is felt to possess physical properties which are comprehensible in terrestrial terms. In the past it was a common practice for a domestic group member to open a window or remove a roof tile at the moment of death so that the soul could leave (see appendix). This custom has fallen into disuse, but many still believe that the soul may frequent the household or neighborhood before finally departing (see appendix).

The bread and candle offerings which are common throughout the Basque country were not always viewed solely as symbolic offerings to the Church. They were given so that the deceased might have food to eat and light to illuminate his way into the next world (see appendix). This desire to provide for the material needs of the deceased is partially reflected in the high esteem accorded to the household bees. In much of the Basque country, although not in Murélaga, the bees are informed when there is a death in the domestic group. If they are not told, they will die; and there will be no wax for candle making (see appendix). If the *echekojaun* dies, the bees are informed in ritualistic fashion. A member of the *echekoak* raps lightly on each hive and says in lowered voice:

> Erletxuak, erletxuak
> egi zute argizaria.

Nagusia il da, ta
bear da elizan argia.

[Little bees, little bees
make wax.
The owner has died
and in the church there is need of light.]

While Catholic theology emphasizes that the living are the ones who can and must activate the relationship with the souls in Purgatory, the villagers in Murélaga believe that the reverse can happen.[39] There are ghost stories in which a dead person appears to someone in the village. Stories of apparitions are less common now than earlier in the century, in part, no doubt, because the religious authorities actively oppose such beliefs. The stories demonstrate the perceived relationship between the living and the dead, a relationship in which the latter depend upon the former for assistance. Apparitions of deceased persons usually follow a set format:

> While walking alone, a villager is confronted with a person who is recently deceased. He recognizes the apparition because there was a specific tie between them when the deceased was alive (for example, a neighbor, a relative, a person with whom he had an economic or personal tie). They speak to each other. The deceased explains that he is suffering in Purgatory for a wrong committed during his lifetime. He asks the other either to atone for this wrong (pay off an outstanding debt, ask the wronged person to forgive him, and so forth) or to offer Masses for his soul. If the villager fails to comply, he will most likely be the object of further visitations. When he fulfills the request, the apparitions cease (see appendix).

Each case may differ in the particulars, but the above is a general model. The two salient characteristics are that the ghosts appear to

---

[39] Actually, the Church also admits the validity of apparitions and visitations from the realm of the dead. However, it considers such instances to be extremely rare and related to a grand design. In fact, such occurrences are taken to be so rare and therefore of such significance that the demonstrated ability of an individual to experience a visitation is a strong recommendation for his canonization as a saint.

people with whom they have a personal tie, that is, they are not anonymous ghosts; secondly, the ghosts are invariably persons who are still in the transitional or purgatorial stage. Souls who are in either Heaven or Hell do not appear to the living. The apparition involves a relationship between the living and dead precisely at the point at which the living are able to lend assistance.

While the overriding emphasis in the various ritual activities initiated by the living is to benefit or assist the departed, it is also clear that the villagers believe that the dead can benefit the living. This attitude is reflected in the fact that the majority of *iru urrune* offerings given in the village are occasioned by a crisis or a "special intention" affecting the life of the donor. The offering is clearly a means of convincing the dead to take one's part. In this context, "the dead" refers to the souls that are in Heaven and are therefore in a position to serve as intermediaries between the living and the Deity. Thus, some villagers profess a belief that the deceased who are in Heaven are capable of serving as intercessors for the living, but this belief is by no means general. Other villagers emphasize that they pray *for* the dead, never *to* them.

A further manifestation of the perceived bond between the living and dead is seen in the conception of the afterworld itself. The conviction that families will be reunited in the hereafter is common in many parts of the Basque country (Azkue 1959:228). An inscription on a tombstone in the cemetery in Murélaga reads: *"Ama! ez gara aztuko; gero arte"* (Mother! We shall not forget; until later).

The second attitude toward death made explicit in funerary practices is that of fear. The major manifestation of this is seen in the *rogativas* ceremony, where the death theme permeates the practices which are obstensibly performed to promote birth and maturation. The custom whereby domestic groups suffering a death in the past year send representatives to every *auzoa* in the village to collect the blessed salt for the fields would appear to be a cleansing ceremony against those aspects of death which are ritually impure.

We may now turn our attention to an examination of the various levels of social organization in Murélaga. These include the *familizhe* and *echekoak,* the *auzoa,* the kindred, and voluntary associations. Throughout the following chapters, the emphasis is upon the significance of the death theme as both a defining and an activating agent for the social units.

3

Family, Household, and Domestic Group

*T*HROUGHOUT much of the anthropological literature on social organization, there is a tendency to employ the terms "family," "household," and "domestic group" in rather loose or uncritical fashion.[1] In part the confusion stems from the fact that both "family" and "household" evoke for the English speaker a broad range of everyday or common-sense meanings which may or may not coincide with the more narrowly defined use of the same terms as ethnological concepts. As a consequence the terms enter the literature at both levels, and it is often difficult to distinguish with precision the author's meaning. A second source of confusion arises when authors carefully define and thereby distinguish between the concepts and then, in the course of their writings, fail to maintain the distinctions. We frequently find that "family" and "household" or "household" and "domestic group" come to be used interchangeably.

To confuse the concepts leads us to statements like this: "Rural

---

[1] See Fallers and Levy (1959) for a consideration of the confusion that stems from the use of "family" as an ethnological concept for the purposes of cross-cultural comparison. The problem arises from the fact that for the English-speaking social scientist "family" has both emic and etic connotations.

Basque society is characterized by the stem-family household"—a view that has been held since the last century when the French sociologist Frederic Le Play cited the Basques as an example in establishing the *famille souche* as a social type (Le Play, 1895). In this view the stem family is a co-residential grouping consisting of ego and spouse, their unmarried offspring, ego's parents, and possibly ego's unmarried siblings. That is, ego's married offspring and siblings are excluded. The problem is that the clearly defined family concept (*familizhe*) which exists in the Basque terminological system and world view does not conform to the stem-family model. In Basque society ego's married siblings and offspring are *not* excluded from his family concept (which is not to say that they are regarded as a part of his domestic grouping). Thus, in analyzing Basque society a problem arises when we try to impose coresidence of the membership onto the family concept or, conversely, when we try to define a coresidential group in terms of family relationships. In rural Basque society the family concept is both *more* inclusive and *less* inclusive in terms of personnel than the ideal domestic group structure. On the one hand, the Basque family includes members who are *not* present in the domestic group; on the other hand, the Basque domestic group *may* contain members who are not included in the family definition.[2]

As our point of departure we might examine the semantics of three closely related, yet clearly distinguishable, concepts in the world view of rural Basques. They are the concepts of *familizhe* (family), *echea* (household), and *echekoak* (domestic group). The terms in parentheses are the rough English equivalents that I have employed throughout the text.

Familizhe. When discussing their kinship relations, informants distinguish between *familizhe* (family) and *familizhekue* (of the

---

[2] I suspect that much of the literature concerning so-called "stem-family peasantries" in Europe and elsewhere might be re-examined profitably in light of these analytical distinctions. The details are, of course, an empirical problem specific to each ethnographic context.

family). The *familizhekue* is an example of the kindred and will be examined in detail in Chapter 5. Of present concern is the *familizhe,* which ego defines as his (or her) spouse, siblings, offspring, and parents.[3] A number of factors are readily apparent. First, a *familizhe* relationship is not contingent upon continued coresidence of the definer and defined. A sibling of ego who is residing in the New World does not, by virtue of his absence, cease to be a member of ego's *familizhe.* Second, a *familizhe* relationship is not (with the exception of the ego-spouse role dyad) contingent upon the presence or absence of a marital tie. That is, ego's married siblings and offspring are as much a part of his *familizhe* as are his unmarried siblings and offspring. Third, the definition or recognition of a *familizhe* relationship is not affected by the life status of the definer or the defined. That is, ego continues to include his father in his *familizhe* definition even after the latter's death. Ego does not say, "So and so used to be my father but he died." We might recall the inscription on the tombstone cited earlier (see page 81). Finally, the definition of the *familizhe* is ego-specific. No two egos (excepting full siblings) have the same *familizhe.*

What we have, then, is a situation in which the *familizhe* is not a discrete social grouping. Just as with the kindred (see Chapter 5) we are dealing with overlapping rather than discrete (that is, mutually exclusive) definitions of social groupings. With the exception of participating in the funerary proceedings of the defining ego, it is unlikely that the *familizhe* membership will ever engage in a common activity. Rather we are dealing with a category of primary kinsmen within which the defining ego activates a number of dyadic social relationships, for example, ego-spouse, ego-father, ego-mother, ego-brother, ego-sister, ego-son, and ego-daughter. Thus, within the *familizhe,* ego occupies a number of statuses with attendant role behavior. He is son in relation to his parents, and in this capacity he owes strong filial respect and obedience to pa-

---

[3] The Basque term is an obvious loan word from the Latin.

rental authority, regardless of his age, domestic group, and marital status and the age and domestic group status of his parents. With respect to spouse, ego is expected to be a life companion. Loyalty to spouse is regarded as the strongest kinship obligation in Basque society. If ego is placed in a situation in which his filial loyalty to parents or his loyalty to his siblings conflict with his loyalty to spouse, he is expected to favor the latter. With respect to his offspring, ego discharges a parental (protective and educative) role and in return expects the same filial loyalty which he extends to his own parents.

Sibling solidarity is another prominent feature of *familizhe* relations. In rural Basque society siblings are one's closest companions throughout childhood and adolescence. These ties of sibling solidarity often carry over into adult life and serve as the basis for economic and social interaction.[4] If two siblings marry and continue to reside in the same *auzoa,* a reciprocal *auzurriķourrena* tie is likely to develop between their respective domestic groups.[5] Thus, ego is expected to maintain a common front with siblings before outsiders. He is expected to lend advice and assistance if called upon to do so by a sibling, regardless of their respective sex, sibling age order, and marital statuses. Ego and all of his siblings are equal with respect to claims upon parents. That is, regardless of sex and age-order distinctions, siblings are felt to share equally in the parents' care and affections.

In sum, the *familizhe* is an egocentric category of kinsmen within which ego occupies a number of statuses (for example, husband,

---

[4] Conversely, animosity may characterize the relationship between adult siblings. It usually takes a serious misunderstanding to cause a breech between siblings, but once this occurs the parties to the dispute are almost irreconcilable. The important point is that ties between siblings rarely tend to be neutral or characterized by indifference.

[5] The incidence of two or more married siblings residing in the same *auzoa* is fairly high. Of the 115 marriages sampled in Table 2 (see p. 164), 23 (or 20 per cent of the total) involve an affine and heir from the same *auzoa.* In each of these instances the affine has one or more married siblings residing in the same neighborhood.

son, brother, father), whereas the other members occupy a single *familizhe* status with respect to the defining ego.

Echea is a Basque term which I have translated as "household." *Echea* may be used to refer solely to the dwelling, in which case it is equivalent to the English term "house." However, when a Basque refers to *"nere echea"* ("my *echea*") he is normally referring to more than the physical dwelling. He is introducing a broader concept which is roughly equivalent to the English concept of "home." In this sense the actor is referring to the constellation of dwelling, furnishings, agricultural implements, landholdings, and *sepulturie* site on the church floor.[6]

The *echea* has a name which is also resistant to change. Within the context of the rural society the actor takes his social identity from the name of his *echea* of residence (see pages 6–7). The practice of identifying the individual by the name of his *echea* is apparently quite ancient among the Basques. It was noted by the famous jurist Pierre de Lancre who, at the beginning of the seventeenth century, presided at the criminal proceedings initiated in the French Basque country against persons accused of witchcraft. In his book *Tableau de l'Inconstance des mauvais Anges et Demons,* De Lancre details the practices of Basque witches while at the same time expressing his obvious dislike for the Basque people. With reference to the naming practices, De Lancre states,

I don't want to forget that in Labourde, the most impoverished villagers are called lord or lady of such and such a house, which are the dwellings they have in the village, when these are nothing but pigstyes. ... They ordinarily drop their surnames ... and even the women [drop] the names of their husbands to take that of their houses ... and in this manner they accommodate themselves to the humor of the devil, seeing that they want to change in all things like him, and to disguise themselves not to be recognized ... all men of good sense try to perpetuate their name, family and house, and they, on the contrary, bring their name

---

[6] The term *baserria* refers to the rural *echea* (that is, to a household which is removed from the village nucleus).

and the memory of their family into the ruin of an odious village dwelling [De Lancre 1612:42; my translation].

There is a sense in which the domestic group (*echekoak*) enters into the *echea* definition; however, the concept primarily encompasses the constellation of physical objects ordered on the landscape in set fashion which is ideally immutable over time. Certain of the household furnishings and agricultural implements are seen as "belonging" to the *echea* and in some cases may be left behind if the domestic group changes residence. The furnishings and implements are carefully maintained, normally lasting for several generations, and are never disposed of through sales or by giving them to departing (for example, out-marrying) domestic group members as part of their dowry payment.

Morally, an owner domestic group is free to sell its *baserria* as a whole, although it may not dismember it through divisive land sales or divisive inheritance practices. Thus the *echea* is not viewed as fixed in a particular family line of descent. The present occupants of the farmstead have usufruct (despite the fact that they may have clear legal title of the *baserria*) of the household resources; they are the present custodians of a social heritage. That is, they are the beneficiaries of the care of household resources exercised by former occupants and, through their careful use of resources, they are the benefactors of future generations of domestic groups. On moral grounds the present occupants are constrained from jeopardizing the transmission of the *echea* intact to the next generation of farmers. It is in this context that we can understand the strong emphasis upon single heir transmission of the farmstead, the rules of dowering wherein the siblings of the heir are compensated only to the extent that the domestic group can pay *without undermining the economic viability of the echea,* and the system of land sales wherein the entire *baserria* including the *sepulturie* changes ownership. In rural Basque society social continuity is provided not by descent groups but rather by the immutability of households (*echeak*).

Life on an independent, autonomous, isolated *baserria* is eulogized in Basque mythology and folklore as being an ideal form of human existence. Throughout the Basque country there are variations of a founder's myth which accounts for the establishment of the first farmstead in a particular area. As the story goes, a domestic group establishes a *baserria* in a previously uninhabited valley. Later they learn that a second domestic group has settled the area, although at a distance of several kilometers from the first. The *echekojaun* of the founder domestic group regards this as a threat and states, "They have settled too near for us to be good neighbors."

Idealization of life on the isolated *baserria* is clearly reflected in the verses of the folk song, "Nere Etchea," by the French Basque bard Jean Baptiste Elissamburu. In the opening stanza we are told,

> Ikhusten duzu goizean,
> argia hasten denean,
> menditho baten gainean.
> Etche thikitho, aintzin xuri bat
> lau haitz andiren artean,
> tchakur xuri bat athean,
> ithurriño bat aldean.
> Han bizi naiz ni, bakean.[7]

> [Look up at the break of day
> and see the white house on
> the hilltop.
> Set in the midst of four large oaks
> with a white dog in the doorway
> and a clear spring nearby.
> There I live in peace.]

Through written records most *echeak* in Murélaga may be traced back in time as identifiable units on the landscape for at least three centuries, and a number of households, existing today, are mentioned in documentation from the fourteenth century (Mugartegui,

---

[7] This song is popular throughout the Basque country and is sung in all the local dialects. The original (reproduced here) is in the Labourdin dialect. Consequently, there are a number of phonetic, and hence orthographic, differences with respect to the dialect of Murélaga.

1932). As we shall see in the chapters on the *auzoa* and the kindred, this emphasis upon the independent and immutable nature of the household and upon the distribution of households upon the landscape, conditions the social relationships between actors and domestic group memberships. That is, in rural Basque society, the "social landscape" is structured, at least in part, with respect to the distribution of *echeak* on the physical landscape.

Echekoak. I am translating this word as "domestic group," but it means literally "those of the *echea*." The concept of *echekoak* encompasses the persons who inhabit an *echea* and, hence, share the same life space, or persons who, while absent, retain the right to return and take up residence. Membership in the *echekoak* grouping may be obtained in one of four fashions: (1) descent, (2) marriage, (3) fictive kinship ties, and (4) consent.

Membership by virtue of descent refers to the fact that anyone born into an existing domestic group acquires rights in its *echea* or household of residence. These rights include the right to continued residence and the right to be compensated with a dowry payment upon marrying out. The right to continued residence is retained by all members born into the group insofar as the person remains celibate and is willing to be subordinated to the authority of the active *echekojaun* and *echekoandria*.

Membership in the domestic group by virtue of marriage refers to the fact that the inmarrying spouse of the selected household heir (or heiress) in each generation is incorporated fully within the domestic group structure. At the same time the inmarrying spouse loses all jural rights in his or her natal domestic group. This change of allegiances is reflected in the naming system wherein the inmarrying spouse is identified in local parlance by the name of his or her *echea* of postmarital residence.

Membership by virtue of fictive kinship ties refers to the fact that a domestic group may adopt new members. A frequent cause for adoption is the childless marital union. The *echekojaun* and *echekoandria* who fail to produce offspring may adopt a child to be raised as the heir to the *echea*. They may adopt a child who stands in a *familizheḵue* relationship to one of them (for example, a nephew or niece) or may simply adopt a nonkinsman from an orphanage. On the other hand, adoption does not result only with respect to resolving the problem of succession raised by the barren marriage. Persons with natural offspring may adopt one or more additional children (either *familizheḵue* members or nonkinsmen). One circumstance leading to such adoptions is when one or both parents of a niece or nephew dies prematurely, leaving young orphans. Finally, adoptions sometimes occur when an infant dies, in which case another infant is adopted so as "not to waste the milk." In all such cases the adopted person is regarded as having full *echeḵoaḵ* status.

Finally, there are two avenues whereby persons gain *echeḵoaḵ* membership by consent. The first is with reference to the infrequent practice of taking in a destitute kinsman or even an unrelated person who is then accorded a large measure of *echeḵoaḵ* status. We might cite the example of a widowed, childless old woman who resides in her married sister's domestic group in Murélaga. The married sister in this case is the inmarrying spouse and hence has no birthright in the *echea*. That the old woman is regarded as having *echeḵoaḵ* status is reflected in the fact that the domestic group fully expects to meet funerary obligations at her death. In local parlance she is identified by the name of her *baserria* of residence. The second source of membership by consent stems from the fact that there may be a hired domestic servant or field hand residing on the farm. This person is treated as if he (or she) were a domestic group member. There have even been cases of domestic groups providing such persons with a kind of dowry payment upon termination of their employment.

It is the domestic group unit which has frequently been referred to as the "stem family." Yet, as we have seen, there is nothing stem-like in the Basque family concept, and the *echeḵoaḵ* or domestic group does not result from simply activating *familizhe* re-

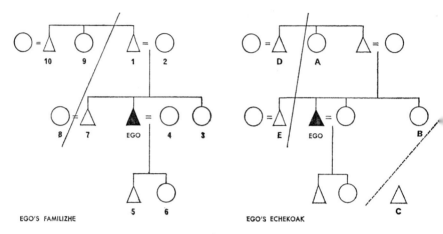

EGO'S FAMILIZHE EGO'S ECHEKOAK

Figure 3

lationships. Figure 3 is a diagram of both the *familizhe* and the *echekoak* of a particular ego. In the *familizhe* are included ego's parents, spouse, siblings, and offspring but not the spouse of a sibling or the siblings of parents (indicated on the diagram by numbers 8 through 10 and excluded from the *familizhe* membership by the solid diagonal line). In the *echekoak* are included ego's parents, the unmarried sibling of the former heir (indicated on the diagram by the letter A), ego's spouse, his unmarried sibling (letter B), his unmarried offspring, and an unrelated servant (who is indicated on the diagram by the letter C and whose semimembership is indicated by the broken line). Excluded from ego's *echekoak* are the married sibling of the former heir (letter D) and ego's married sibling (letter E). Note that ego's father's sibling (number 9 on the *familizhe* diagram and letter A on the *echekoak* diagram) is excluded from ego's *familizhe* but is a member of his *echekoak*. Conversely, ego's married sibling (number 7 on the *familizhe* diagram and letter E on the *echekoak* diagram) is included in ego's *familizhe* but excluded from his *echekoak*. Obviously in terms of personnel there is a large measure of overlapping between ego's *fami-*

lizhe and *echekoak*. If we map the *familizhe* onto the *echekoak* we include all persons indicated on the *familizhe* diagram by the numbers 1 through 6. The only person excluded would be ego's married sibling (number 7).

However, while there is a large measure of overlapping in terms of personnel, there is no overlapping between the *familizhe* and *echekoak* in terms of role structure. The point can be illustrated by examining the relationships that ego has with his father in terms of his *familizhe* role of son on the one hand and as active married male within the *echekoak* structure (*echekojaun*) on the other. With respect to his *familizhe* role of son, ego owes filial respect and obedience to his father. However, with respect to his role of *echekojaun,* ego is the main authority figure within the domestic group and makes the economic decisions affecting the well-being of the household. Thus, in the *echekoak* context, ego's father, in his capacity of retired *echekojaun,* is subordinated to ego's authority. If confusion is to be avoided in interpreting interpersonal relations between primary kinsmen in rural Basque society, it is necessary to determine whether actors are discharging *familizhe* or *echekoak* roles (or both) in a particular behavioral context. The distinction is particularly important in the quest of transmission of property rights between the generations. Ego has both a *familizhe* and *echekoak* claim on his parents' possessions. That is, ego in his capacity of son has a *familizhe* claim on his father's personal wealth which, in keeping with the *familizhe* principle of the equivalence of siblings in relation to their parents, is the same as the claims of the father's other offspring. Thus, at father's death all legitimate offspring have more or less equal claim on his personal estate. However, in his capacity of *echekojaun* or selected heir to the patrimony, ego has a special claim on the former *echekojaun,* one that is greater than that of his siblings. He receives legal ownership of the *echea,* whereas his siblings receive dowry payments out of liquid household cash reserves. The dowry payments are not normally equivalent in value to ownership of the *echea*. Ego receives this legal ownership of the farmstead at his marriage rather than at the death of the former legal owner.

The *echekoak* in Murélaga is an integrated, self-sufficient labor force whose primary economic activity is agriculture. Ideally, the domestic group should be able to meet all agricultural labor demands without recourse to outside assistance. In practice, there are several contexts in which the domestic group cooperates with others on the basis of a kinship tie or a bond of common residence (the *auzoa*) between their memberships. These instances of extra household involvement will be treated in subsequent chapters.

Whereas ideally there is a balance between the domestic group and the *baserria* or agricultural resources, the relationship is never stable when viewed over time. The domestic group undergoes a developmental cycle as individuals are born, mature, marry, and die (Fortes 1958). This means that the amount of human capital available on the farm is rarely the same at any two points in time. Domestic groups expand beyond the carrying capacity of their available agricultural resources; other domestic groups contract to a point where they are unable to utilize their *baserria* properly or efficiently. The contracted domestic group is able to adjust by renting out some of its fields on a short-term basis and by decreasing its direct involvement in agriculture. The expanded domestic group adjusts by renting fields from handicapped domestic groups, by sending some of its members to the marble quarries or nearby factories, or by encouraging excess members to migrate to urban areas or emigrate to the New World or Australia.[8]

While, as we have seen, the domestic group membership may

---

[8] These adjustments are of a cyclical nature and suggest that the expanded or contracted domestic group may eventually reach a condition more in keeping with its *baserria* resources. This view of cyclical adjustment in the organization of agriculture is an oversimplification. There are directional processes present in the rural society and economy as well. There are constant technological innovations and new cropping technique inputs into the household economy. Marketing conditions vary greatly, and largely without reference to local developments. The desirability of continuing in agriculture is partly

include adopted members (kinsmen or otherwise) and hired hands, it is equally true that descent and marriage are regarded as the "normal" channels for acquiring membership. In the world view of the rural Basque, the ideal *echekoak* structure consists of an elder married couple (retired or semiretired from economic activities), a young or active married couple, and the unmarried offspring of both. Included in the membership, then, are the unmarried siblings of the selected heir who fail to leave their natal domestic group of their own volition. Similarly, it is possible that the domestic group will contain an aged, unmarried uncle or aunt of the active heir (that is, a sibling of the former selected heir), a person who does not qualify as a member of the actual heir's *familizhe,* who resides on the *baserria* and is accorded full membership in the *echekoak*.

While the ideal domestic group is three-generational, only a minority of households in the village have such domestic groups at a specific moment in time. In 1966, of 143 domestic groups residing on *baserriak* only 32 conformed to the three-generation pattern. Eighty-nine of the domestic groups were two-generational. The two-generation domestic group is formed in a variety of ways: the junior married couple may have a barren union; after having achieved successful social reproduction in the accepted manner (that is, marriage of a selected heir and the presence of offspring from this marriage), the three-generation domestic group may be reduced through the subsequent deaths of the retired donor couple; or two persons who are excluded from the heirship in their respective natal households may contract marriage and take up neolocal residence on a vacated farm. In this instance neither set of parents will reside with the couple.

In Murélaga in 1966 there were twenty-two instances of one-

conditioned by the economics of alternative forms of employment and opportunities for emigrating. Finally, the economic aspirations of the farmers are not constant in themselves and force the villagers to seek alternative solutions when traditional means are insufficient to attain present-day goals. For a detailed treatment of the interplay between cyclical and directional change processes in the rural household of Murélaga, see Douglass 1967.

generation domestic groups residing on farms. There may be several reasons for this arrangement. A young couple that takes up neolocal residence may have a barren union. Similarly, a young couple may take up residence on the natal farm of one of them, their union may prove to be barren, and the elder donor couple be removed by death. However, celibacy is a more common source of one-generation domestic groups. If in a given generation none of the offspring is willing to marry and remain on the farm, the result is the demise of the family line on the territorial unit. In some cases, a retired couple faced with this prospect simply abandons the *baserria* and moves to the village nucleus or to an urban area. However, more commonly, an aged couple is left with two or more celibate middle-aged offspring. After the elderly donors die, their unmarried offspring continue to live together on the farm:

Two bachelor brothers and their spinster sister maintain common residence on a farm in Murélaga. They are all over seventy years of age. The persons involved have undergone a minimum of hardship, since the sister handles the domestic tasks, and the two men work the farm.

The only real crisis facing this domestic group is one of succession and, by implication, economic security in their old age. In other instances of one-generation domestic groups, the persons involved are clearly handicapped by the arrangement and are unable to carry out a "normal" existence:

On one farm two middle-aged brothers live alone. They complain of the drudgery of cooking and housework, and their dwelling is poorly kept in spite of the fact that their married sister, who resides in the area, makes frequent trips to the farm to tidy up the dwelling.

More extreme cases may be cited. On each of five farms in Murélaga a middle-aged man lives by himself. In three cases a middle-aged woman lives alone. The five solitary males all engage in agriculture. However, they are personally unkempt, their homes are not kept up, and in some instances they are poorly nourished (more as a result of eating improperly prepared food than of economic privation). The three solitary females, while residing on farms, do not engage in agriculture (with the exception of raising poultry and maintaining a household garden).

Thus, the three-generation domestic group normally results only when there is an identification of a family line with the same territorial unit over at least two generations of adults. In the event that the active married couple is residing neolocally, the three-generation *echekoak* is ruled out. That is, the three-generation domestic group results when a donor couple selects an heir to the farm from among their legitimate offspring *with* the implication that the donors and recipient (and spouse) will form a common residential unit.[9] Therefore, the three-generation domestic group is defined with reference to the selected heir who is the active male or female head of the *echekoak* at a particular point in time.

Transmission of the *baserria* between the generations turns on the ecological fact that the farm is basically indivisible if it is to remain a viable enterprise over time. The amount of arable land and meadows pertaining to a *baserria* is approximately three hectares. These are often poor quality lands situated on steep slopes. Dividing the farm into two or more units would make individual landholdings so small that they would be incapable of supporting a domestic group. Furthermore, there is no possibility of expanding the land-resource base because all available land is occupied and has been for several centuries. The inheritance system provides for the integral transmission of the *baserria* over time through the selection of a single heir in each generation.[10]

The selection of a single heir runs counter to the Spanish Civil Code, which dictates that all legitimate offspring share equally in

[9] Theoretically, an established *echekoak* could move from one territorial unit to another. In this event the active married couple would be residing neolocally but still caring for the parents of one of them. While not unheard of, postmarital change of residence is extremely uncommon in Murélaga.

[10] R. K. Burns notes that a similar system of domestic group organization and inheritance obtains in most of the mountainous regions of Europe (Burns 1963).

the estate. However, in the rural areas of Vizcaya the local laws or *fueros* take precedence over the Civil Code in the question of inheritance.[11] The *fuero* guarantees the donor couple's right to name a single heir to the *baserria,* but it does not specify which of the legitimate offspring is to inherit nor does it specify that the donors' remaining offspring be compensated.[12] Local custom resolves both of these issues. In Murélaga there is preference for male primogeniture; the remaining siblings of the heir are compensated with dowries.

Male primogeniture in Murélaga is preferential not prescriptive. When the first child is born to a couple, the infant is referred to in the wider society as the *erederue* (heir) of the farm, regardless of the infant's sex. However, crosscutting this consideration is an acknowledged preference for a male heir. And there is a further complication, since informants insist that the heir should be the most "suitable" offspring of the donor couple. That is, the heir should be the most serious, hard working, dedicated, and intelligent of the offspring. Finally, in order to qualify as heir to the *baserria,* the candidate must contract marriage. The choice of spouse may influence the individual's chances of inheriting the *baserria,* since the spouse should also be "suitable" in the donors' eyes (that is, mirror the qualities esteemed in the heir). Obviously, it is not always possible to meet all of the criteria when selecting the heir. Therefore, while a preferred practice, male primogeniture with corresponding virilocal postmarital residence occurs in a minority of instances.

A sampling of 138 marriages reveals that in 79 instances residence is virilocal, in 38 instances residence is uxorilocal, and in 21

---

[11] Rural areas are defined as those sectors of Vizcaya which are not population centers large enough to be termed "urban" or those sectors of urban municipalities which, while affiliated with the larger population center for administrative purposes, are made up of rural farms (*Leyes Forales* 1962:284–85).

[12] It does state that the heir be selected from among the donors' legal offspring and not from among strangers (Vicario de la Peña 1901:150).

instances residence is neolocal. Of the seventy-nine virilocal marriages, thirty-seven involve the eldest male offspring of the donor couple, twenty-eight an intermediate male offspring, and fourteen the youngest male offspring in their natal domestic group. In the case of the thirty-eight uxorilocal marriages, fifteen heiresses were the eldest female offspring, eighteen were intermediate offspring, and five were the youngest female offspring in their natal domestic group.

Therefore, of the 138 marriages sampled, 101 deviate from the male primogeniture norm. There are a number of possible reasons for this:

1. There are no male offspring.

2. The eldest male child remains celibate.

3. The eldest male child insists upon migrating or entering the religious life.

4. The conflicting norm of strict primogeniture prevails, with the eldest child being a daughter.

5. As a corollary of 4, the firstborn child may be a daughter, but the donors' desire for a male heir dictates the selection of an intermediary or youngest male offspring.

6. The eldest child is deemed unfit because of physical or moral defects.

7. In the event that the expected heirs of two households contract marriage, the claim of one or the other must be relinquished. Normally this is the spouse that can leave behind other suitable candidates in his (or her) natal domestic group.

The selection of the heir may be conditioned by one or a combination of the above factors. The system admits a fair degree of flexibility of choice on the part of both the donors and the recipient. Just as the donors may pass over the logical candidate, the logical recipient may refuse to inherit:

An unmarried man (in his middle thirties) resided on a *baserria* with his aged mother, spinster sister, and mentally retarded brother. His mother deemed him to be the only one of her children fit to inherit so she pressured him to accept legal ownership of the farm. For a number of years he was undecided and reluctant since ownership of the *baserria* entailed assuming the burden of supporting this weakened domestic group.

Sometimes the selection is made by circumstance or a process of elimination rather than by the design of the donors:

A married couple resided on a farm with their five offspring. The eldest child, a son, died before contracting marriage. The second child, a daughter, was committed to an insane asylum. The third child, a son, entered a religious order, as did the fifth child, a daughter. This left the fourth child, a son, to inherit the *baserria*.

Although the element of choice enters into the selection, and in spite of the fact that the statistical incidence of the preferred eldest male sibling heirs is decidedly in the minority, selection of the heir is far from random or haphazard. In a real sense the logical candidate to the heirship is socialized into the role of heir and raised with the expectation of inheriting and remaining on the *baserria*. Similarly, the siblings of the candidate are socialized into the role of non-heir and, at an early age, are impressed with the fact that their future lies elsewhere (unless they are willing to remain celibate and subordinated to the authority of the heir). Commonly the sober attitudes and behavior of an adult are forced upon the eldest male child during early adolescence, whereas younger male children in the same domestic group are permitted a much slower development. Thus it is more than coincidental that the logical candidate is likely to manifest the behavior deemed desirable for a future heir. Both his parents and the wider society impose upon him rigorous expectations and responsibilities.

Legal transmission of ownership of the *baserria* resources from the elder or donor couple to the new heir is made at the marriage of the latter. The transaction is formalized in a legal document or marital contract which is prepared by a notary public and signed in his presence by both the donor and recipient couples. The contract stipulates that the donors relinquish control of the *baserria* in return for the inmarrying spouse's dowry. This dowry enables the donor couple to meet their dowry obligations to their remaining offspring. An alternative to conceding the dowry to the donor couple is to stipulate that the recipients make dowry payments to the unmarried siblings of the heir. In this event, the amount of the dowry payments may or may not be listed in the document. The actual payment of the dowries may take place at the signing of the marital contract or be deferred until such time as the heir's siblings marry or express their intention to leave the domestic group. The dowry payment enables the siblings of the heir to contract a suitable marriage in another farming household, migrate to an urban area, or emigrate to the New World or Australia.[13]

The marital contract also provides the newly aligned domestic group with a blueprint for future social relations between the donor and recipient couples. It specifies that they are to establish common residence. It directs them to live amicably and enjoins the young couple to treat the old couple with respect and affection. It may specify that the donors have no obligation to continue working in the household economy. It may stipulate that the old couple receive

---

[13] Emigration from Murélega is three-directional. Persons leave for Latin America where they commonly establish a small business. Those who go to North America work as sheepherders in the Far West. The most recent object of emigration, dating from the 1930s, is Australia, where villagers work as cane-cutters in the sugar industry. The problem of dowry payments to departing unmarried siblings is often ill-defined. If an unmarried sibling leaves for a foreign area, he is provided with passage money and a cash "nest egg." Whether or not this is to be construed as his final dowry payment is dependent upon the course of future events. If he contracts marriage in the foreign area or remains there for the rest of his life, the passage money is considered to be his dowry, and the matter is closed. However, the emigrant who remains celibate retains the right to return to his natal domestic group and resume permanent residence. In this event, the returnee may be expected to compensate the *echekoak* for the original passage money as a condition for reincorporation into the domestic group.

a daily cash stipend for their personal use. Commonly, the donors reserve the right to one-half of the cash profits accruing to the farm. The contract also stipulates that the young couple provide the donors with a decent burial and perform the attendant household funerary obligations.

The marital contract provides for a solution in the event that the couples prove incompatible. A common means of handling irreconcilable discord is for one of the couples to leave for another dwelling (the contract may specify which couple is to leave). In this event each of the couples names a representative from among the *auzoa* membership, and these persons effect a division of the common property. The departing couple takes with it one-half of the movable property (including livestock, utensils, and crops). An alternative solution is for the old couple to move to another dwelling, leaving the young couple with all of the *baserria* resources. The latter then provide the old couple with a specified income. A final means of handling discord is for the two couples to partition their common dwelling. In this event each maintains a separate kitchen. If the elder couple has other unmarried offspring capable and willing to participate in agriculture, they might insist that the fields, agricultural implements, and livestock be divided as well. They then establish a separate, self-sufficient agricultural household (but under the same roof as the appointed heir).[14]

---

[14] It should be noted that discord leading to dissolution of the three-generation domestic group is a rare occurrence. There are many social and economic pressures which militate against it. Public opinion heavily censures all parties. Economic pressure is also intense, since the already small farm units are not readily divisible into two agriculturally viable units. The donor couple is interested in avoiding partition because they are in their declining years and hope to receive their economic and social old-age security from the heir and spouse. The active married couple is also interested in avoiding discord. Partition of the household places a heavy financial burden upon them. As long as they remain in common residence, the old couple represents a minimal drain on household cash reserves. Their wants are simple and few. Once a division becomes formalized and the old people move out, they make a constant and heavy cash demand upon the young couple, who are faced with the prospect of providing the economic support for two independent households.

The Basques emphasize strict allegiance of the individual to his domestic group and *baserria* of residence. The salient socioeconomic unit of the rural society is the domestic group (identified with a particular farm), rather than the individual actor or married couple. Thus, the manner in which the individual filiates with a particular household—that is, the ways in which membership is attained, maintained, and altered—is of paramount importance in Basque society. A simple rule of thumb is that the loyalties of the individual are always to his *echekoak*. The actor may filiate with one and only one domestic group at any moment in time.[15]

To the degree that it is determined by descent, filiation in Basque society is utrolateral. The domestic group, associated with a particular *baserria,* constitutes a local landed three-generational descent group. Persons who are born on the farm receive full jural membership. While theoretically the individual may filiate with the birth group of his mother *or* his father, in actual practice, there is no choice. The child filiates with the birth group of the parent who is residing on his or her natal *baserria*. Since there is a preference for a male heir which translates into a high statistical incidence of virilocal marital residence, it is more common for children to filiate with their father's birth group. However, in the event that father is residing on mother's natal *baserria,* the children filiate with mother's birth group. Offspring of couples that are residing neolocally do not normally filiate with the birth group of either parent (except in the rare instance where an established three-generation domestic group takes up neolocal residence as a unit after the marriage of the selected heir).

[15] J. D. Freeman encountered a similar situation among the Iban of Borneo. In the Iban *bilek* household, "filiation is of a special kind, for it may be either to an individual's mother's *bilek* or to an individual's father's *bilek* but not to both at the same time" (Freeman 1958:27). Freeman calls this type of filiation *utrolateral*. He states, "By the term *utrolateral* . . . I mean to denote a system of filiation in which an individual can possess membership of either his father's or his mother's birth group (i.e., the *bilek* family among the Iban), but not of both at the same time" (*ibid.*).

Membership in the *echekoak* for the child or adolescent is defined on the basis of descent and maintained by continued residence. For the adult, domestic group membership is affected by the added criterion of the marital tie. Thus, the spouse of the selected heir is, by virtue of the marriage, accorded full jural status in the domestic group. In accordance with the norm that the individual may filiate with only one domestic group (that being the *echekoak* of residence), the inmarrying affine relinquishes membership in her (or his) natal household. The heir's siblings, who originally define their membership in the domestic group on the basis of descent and residence, retain adult membership only insofar as they do not marry or profess religious vows (a functional equivalent of marriage). The adult unmarried sibling who remains in residence is not accorded social adulthood. The Basque term for the bachelor is *mutil zarra* (old boy), and the spinster is referred to as *neska zarra* (old girl). These persons, as long as they remain celibate and in residence, retain full jural rights in the domestic group. Unmarried siblings residing elsewhere retain latent jural rights in the domestic group and continue to filiate with it. They have the right to return and resume permanent residence (even after many years' absence).[16] Once a sibling of the selected heir contracts matrimony, he loses all jural rights in his natal domestic group.

Thus, for adults, the presence or absence of a marital tie defines domestic group membership. Marriage with the selected heir affords full membership to the inmarrying affine, whereas marriage effectively terminates all claims of the disinherited siblings upon their natal household. Adult acquisition or loss of membership is formalized in the dowry payments. Every adult who enters or leaves the

---

[16] In extreme cases an unmarried sibling may spend forty years or more in the New World and then return to the Basque country to retire on his natal farm. This may entail returning to a farm which is now owned by a nephew whom he has never met. However, in spite of his being absent for the majority of his life, the old man retains the right to resume residence.

domestic group brings or takes with him a dowry. In this respect the dowry system may be construed as a means whereby the agrarian population compensates some of its membership for leaving agriculture in a setting where further proliferation of farming domestic groups is virtually impossible. Dowry payments made in the course of marriages involving heirs to farms (that is, the marriages which provide the farmers of the next generation) do not remain in the domestic groups to which they are taken. They are, in turn, used to provide the dowries of the departing siblings of the heir. Those who benefit directly from their dowry are persons who emigrate, contract marriage and take up neolocal residence on a vacated farm, or who move to the village nucleus or urban areas to enter industry or commerce. That is, a marriage between two persons who are both excluded from the heirship in their respective households produces a union with the economic means to establish neolocal residence. They are in a position to use their combined dowries to purchase a small business, a vacated farm, or an apartment in an urban-industrialized area.

THE INDIVIDUAL AS MEMBER OF A DOMESTIC GROUP

The individual plays a variety of roles within the domestic group. In Basque society these roles are regarded as his most important ones. This is particularly so because in the farming economy the majority of economic roles center upon activity at the household level.

At the core of the domestic group structure is the *echekojaun-echekoandria* role set. The authority structure of the domestic group turns upon the joint decisions of the active selected heir and spouse. The active married male or *echekojaun* is the nominal male authority figure within the domestic group structure, but in the majority of instances he is not in a position to exert authority without consulting with the *echekoandria*. In partnership with the *echekoandria,* the *echekojaun* is responsible for making the economic decisions which affect the welfare of the domestic group. He also represents the domestic group before the wider society in legal matters. Finally, he organizes agricultural activities on the farm and personally performs many of the heavier tasks.

The ideal *echekojaun* is serious, hard working, and little given to recreation. In the words of one Basque saying, *"Jokua ezta errenta"* (Play is not rent). Probably the form of deviant behavior most censured by public opinion in Murélaga is that of the *echekojaun* who is less than energetic in the performance of his economic roles. His primary obligation is successful management of the farm resources. The *echekojaun* who fails to take this obligation seriously or is lax in his duty because of character flaws such as gambling or alcoholism is heavily criticized.

The economic roles of the *echekoandria* complement those of the *echekojaun*. Her primary goal is the successful management of the domestic cycle. She makes the majority of everyday purchases—items such as food, clothing, kitchen gadgetry, and the like. Furthermore, she often represents the domestic group in economic transactions involving the sale of household produce such as eggs, poultry, garden vegetables, fruits, and nuts. Because the *echekoandria* concludes the majority of economic transactions for the group, she often controls the purse strings. It is not uncommon for an *echekojaun* to go to his wife and ask for money. Ideally, equal weighting is given to the opinion of both the *echekojaun* and *echekoandria* whenever a major decision affecting the welfare of the household must be made. The sale of livestock is normally concluded by the *echekojaun,* either through dealing with a livestock buyer who visits the farm or by taking the animal to a nearby market. However, the actual decision to sell may not be taken without the consent of the *echekoandria.* The influence of the *echekoandria* upon the decision is seldom sub rosa. Women are not felt to be excluded from the realm of higher finances. The husband and wife openly discuss the matter, and if they fail to agree, the decision is postponed until one is able to convince the other. While it is normally the *echekojaun* who represents the household before the livestock buyer, exceptions are so common as to scarcely constitute exceptions.

The *echekoandria* should mirror the qualities listed above for the "good" *echekojaun*. She should be serious, dedicated to her tasks, and hard working. She should be a shrewd manager of household affairs and finances. The *echekoandria* who is unable to run an efficient household, or who is an alcoholic, is roundly censured in public gossip. Villagers are more willing to attribute the financial ruin of a household to the shortcomings of the *echekoandria* than to those of her spouse. She controls everyday finances, and it is in this area that the household economy is felt to be vulnerable.

While the *echekojaun* is responsible for the organization of agriculture and the *echekoandria* is charged with managing the activities of the domestic cycle, the division of labor between them is far from absolute. Men seldom engage in domestic tasks such as cooking, cleaning, or child care; but women freely enter the agricultural sphere.[17] In fact, it is a rare *echekoandria* who does not help her husband in the fields, doing such heavy labor as scything meadows, assisting with the plowing, and weeding the cereal lands. The lighter tasks—such as milking, caring for poultry, and maintaining the household garden—are often carried out exclusively by her. In instances where there is no adult male present in the domestic group, the *echekoandria* may assume the economic roles of the *echekojaun*. There are some extreme examples: In 1965 on one of the most isolated farms in Murélaga a woman lived with her two young children. Her husband was in Idaho on a three-year sheep-herding contract. This woman carried out normal farming operations and managed to support two cows, five milk calves, and sixty

[17] There is little indication, however, that men entering the domestic cycle impair their "manliness." We have noted cases (see pp. 96–97) where one or more unmarried men maintain independent residence and are, therefore, forced to fend for themselves.

sheep. The presence of sheep is particularly noteworthy since many domestic groups in the village have abandoned sheep raising because it is time consuming to keep track of their movements.

There is little indication that women are deemed to be inferior or that they hold less important roles in the society. Even in the political sphere there is marked egalitarianism between the sexes. Women hold and express political opinions. This is seen clearly in the political process at the *auzoa* level of social organization. The post of *mayordomo* rotates on a household basis, but the discharge of the duties of office normally requires the concerted effort of both the *echekojaun* and *echekoandria*. While he is the nominal authority figure, it is she who cares for the chapel and religious vestments. At *auzoa* public meetings where decisions are made, the women attend and speak their views on the topics under consideration. The fact that a domestic group lacks an *echekojaun* does not exempt it from holding the *mayordomo* post. In the organization of communal labor projects (*auzolan*), each domestic group is required to send a representative, normally, an adult male. However, a woman may be sent in his place, and her labor counts equally with that of the male representatives of the other domestic groups.

The complementarity of the *echekojaun* and *echekoandria* roles is apparent in the cycle of funerary ritual. At every point in the proceedings, each plays a role which complements that of the other. The egalitarianism between the sexes is reinforced by the fact that funerary proceedings are the same regardless of the sex of the deceased.[18]

One final bit of evidence of sexual egalitarianism may be cited. The double standard in sexual behavior which characterizes much of southern Europe is totally absent in Basque society. Premarital sexual relations are felt to be morally reprehensible to an equal degree for both sexes. Extramarital sexual relations are strongly

---

[18] There are two exceptions: (1) the church bells are rung differentially according to the sex of the deceased; (2) the presence of the Hijas de María for a woman or the Luises for a man is determined by the sex of the deceased.

censured, and to an equal degree for both partners. The unmarried girl who bears a child is more pitied than censured. The child is not stigmatized by the circumstance of its birth, and the mother's marital chances are not seriously impaired by her indiscretion.[19]

Although there is marked egalitarianism between the sexes in a wide variety of contexts, it is equally true that the *echekojaun* enjoys more personal freedom and enters into more extradomestic group social contexts than does the *echekoandria*. He may emigrate to the New World to spend several years even after marrying.[20] He may, while residing on the *baserria,* commute daily to a job in one of the marble quarries or to a factory in a nearby town. In these contexts he mixes with men from other *baserriak, auzoak,* and villages. Married men have more opportunities for recreation than do married women. Every Sunday morning after Mass there is a flurry of activity in the church square and in nearby taverns. Men form into small groups to exchange gossip, drink, and play cards. Women also form conversation groups, but these break up rapidly as each leaves to make her purchases in one of the stores before hurrying home to prepare the midday meal. On Sunday afternoon a number of married men converge on the nucleus to resume card playing and drinking or to attend a handball match in the village *frontón.* Married men also engage in seasonal recreational activities, such

[19] This is not to say that premarital sexual delicts are taken lightly. This behavior is condemned by the clergy and thoroughly disapproved of by public opinion. However, the individual's and the family's honor is not at stake in the public revelation of improper sexual conduct. Honor and chastity are only remotely related. Therefore, in Basque society there is little chaperonage of unmarried girls.

[20] At any given moment in time there are between ten and twenty *echekojaunak* residing in the New World. Some cases of absent fathers are extreme. For example, one *echekojaun,* presently in Utah, has spent ten of his thirteen married years in the United States. The relative ease with which the *echekojaun* leaves, if there is a strong economic incentive, underlines the importance of his *echekoak* economic role as opposed to his *familizhe* roles (husband, father figure, agent of socialization for the children, and the like). Even when both the *echekojaun* and *echekoandria* are present in the domestic group, the *familizhe* burden of socializing offspring is mainly her concern.

as hunting and fishing or trips to the mountains to search for mush-rooms. Men are also more prone to leave the village expressly for recreational purposes. Each Monday a few married men journey to Guernica to have a meal in a restaurant and see a professional *jai alai* match. Many married men from Murélaga attend the monthly livestock fair in Marquina. While some are there on busi-ness, the majority view it as an outing where they can meet men from other areas, determine the going rates for livestock, and drink wine in the taverns. Women who leave Murélaga for other areas do so to visit a medical specialist, sell household produce, or make purchases. In the course of such trips they may allow themselves the pleasure of visiting relatives, but the purpose of the excursion is usually of a more serious nature.

The former *echekojaun* and *echekoandria* are also evaluated in terms of their economic roles. The influence that the elder couple exerts on domestic group decision making is largely commensurate with the degree that they remain active in the household economy.[21] Senility is defined as the inability to perform economic service for the domestic group.

The former *echekojaun* normally accompanies the active *echeko-jaun* in agricultural tasks. However, little pressure is exerted upon him because technically he is retired. The old man is allowed to participate to the extent that he wishes, and the young *echekojaun* seldom attempts to direct his efforts. The majority of old men remain active until physical failings force their retirement. This is not surprising, since it is difficult for a man who has been active all his life and has defined his personal pride in terms of his capacity for hard work to disengage himself. Supposedly retired old men actually seem to be overactive in agriculture, and as such they may be a source of worry to the active married couple. The former

---

[21] And not to the degree that they retain legal control of a portion of the household income—see pp. 101–2.

echekojaun is considered to be a reservoir of agricultural lore,[22] and is frequently consulted. In his waning years, when the old man is no longer able to follow the *echekojaun* to the fields, he busies himself with lighter tasks around the dwelling. He may spend the morning collecting firewood for the stove, or he may take the livestock to drink at a nearby spring. Finally, he withdraws altogether and remains in the kitchen with the women or, on nice days, whiles away his time seated in the doorway of the dwelling.

The elderly *echekoandria* retires from the domestic cycle of activities in much the same manner. As long as she retains her physical faculties, she helps with cooking, cleaning, and child care. In this capacity she frees the *echekoandria,* who is then able to join her husband in the fields. However, as her strength wanes, she spends most of her time in the kitchen seated by the fire. At this point she represents a burden to the domestic group because she may require special care.

The point is that the old people are generally treated with respect and are allowed a degree of influence over household affairs. They seldom leave the domestic group to enter an institution for the aged or a hospital, even if in the advanced stages of senility or when suffering from a terminal disease.

Ideally, unmarried siblings of the heir who remain in residence must subordinate themselves to the authority of the *echekojaun* and *echekoandria.* This is most evident in economic matters. In return for daily sustenance and a claim to a dowry payment, the unmarried sibling owes his or her labor to the domestic group. In re-

---

[22] Recently there has been a widening gap between the generations. Within the space of about forty years, agriculture has undergone radical changes from a subsistence-oriented household variety to commercial farming. This has entailed a break with "tradition" at many points in the organization of agricultural activities. The break with tradition may lead to friction between the active and former *echekojaun.* However, it is equally true that the Basque farmer values experience. For this reason, the opinion of the retired *echekojaun* is still to be contended with, even if it is ultimately overruled.

cent years, it is increasingly common for the unmarried siblings to engage in wage employment in lieu of working on the farm. When this is the case, the traditional definition of their rights and obligations is modified. The individual gives money to the active married couple, which is an out-and-out payment for room and board. Upon marriage, this sibling is given a smaller dowry (or none at all) than those who remain in agriculture. The sibling who remains on the farm, subordinated to the active married couple, receives clothing and spending money in addition to his room and board.[23]

The unmarried sibling role contains a structural feature which often leads to conflict. The unmarried sibling retains the right to continued residence in return for his labor in the household economy; however, if he refuses to contribute to household production, he still may not be expelled. It is not uncommon for the *echekojaun* and *echekoandria* to complain that they are taken advantage of by a lazy subordinate member or by one employed in wage labor who retains all of his income.

The system of dowry payments is a further source of tension between the heir and his unmarried siblings. While the sibling may expect to receive a dowry, the amount is set by either the active married couple, the retired married couple, or both. That is, the amount of the dowry payment is determined by the donors and is not negotiated with either the recipient or the future domestic group of the recipient. Honor demands that the amount of the dowry payment be commensurate with the donors' ability to pay (that is, without impairing the economic viability of the farm in light of the number of other candidates for dowry payments still residing in the domestic group). The circumstances of the proposed marriage are also taken into account. If the departing sibling is marrying into a "strong" household, he should receive more than if he plans to marry into a "weak" household. But the recipient

---

[23] For a fuller treatment of the position of the unmarried sibling in his natal household, see Douglass 1967, chap. xiii.

lacks leverage in the matter, and in the final analysis is at the mercy of the donors. The element of negotiation, which characterizes the dowry system in other peasant societies, is largely absent in Murélaga (see Arensberg 1938:73–79; Friedl 1963:123–35).

The dowry system lends a strong economic overtone to personal relations between domestic group members. In each generation the marriage of the selected heir signals the distribution of a pool of economic resources. Items defined as being at the core of the household's ability to continue in agriculture—the lands, dwelling, livestock, stored crops, and agricultural implements—do not enter into the calculations. However, the cash profits of a generation of agricultural effort are distributed among the heir's departing siblings in the form of money payments and purchased items such as household furnishings and clothing. The dowry system encompasses the entire membership of the domestic group, in the role of either donor or recipient. Each member is aware of the nature of the dowry system, at the same time perceiving that there is a great deal of flexibility in the determination of the amounts. Competition between siblings is frequent; each seeks to manipulate the system to maximize his advantages. It is but a short step from competition to conflict.

The dowry system provides the *echekojaun* and *echekoandria* with a fulcrum in domestic group affairs. The active married couple is often able to exert control over the subordinated domestic group members by threatening to refuse them a dowry payment. In this manner the dependent member is constantly forced to "merit" his dowry by conforming to the wills of the *echekoak* heads. The potential for conflict and tension over dowry payments often translates into overt hostility once the former dependent member collects his dowry and leaves the domestic group. The individual may feel that he has been "shortchanged" and direct his antagonisms toward his other siblings who received larger dowry payments or toward the donors. Here we have a clear distinction between the *familizhe* sibling role of the actors (a role in which sibling affection and solidarity is emphasized) and the same actors' *echekoak* roles in which they compete with one another with respect to dowry payments.

In the context of the domestic group, even children play economic roles. Approval of the child is contingent upon the degree to which he manifests the qualities deemed desirable in a future *echekojaun*. The desirable child is quiet and retiring, willing to work, and physically strong for his age. Formal education is esteemed more as an exercise in discipline than for the knowledge that it imparts. The loud, playful, and precocious child is more a source of consternation than of pride.

From about the age of seven, young boys are expected to assist their father in lighter agricultural tasks. By the time the boy is fourteen, he takes his place as a full participant in agriculture. The young girl is expected to assist with the housework from about seven years of age. Throughout much of her childhood and adolescence, she learns agricultural skills by helping her parents and brothers in the fields. By the time the young girl leaves school (at fourteen) she works full time in both agriculture and domestic tasks. She continues to work in this capacity until she marries or leaves for an urban area for employment as a maid (usually any time after her sixteenth birthday).

Outside the domestic group context, the number of roles the individual plays and the intensity with which he discharges them diminish considerably. The heavy emphasis placed upon domestic group loyalties may be maintained only at the expense of less intensive involvement in wider social contexts. Even within the *auzoa* and the kindred contexts, interaction is generally between actors representing domestic groups, rather than between individuals acting on their own behalf. Furthermore, the interaction between *echekoak* is largely restricted to life-crisis rituals or to formal contexts where economic cooperation is suggested and sanctioned by tradition.

It is scarcely an overstatement to contend that the individual in rural Basque society maintains a social personality only within the context of the domestic group.[24] That is, when the individual is interacting with persons who are not members of his domestic group, he is viewed as being a representative of his *echekoak*. This identification is particularly apparent in the naming system whereby the individual takes his social identity from his farm of residence. If he is deviant in his behavior, he may be sure that his transgression will reflect upon his domestic group as well—albeit indirectly and to a lesser degree.

Because of the nature of the Basque *echekoak* (placed in the wider context of rural Basque society), the impact of death, that is, the forceful removal of a member, is greatest at the domestic group level of social organization. From a societal viewpoint the loss of an individual is not a disturbing event, nor does it trigger an inordinate number of economic and social adjustments. The deceased, who participated in *auzoa* and kindred affairs, did so as a representative of an *echekoak*. His place may be taken by another member. For the bereaved domestic group, replacement of the deceased member may be extremely difficult or impossible. Death may strike deeply at the very existence of the domestic group as an integrated labor force. Each member plays a variety of roles in the domestic group, many of which are functions of his personal attributes (sex, age, marital status, physical strength, moral rectitude, and so forth). Furthermore, personal relations within the domestic group are overlain with a great deal of affect. Thus, the immediate survivors clearly face the problem of psychological adjustments to the loss of their loved one. We may therefore examine in more detail the impact of death on the structuring of the domestic group.

---

[24] I emphasize that I am here referring to persons engaged in the agricultural way of life. Young men who enter industry or the marble quarries become involved in more extradomestic group contexts and begin to define their allegiances in personal rather than domestic group terms.

THE IMPACT OF DEATH ON THE
DOMESTIC GROUP STRUCTURE

The adjustments occasioned in the domestic group by the death of a member are likely to be of psychological, economic, and social nature. If the deceased is a child, the death does not produce an immediate or radical rearrangement of the role players, since the child is more a potential than an actual economic and social role player. The short-term effects of the junior member's death are unimportant, and this relative unimportance is reflected in the paucity of funerary ritual occasioned by such a death.[25] The long-term effects of the death may be quite significant. If the deceased was the logical candidate for the heirship, his removal by death forces the domestic group to select an alternative heir. Of course, if the deceased was an only child, then his removal by death poses a problem of succession of the same family line on the farm. Such a death forces the married couple to seek an alternative means of providing succession through adoption. Failing this, they may plan to leave the farm when faced with advancing old age.

The child's death removes his potential labor contribution, which in itself may portend future hard times for the domestic group. However, the death of the child does provide some short-term economic relief, since young children are an economic drain on household resources.

The death of an unmarried sibling who is residing elsewhere (but retaining the jural right to return to his natal farm) will have only an indirect effect upon the structuring of the domestic group. The absent individual was, at the time of his death, not in residence and therefore not a contributor to the well-being of the household. Although he did not contribute to the household economy, neither

---

[25] Although there is a religious rationale as well, that is, from a doctrinal viewpoint the child is "innocent" and therefore an immediate candidate for heaven. Consequently, he does not require the spiritual supportive aspects of funerary ritual.

did he make immediate economic demands upon it. The death of this person may actually strengthen the economy of his natal household. He is no longer a dowry claimant (assuming that he had not collected his dowry before his death). And any worldly goods that he possesses revert to his natal domestic group and his siblings residing elsewhere. In some cases the savings of the deceased may amount to a large sum of money and enrich those who collect the inheritance.

If an unmarried sibling of the heir dies while residing on the *baserria,* there are immediate repercussions on the structuring and well-being of the domestic group, for the strength of the household labor force is reduced. However, the economic consequences are not all negative. Whereas the deceased no longer contributes to the household economy, neither does he make demands upon it for his daily sustenance and his dowry payment.

The death of the former *echekojaun* or *echekoandria* is of greater significance. Both are normally in residence on the *baserria* at the time of their deaths, and their deaths constitute either a strengthening or weakening of the ability of the domestic group to exploit its resources, depending on the degree to which they played an active role in the household economy. If the deceased was so senile as to require a great deal of care, his death will actually strengthen the group. Similarly, his death may reinforce the authority wielded by the younger couple, because the young people, out of respect for the elder couple, may often fail to exert full authority in order to avoid conflict with the desires of the latter. The deaths of the elder couple permit the full assumption of authority by the young *echekojaun* and *echekoandria.*

If only one of the elderly people dies, there is no clear-cut transmission of authority between the generations. This transmission is a process initiated with the marital contract and completed gradually as the former authority figures decline in vitality and finally pass away. In most cases, as long as both the former *echekojaun* and *echekoandria* are present, they will exert considerable influence.

Their allegiance is to one another, and they are accustomed to operating jointly when making decisions. When one of them dies, the other becomes much more pliant and subservient to the younger couple. The survivor no longer enjoys the spouse's support and is now completely dependent upon the young couple. His influence over major decision making diminishes, but ideally he retains the respect that is due his age and the role he formerly fulfilled. With his death the transmission of authority between the generations is completed.

Here again we are dealing with a distinction between the structuring of roles in the *familizhe* and the *echekoak*. In terms of their *familizhe* roles, the old people are parental authority figures. With respect to their *echekoak* roles, they are subordinated to the authority of the active heir and spouse, particularly in economic matters. That these two essentially conflicting role definitions are sometimes difficult to reconcile lends a degree of indeterminancy to interaction between the generations. The young *echekojaun* seldom orders his father around in agricultural projects, although, theoretically, he has the right to do so. The old man is allowed to decide to what degree and in what ways he will enter into the household economy. The attempt on the part of the young couple to exert their *echekoak* authority in dictatorial fashion may trigger open conflict leading ultimately to the dismantling of the three-generation domestic grouping. The attempt on the part of the old couple to exert their *familizhe* authority over the heir to the detriment of the latter's ability to discharge his *echekoak* role may just as quickly lead to a schism within the domestic group. Potentially, the greatest source of conflict between domestic group members lies in the relationship between the inmarrying spouse and the heir's parent of the same sex. The inmarrying spouse expects to assume his or her *echekoak* authority role, yet, at the same time, does not assume a tempering *familizhe* role with respect to the old couple.

The death of the elder couple may also signal a redistribution of jural rights over property. If the elder couple retained the right to share in one-half of the profits from the farm, then the death of the surviving spouse will call for the transfer of full economic control over the *baserria* to the younger couple (unless some other arrangement was specified in the marital contract).[26]

The elder couple will usually have a legal arrangement between themselves (termed the *alkar poderoso*) which is specified in the marital contract. This empowers the one to act in place of the other (that is, a right of survivorship) in questions of naming an heir or distributing the benefits of the *baserria* produce. Thus, in some instances the full transmission of jural rights from one generation to the other may take place only after both donor spouses are dead.

In the majority of cases the retired *echekojaun* and *echekoandria* have, in addition to their *alkar poderoso* agreement, a *testamentue* or will. In this will, they may dispose of any personal cash reserves and property, such as pine trees, stocks, and buildings other than the *baserria* (in some instances possibly even other *baserriak* or apartments in urban areas). In this last will and testament, they divide up their personal belongings more or less equally among their children. Therefore, while the death of the former *echekojaun* and *echekoandria* will not directly affect the economic base of the *baserria* (since this was transferred *in vitam* to the heir), potentially it will have a significant indirect impact, depending on the degree to which the household received economic benefits as a result of the income controlled by the elder couple. That is, while the former *echekojaun* and *echekoandria* live on the farm, the domestic group as a whole benefits from their personal wealth. Upon their deaths a forceful redistribution of this wealth (in which the present

---

[26] In some instances the marital contract may stipulate that one or more unmarried siblings residing on the *baserria* receive the elder couple's right to share in profits when the two spouses die. However, in such cases the time during which the unmarried siblings retain this right is limited (usually about three years). If they wish to continue to live on the *baserria* beyond this time, they revert to their former status of nonparticipants with respect to the direct control of economic benefits.

echekojaun and *echekoandria* usually participate) takes place, and the majority of this wealth will most likely leave the sphere of the domestic group and move into the hands of the heir's siblings.

Once again the distinction between the *familizhe* and *echekoak* role structures is apparent. In their *echekoak* capacity of caretakers of the *echea,* the former heir and spouse transmit the patrimony intact to a single heir at the latter's marriage. Their remaining off-spring receive dowry payments only insofar as the economic viability of the *echea* is not thereby threatened. Normally, a dowry payment is substantially lower in value than the economic worth of the *echea.* However, in their *familizhe* parental capacities the elderly couple treat *all* of their offspring more or less equally with respect to division of their personal wealth. This transmission takes place at the death of the donors.

If the active *echekojaun* or *echekoandria* dies, the impact upon the structuring of the domestic group is paramount. In this event, an important factor in the redistribution of rights is the presence or absence of children. This death is no longer the affair of a single domestic group; marriage is not only an arrangement between two individuals but also between two domestic groups. A marriage pay-ment in the form of the inmarrying spouse's dowry is made prior to the marriage ceremony. Therefore, the dissolution of the mar-riage partnership through the removal by death of one of the individuals calls for a reassessment of the original agreement. I reproduce several clauses taken from a marital contract in order to illustrate the nature of this adjustment:

1. The inmarrying wife brings with her 2,750 *pesetas* and her clothing.
2. Each marriage partner wills 10 per cent of his or her belongings to the other in the event of the death of one or the other without descent.
3. If he (the household heir) dies without descent, then the *baserria* reverts to his father (in this case the donor).
4. In the event of Article 3, the father is required to return the de-ceased's wife's dowry. He must further give her that which corresponds to her from Article 2.
5. Until such time as she receives that corresponding to her under Ar-

ticle 4, she has the right to continue residing on the *baserria* and share in one-half of the earnings.

6. If she dies without descent, then her dowry (less the 10 per cent corresponding to her husband under Article 2) reverts to her natal domestic group.

From the above we see clearly that the jural rights of the affine with respect to the *baserria* are not finalized until the marriage produces offspring. The death of either spouse in a childless union nullifies the agreement.[27] Data furnished by a notary public round out the picture. He notes that legally, in the event of the death of the affine (without descent), her domestic group has a right to claim not only her dowry but also one-half of any earnings that she and her husband made jointly—insofar as these earnings were not employed to make immovable improvements to the *baserria*. If it is the household heir who dies, the affine theoretically retains the right to continue in residence as a participant in the household economy for one year and one day. However, if the bereaved domestic group is unwilling or unable to return the dowry, the affine may reside in the household indefinitely, sharing fully in the profits until such time as the payment is made, along with accrued interest on the dowry itself.[28]

The sample marital contract also provides that in the event of the death of either of the marriage partners (without leaving offspring) the *baserria* reverts once again to the donor. This is an escape clause which allows the donor a second chance to ensure continuity of his descendants on the farm. The donor may then name another heir from among his offspring, or rename the original heir upon his or her marriage to a second spouse. The underlying purpose is to ensure social continuity on the *baserria*. This suggests that in rural

---

[27] Informants recall cases in which after the affine died her domestic group confronted the bereaved husband during the burial service to demand that the dowry be returned without undue delay. Such behavior is felt to be callous and is rare. Usually the arrangements are made more amicably and at a later date.

[28] This rarely occurs because the affine is usually anxious to leave the unpleasant situation and return to his or her natal household.

Basque society marriage is a *process* rather than an *event*. That is, rural Basques do not get married all at once, as in the American view, but by degrees. The signing of the marital contract is one step, the church ceremony another, the birth of the first child a third. As persons become progressively married, the jural arrangements occasioned by the death of one of the partners change.

An eventuality that is not resolved by the marital contract is that of a barren union in which neither partner dies. Public opinion regards such a marriage as pitiful and disturbing. Barren unions strike deeply at the very basis of the approved system of transmission between generations. Various solutions are possible in these cases. The married couple may sign over the *baserria* to one of the married siblings of the heir, in which case the barren couple may leave and take up neolocal residence, or the dwelling may be partitioned between the two domestic groups, with the whole then transmitted in the next generation to an heir selected from the offspring of the fertile union. Another solution is for the barren couple to adopt a nephew or niece to raise as the heir to the *echea*.

In the event that the young *echekojaun* or *echekoandria* dies after producing offspring, the widowed spouse is guaranteed permanent residence in the domestic group. This spouse will have full jural rights to the usufruct of the farm and, if the *alkar poderoso* existed, will also be the one to name the future heir from among the offspring. Even lacking the *alkar poderoso* agreement, the surviving spouse retains full jural rights to one-half of the *baserria* resources. In this event, if the deceased failed to designate a single heir to the other half, it is divided equally among all of the legitimate children. This is an instance of a potentially divisive redistribution of jural rights over property, and therefore a threat to the continuity of the *baserria* as an integral unit. Practically, this is not as divisive as it appears. The remaining spouse retains one-half ownership of the *baserria,* which he may then transfer to a single heir. This heir, having received his equal share from the deceased spouse, controls the majority share. His siblings have only small shares compared with his and are usually happy to sell out to him. The sale price is not unlike the normal dowry payment. The end result is the same as if the *baserria* had been transmitted through normal channels.

The problem of succession is more complicated in cases where a widowed spouse with children remarries. In this event succession differs according to whether the person surviving the first union resides on the farm as an heir or an affine. Each contingency may be examined in detail.

At the death of one of the spouses in a marital union, jural rights over immovable property are affected. If the surviving spouse is the original heir to the farm, then the death of his first spouse means that her share in the *baserria* is treated in one of the following manners:

1. A single heir designated by the deceased from among her legitimate offspring receives ownership of one-half of the total (with the surviving spouse retaining control over the other half).

2. If there is an *alkar poderoso* agreement, the survivor is free to name a single heir to the entire holdings.

3. If the deceased failed to designate a single heir and also failed to grant *alkar poderoso* to the surviving spouse, then ownership of one-half of the total is conferred in equal shares to all of the legitimate offspring produced by the marriage.

The remarriage of the survivor which leads to new offspring conditions the ways in which he can transmit ownership of his share of the property. In this second union he controls one-fourth of the total (since his first wife controlled one-half of the total and his second wife controls one-half of the remaining half). He can transmit his share in one of the following manners:

1. He can designate a single heir from among his legitimate offspring from *either* union.

2. If he has conferred *alkar poderoso* to his second spouse then

she is free to select a single heir, but only from among the off-spring of the second union.

3. If he dies without designating an heir and without con-ferring right of survivorship to his second spouse, then his one-fourth share in the total is divided in equal parts among all of his legitimate offspring from *both* unions.

If it is the affine who survives the first marriage and then re-marries (with both unions producing offspring), succession to the *baserria* resources is handled as follows:

1. One child from the first union may, if designated by the deceased, inherit one-half of the total. If the deceased did not designate a single heir, then one-half of the total is divided in equal shares among all the legitimate children of the first union.

2. The surviving affine retains one-half control over the re-mainder but is not in a position to transmit her share to the off-spring from the second union (since a principle of truncality governs succession and neither spouse of the second union is affiliated with the patrimony by virtue of descent). Thus the affine's ownership of one-half of the *baserria* is actually a right of usufruct. At her remarriage she surrenders this right unless her offspring from the first union agree to allow her to continue in residence on the farm (along with her second husband and off-spring). If this permission is denied, then either she or her chil-dren from the first union invoke legal division of the *baserria* into shares. However, in the majority of cases magistrates rule that such a division would destroy the *baserria* as a viable eco-nomic entity. The magistrate therefore orders a public auction of the farm (either contending party is free to bid at the auction). Through the auction immovable property is converted into money. The affine is then free to dispose of this as she sees fit.

While the above circumstances represent serious fragmentation of jural rights over immovable property, the ideal of integral transmission is not unattainable. There is the likelihood that one child of the first union will receive one-half of the total. In the event that it is the original heir who survives and remarries there is the possibility that he will confer one-fourth of the total to the same heir. Thus a single heir could control three-fourths of the total. Where one heir receives a larger share of the total, the remaining heirs are likely to sell him their shares. In this manner the integrity of the *baserria* is protected as fully as if the transmission took place through normal channels.

Probably the most disruptive situation of all is the death of both the *echekojaun* and *echekoandria* before an heir has been named. In this event the provincial *fuero* is no longer applicable, and the Spanish Civil Code takes effect. The Civil Code dictates that the division be made between all of the heirs on the basis of equal shares. This presents a real problem for the continuity of the same family line on the *baserria*. None of the heirs will hold majority rights. Continuity is threatened unless one of them is in a financial position to buy out the others. Where one heir does not purchase the whole, the *baserria* may be sold and the cash divided equally, it may be rented to a different domestic group with the heirs dividing the rent, or it may be put entirely to pines, with the heirs sharing equally in the long-range benefits.

The death of the active *echekojaun* or *echekoandria* has more than jural impact upon the domestic group. Death at this level removes one of the two most important persons in the household labor force. The group is left without its prime authority figure, and major adjustments must be made.

If the deceased is the *echekojaun,* other males in the group must assume his economic roles. If the former *echekojaun* is still present and active, he is likely to become the male authority figure. If there are unmarried adult male siblings present, they must assume fuller obligations. If the deceased is survived by an adolescent son capable of heavy farm labor, this boy may assume a more important economic role. The *echekoandria* herself may compensate partially for her husband's absence by engaging full time in the agricultural cycle and delegating domestic duties to the former *echekoandria* or an unmarried female sibling of the heir.

The death of the *echekoandria* requires an adjustment in the domestic cycle. The former *echekoandria* or unmarried female siblings assume her duties. Males seldom assume the domestic tasks of cooking and cleaning.

Where there are three generations present in the domestic group as well as unmarried adult male and female siblings of the heir, a restructuring of economic roles within the membership can meet the problems posed by the death of the *echekojaun* or *echekoandria*. However, if the domestic group is residing neolocally or if it is a simple nuclear family, it is unlikely that it will be able to cope with the loss through an internal adjustment.

The death of the *echekoandria* who leaves her husband with small children and no adult female present is most disruptive. Often the children are given to either set of grandparents or given in adoption to a married sibling of one of the parents. If the *echekojaun* dies, leaving the widow alone with small children, a number of solutions may be employed. She may bring one of her (or her husband's) unmarried adult male siblings to reside on the farm with her. She may give up the farm and move to the nucleus or to another area to engage in wage labor. In rare instances, she may give the children to her parents or permit relatives to adopt them.

The over-all impact of death on the domestic group is best understood in light of the strict correspondence between one *baserria* and one domestic group with respect to economic activity. Since, for the most part, the *baserria* resources are fixed and are exploited solely by the domestic group membership, the relative strength of the domestic group at any moment in time determines the intensity with which these resources are exploited. The relative economic well-being of the domestic group, and the status of the household within the economic structure of the village, is in part determined by the size and condition of the domestic group. As the domestic group waxes and wanes with respect to size, health, and dedication of its members, the fortunes of the *baserria* fluctuate. Loss of members through death is certainly a significant factor in these fluctuations.

DEATH AND THE DEFINITION OF THE
DOMESTIC GROUP

In the last section we examined the ways in which a death may necessitate a rearrangement of the roles and role players within the domestic group structure. In this section we shall consider the ways in which the definition of the domestic group membership is reflected in funerary proceedings. Since it is the domestic group of the deceased which has the obligation to sponsor the proceedings, a means of defining the domestic group is to ask for whom the household is obligated to provide a funeral.

Given the territorial or common-residence definition of the domestic group, it is not surprising that the group initiates funerary proceedings for any individual who dies while residing on the farm.[29] The spouses residing on the *baserria* as affines are given a full burial by the domestic group.

In the last section we discussed the affinal spouse's full jural rights in the *baserria* once offspring are present. The integration of the affine into the domestic group is complete in every way. The affine assumes one of the most important economic roles within the unit, becomes an authority figure, may make the ultimate decision as to who will inherit the *baserria* in the next generation, and is a representative of the domestic group before the society as a whole.

The complete identification of the affine with the territorial unit is apparent in the naming system. We have seen that persons born on

---

[29] Formerly, it was common to have an unmarried servant on some farms. This was normally a member from a neighboring, overly expanded domestic group. The death of this servant was the concern of his natal household, but in some instances, if the servant lacked kinsmen, the funerary obligations were met by the employer domestic group.

a *baserria* take their social identity from it. Thus Pedro Armaolea of the *baserria* Cearra becomes "Cearrako Pedro." Nevertheless, an identification and a name will not necessarily last throughout one's lifetime. If the individual marries into another *baserria,* he (or she) becomes identified with it. This identification does not take place immediately. When Cearrako Pedro married onto the *baserria* Zuberogoitia, several years went by before the society referred to him as "Zuberogoitiko Pedro." [30] But once made, the new identification is absolute. All of the affine's formal *echekoak* ties with his natal group are broken, and he assumes full membership status in the new domestic group. His death is primarily the concern of his domestic group of residence, who will initiate the funeral proceedings, activate the *sepulturie,* send a representative to the *luto bankue,* and observe the period of mourning. The equal treatment of affines and consanguines with regard to funerary obligations underlines the fact that once they have produced offspring, the affines are deemed to be full jural members of the domestic group. In the case of barren marriages, lengthy residence in the domestic group may equally qualify the affine for full jural status. His death will be as much a domestic group concern as if the union had not been childless.

Unmarried siblings of the *echekojaun* or *echekoandria* who are born on the *baserria* and are still residing on it are accorded full jural status with respect to funerals. They retain their rights by virtue of their continued residence in the household and by the absence of a marriage tie which would align them with a different domestic group. Significantly, domestic group members who fail to marry but are residing in other areas (for example, the New World) are also accorded full rights with regard to funerals. Even if they die on another continent and after many years of absence from the village, their deaths are the concern of the domestic group. That is, the

[30] The length of the time lag before there is total identification of the affine with his new place of residence is partially dependent on the presence or absence of offspring. Full jural rights in a domestic group are not acquired by an affine until a child is born.

domestic group is obligated to provide a complete funeral for the deceased. This tradition is common throughout the Basque country (Echegaray 1922:329). There is neither a *gauela* nor a funerary procession because there is no corpse. However, every other aspect of the funerary cycle (the burial service,[31] *artu-emon, bederatziurrune, argia,* funerary banquet, *lutue,* and *ogistie*) is carried out. Attendance at such affairs by all having *artu-emon* relationships with the bereaved domestic group is the same as if he had died in the village.

The perceived degree of domestic group responsibility is illustrated by the statements of an elderly *echekojaun* and *echekoandria* in which they discuss their obligations toward their seven adult children:

Matilde, our eldest daughter, is married in Guernica. If she were to die, we would not take part in the funeral beyond simply attending and giving Masses in the *artu-emon.* Mari, who is married and resides in the village nucleus, is in a similar position. Two of our sons, Benedicto and Sabino, live in Idaho. They are both married. If they die, we would not be obligated to have anything done for them. We would give Masses but nothing more. One of our sons, Martin, lives in Venezuela where he drives a truck. He is not married. If he were to die, we would make arrangements for a funeral Mass and would inform our relatives. The Mass would be announced in advance, and all having *artu-emon* with us would come. It is the same as if he died here with us. Our son and daughter (Enrique and Beatriz) live here and are unmarried. Of course, we would be obligated to provide a funeral for them as well.

The criterion for inclusion or exclusion of an adult in the domestic group is the presence or absence of a marriage tie with another domestic group. Thus Enrique, Beatriz, and Martin (who has been in Venezuela for the past eight years) are all jural members of their natal domestic group. Matilde, Mari, Benedicto, and Sabino are not. However, while no *echekoak* obligation exists toward the married offspring, a *familizhe* obligation most certainly remains. It

---

[31] The sacristan will even prepare the table in the church normally used to hold the coffin. A small symbolic coffin is placed on the table and the *kandelak* and *achak* are arranged as if the body were present.

is with respect to the *familizhe* ties that Masses would be offered and the funerals of Matilde and Mari would be attended.

THE DOMESTIC GROUP ROLE IN
FUNERARY RITUAL

The consequences of an individual death are most marked at the domestic group level of social organization, but society is also deprived of a member. While the bereaved domestic group is supported and assisted by the society as a whole, it also assumes certain social obligations, the most obvious of which is to sponsor the funeral. The bereaved domestic group pays the priests, purchases the coffin, and hosts the banquet(s). A further obligation of the bereaved domestic group is to engage in the formal expressions of mourning centered upon the *sepulturie* and *luto bankue*. The domestic group's association with the *luto bankue* is temporary, terminating at the end of the formal period of mourning. Its association with the household *sepulturie* is more complex and long lasting.

Ideally there is strict identification between the *sepulturie* and the *echea:* the two are conceived as being inseparable. Activation of the *sepulturie* during the formal period of mourning is only an intensification of its usual and never-ending role. The *sepulturie* is activated even when there have been no recent deaths in the household. Each Sunday one female member attends High Mass, kneels on the site, lights a single *kandela,* and makes (formerly) an *olata* offering. During the mourning period, this behavior is intensified with the inclusion of a formal bread offering, *responsuek,* and a greater number of *kandelak.*

Until the *sepulturiek* were abolished in 1958, it was felt that every household should have one. In actual practice there were complications. Some *baserriak* lacked a *sepulturie.* There were other instances where two domestic groups that shared a single *baserria* dwelling also shared one *sepulturie.*[32] There are 143 domestic groups

---

[32] The reason that some *baserriak* lacked a *sepulturie* was the limited space on the church floor. The most recently constructed *baserriak* were unable to establish a *sepulturie* site.

residing on 121 *baserriak* in Murélaga today. In twenty-two cases
there are two domestic groups residing on the farmstead. This situation runs counter to the ideal of one *baserria* and one domestic
group.

We have already considered ways in which a *baserria* can be divided into two subunits. If the young *echekojaun* and *echekoandria*
prove to be incompatible with the older couple, the marital contract
stipulates that the *baserria* may be partitioned between them. If the
heir's marriage is barren but both spouses survive, a married sibling
of the heir may be brought in to provide descendants; in this event
the *baserria* is divided between the two domestic groups, and each
maintains a separate residence. A further source of division of *baserria* units is the decision of an absentee landlord to build two living
quarters under the same roof so that he may realize rent from two
sources. This is only feasible when the *baserria* is large. Finally,
when an owner domestic group suffers a decrease in its working
force, it may bring in another family which sets up residence in a
separate part of the dwelling and farms part of the landholdings on
a rental basis. As long as the partitioning obtains, there are two
echekoak and two *echeak*.

While none of the above causes for division occur commonly there
are a few instances of division in each generation. The division of
the *baserria* may be reversed within a few years, that is, the two living quarters may revert again to one dwelling. Occasionally the division becomes formalized. This is attributable to the strength of
the specific norm of one *baserria*–one domestic group which was
broken in the first place. Once having established two subunits
within the larger *baserria* unit, both domestic groups seek to formalize the division. Separate kitchens and living quarters are built under the same roof. Each domestic group builds a stable area. The
fields are rigidly divided, with each group having full control over
one-half of the agricultural resources (rather than a cooperative situation where the two groups might exploit the same land unit together). Particularly large or desirable fields are divided between
the two domestic groups in the presence of witnesses, and boundary

markers are placed to formalize the arrangement. The net result is
the creation of two separate ecological units within the former one.
For all practical purposes they become two separate *baserriak*.

The *sepulturie* was not so flexible. Each *baserria* received a *sepulturie* at some point in time, and the identification between the two
became immutable. If the *baserria* is subsequently divided into two
households, the two domestic groups are forced to share the one
sepulturie. When a sepulture is shared, the bread tithe which is paid
to the *difunterie* is divided equally. The following is an account of
how two domestic groups shared a single *sepulturie:*

> We each maintained a chair on the *sepulturie* and every Sunday we
> both sent a woman to the spot to hear Mass. The *difunterie* placed a sin-
> gle *olata* on the site which sufficed for both of us. We each had our own
> *kandelak*. My people made the *almaiyerue* (a linen cloth which is placed
> on the floor), and they bought the basket for the bread offering. When-
> ever we had a mourning period or wished to have *responsuek*, they let
> us use the entire *sepulturie,* and we did likewise when they had a similar
> need.

The *sepulturie* serves as the focal point of the domestic group's
formal mourning.[33] The obligation, from a societal viewpoint, is
one of simple compliance with traditional practices revolving around
the *sepulturie* and the *luto bankue*—there has been a death, which
requires the performance of traditionally determined rituals. In this
context no reference is made to the personality of the deceased. The
form is the same for any dead person, regardless of age (assuming
that he had at least attained the age of reason), sex, or status within
his domestic group or the wider community. Every member of the
society is treated equally, and the formal expression of mourning by
the bereaved domestic group is always the same.[34]

---

[33] We are speaking in present tense since bereaved domestic groups continue to establish a *sepulturie* site in one of the side aisles of the church. The
site is activated throughout the year of formal mourning.

[34] This last statement must be qualified with respect to the economic differences which may be manifesed in classes of funeral Masses. But even here the

From a societal viewpoint the domestic group is a corporate body, so any member may perform the ritual obligations associated with the *sepulturie* and *luto banḳue*. Any female member may activate the *sepulturie* and any male may represent the deceased in the *luto banḳue*. The important point is that *someone* perform the acts.

The question of who should activate the *sepulturie* and represent the deceased in the *luto banḳue* is viewed differently by the domestic group. It is preferable that the *echeḳojaun* and *echeḳoandria* fulfill the religious roles before the wider society. This is not surprising in light of the fact that the *echeḳojaun* and *echeḳoandria* are the group's representatives in most other important contexts as well. It is also consistent with the authority structure within the *echeḳoaḳ*. However, there may be extenuating circumstances that alter the ideal—particularly with respect to who shall activate the *sepulturie* site. A consideration of such differences serves to illustrate further the internal structuring of the domestic group.

If the deceased is the former *echeḳojaun,* and the former *echeḳoandria* is still living, the active *echeḳoandria* is likely to abdicate her right to represent the group in favor of the older woman. This is true in spite of the fact that the older woman has relinquished her claims to the role of *echeḳoandria*. By standing aside, the younger woman is respecting the intense *familizhe* bond existing between the former *echeḳojaun* and *echeḳoandria*. The older woman has a right to honor her dead husband's memory by activating the *sepulturie*.

The *familizhe* bond between husband and wife is seen as being more intense than the *echeḳoaḳ* bond between the former *echeḳojaun* and the active *echeḳoandria*. Even if the *echeḳoandria* is his daughter (rather than daughter-in-law), the *familizhe* tie between

---

logic is not altered drastically. The sole difference between individuals reflected in different types of funerals is whether or not they pertained to an owner or a renter domestic group. Within each of these broad class distinctions there are no additional emphases placed on the personal attributes of the deceased.

husband and wife takes precedence over that between father and daughter. The husband-wife relationship involves a great deal. They have lived the major part of their adult years together, reared their children, played equal and complementary roles with regard to the internal structuring of the domestic group, and shared in the decisions affecting the continuity of the unit through time. It is therefore fitting, in the villagers' view, that the old *echekoandria* be allowed to activate the *sepulturie*.

If the former *echekoandria* dies, the former *echekojaun* normally exercises the right to be the domestic group representative in the *luto bankue*.

Another alteration of the expected behavioral pattern might occur when the deceased is an unmarried sibling of the *echekojaun* and the young *echekoandria* is an affine. In this circumstance, the young *echekoandria* may defer to the former *echekoandria,* respecting the *familizhe* tie between mother and child. The young *echekoandria* is more likely to stand aside if she has been in the household only for a short time.

A young *echekojaun* or *echekoandria* meets the domestic group obligations with respect to the *sepulturie* or the *luto bankue* at the death of the other. This is certain as long as there are children present. However, if the surviving spouse is an affine and childless, he or she will return to his or her natal household and leave the former *echekoandria* or an unmarried sibling of the deceased to activate the *sepulturie.* Tensions and conflicts between domestic group members may be played out or at least become apparent in the course of meeting funerary obligations to a deceased member. Conflict is particularly common between the parents and the spouse of the selected heir. Another common source of tension is the power struggle between the former and the active married couples.

In the virilocal household, conflict usually centers upon the relationship between the former and actual *echekoandriak*. The older couple transfers control of the *baserria* to the young couple when they marry; and theoretically, the young *echekoandria* assumes full authority within the domestic group. Immediately, the young woman has a more important voice in household affairs than the former *echekoandria*. Yet, the latter has been exercising similar authority throughout most of her adult life. The *echekoandria* who instills into her own daughter the expectation that she will assume control over the domestic cycle in the household into which she marries often resents this same behavior when it is manifested by her daughter-in-law.

There are no clear-cut guidelines for resolution of the conflict. Indeed it is a common occurrence for the husband's mother and his wife to be on very bad terms. Often this places the husband in the middle as both women seek to influence him.[35]

Conflict between the actual and the former *echekoandriak* is the usual reason for the partitioning of the household unit. If the dispute becomes so bitter as to alienate the husband from his parents, the two couples are likely to invoke the marital contract clause providing for the resolution of conflict. One of the two couples may have to move out, or the *baserria* itself may be partitioned into two subunits. Each couple names a disinterested spokesman to represent them. The spokesmen in turn name a third. The three mediators then decide how the property and possessions are to be divided (Echegaray 1922:294–96).

The relationship between the former *echekojaun* and *echekoandria* and their heir is much less volatile. While the marriage of the heir theoretically signals his assumption of authority within the domestic group, the transmission is not so abrupt. First, the older couple anticipates for several years in advance which of their children is likely to receive the farm. From early adolescence this candidate is given more responsibility in household affairs than his siblings. The older couple is accustomed to working with him. Second,

---

[35] The beleaguered and compromised husband may seek a solution by bringing the priest in to mediate the dispute. In extreme cases the husband may turn his back on the quarrel and emigrate to the New World or to Australia.

they feel assured that their parent-son *familizhe* relationship will allow them to influence his decisions. With the affine they have no such guarantee.

Conflict between the generations, particularly between the two married couples, is potentially present in any domestic group. In many domestic groups the conflict inherent in the structural situation never becomes overt. The personalities apply themselves to the problem of amicable living. The many advantages in maintaining harmonious relations binds both couples to a policy of restraint. The elder couple is economically dependent upon the younger; they are no longer able to perform the rigorous farm tasks. Their old-age security rests with the young couple. However, the door swings both ways. The younger couple is often partially dependent upon the older in financial matters because the latter may still control half of the farm income. Fear of public scandal and gossip also encourages the young people to be concerned with their obligations toward their elders.

The key figure in the resolution of conflict between the generations is the heir. He is in a *familizhe* relationship with both his parents and his spouse, and he may manipulate his *familizhe* role performance so as to ameliorate tensions in the *echekoak*. Harmonious domestic group relations are generally a reflection of the degree to which the *echekojaun* is a successful mediator.

The activation of the *sepulturie* is an opportune occasion for conflict to arise. For instance, if the old *echekojaun* dies and the former *echekoandria* wishes to go to the *sepulturie,* the young *echekoandria* might be willing to step aside in the interest of harmony; but if she is quarreling with her mother-in-law, she may use the occasion as a means to aggravate the conflict by insisting that she herself go to the *sepulturie.* Such factors as the length of her residence in the domestic group, whether or not her husband supports her in family affairs, and her sensitivity to public opinion will all influence her decision.

Even if conflict leads to partitioning of the *baserria* or to the departure of one of the couples, the young couple has an obligation to provide funerals for the older couple. This is made an explicit provision of the marital contract.

The death of any member of the *echekoak* commits the group as a whole to the formal mourning period. This is the same for every domestic group in the society. The personal mourning period is at the discretion of the domestic group members and varies for each. Thus, if the former *echekojaun* dies, the *echekoak* as a unit will go through the formal mourning practices, and during this time all members will observe personal mourning practices as well. Beyond the year of prescribed formal mourning, there are varying degrees to which each member participates in continued mourning. The former *echekoandria* is likely to continue to wear black clothing indefinitely. She might continue to activate the *sepulturie* for a year or more beyond the prescribed mourning period. At her instigation the domestic group may initiate *responsuek* and anniversary services for the deceased. In fact, she may continue self-imposed mourning for the remainder of her life.

The response of other adult members will be less intense. The *echekojaun* and *echekoandria* extend their period of personal mourning for about eighteen months, followed by six months of partial mourning. At the end of this time they resume normal activities. The same may be said for other adult members (unmarried siblings of the heir). The grandchildren of the deceased, especially adolescents, may prove to be the ones least concerned with maintaining a long personal mourning period. The forced withdrawal from recreational activities is particularly difficult for them.[36]

[36] In this respect we might note that there is a growing hiatus between the generations in the perception of mourning obligations. Young informants express dismay at the custom of a long *lutue*. One case that scandalized the older generation in the village was that of a young girl who returned after having studied in England. Her father died three months before her return,

The marital status of the deceased conditions the personal mourning practices of the survivors. The relationship between the *echekojaun* and *echekoandria* is at the core of the domestic group structure. All other individuals present in the household are subordinated to this core couple. The removal of one member of the core is therefore felt to be much more tragic and significant than the loss of an unmarried adult member, child, or one of the retired old people. Therefore, the death of either the *echekojaun* or *echekoandria* produces extreme manifestations of personal mourning for all domestic group members.

Formal or public expressions of mourning are only initiated for members who have jural status within the domestic group. However, the bonds of affectivity expressed through *personal* mourning practices extend to *familizhe* members as well. The former *echekoandria* may choose to enter a period of personal mourning at the death of one of her married offspring. The extension may go even further, since an *echekoandria* who is residing on the farm as the affine may choose to mourn the death of her married sibling-in-law. Through her initiative, the domestic group may sponsor a religious service for the deceased (when in fact there is no formal obligation to do so). The service is termed *memorizhek* and consists of a Mass for the departed soul, terminating with *responsuek* on the household *sepulturie*. While a public service, this is not a formal expression of mourning because there is no social obligation to perform it. It is not performed at the deaths of all former residents, and it does not initiate a chain of *artu-emon* obligations. Only domestic group members are obliged to attend the service, although anyone else who feels a special tie with the deceased is welcome. The service ends with the *responsuek,* and there is no further activation of the household *sepulturie*.

There is a difference here between obligation and desire. For pres-

---

and she arrived in the village dressed in gay colors. When confronted with this fact, she retorted that it was not customary to wear black in England, so she did not see why she had to do so in Murélaga.

ent *echeḳoaḳ* members there is a domestic group obligation, but for former members, the tie may or may not be expressed:

J., a middle-aged *echeḳoandria* who was named the heir to her natal household, had three brothers living in the New World. Two were married, while the third was not. At the death of the unmarried brother the domestic group initiated full funerary proceedings and J. observed a period of personal mourning lasting about eighteen months. At the death of one of her married brothers J. again went into mourning but only over the protests of her daughters, who claimed that she was "always" in mourning. She maintained her personal mourning for this brother for one year. She then received news that her remaining brother had a terminal case of cancer. She talked about how she would have to make a black dress in preparation for this impending mourning. Her daughters were once again voicing objection.

In J.'s case, an individual is caught between her personal feelings of sibling affection and solidarity (*familizhe* obligations) and the cultural norm which restricts formal mourning to the deaths of jural members of the domestic group (*echeḳoaḳ* obligations).

DEATH AND THE ANCESTORS

The sepulture on the church floor is the stage on which the relationship between the domestic group and the dead is expressed. Up to this point the discussion has examined how structural relationships among the living are apparent in the selection of the domestic group representative to the *sepulturie,* but this fails to consider the implications of the fact that the *sepulturie* pertains to the *echea* and *not* to the *echeḳoaḳ.*

In one sense the *sepulturie* complex appears to be a form of ancestor worship or an ancestor remembrance cult. The female members of the domestic group (particularly the *echeḳoandria*) in any given generation are its priestesses. However, some of the evidence suggests that we are not dealing with a genuine ancestor cult. In the first place, there is a strict identification between the territorial unit and the *sepulturie.* Thus, the sepulture is not of necessity linked with a lineally related series of domestic groups. It is identified with the *baserria*. At any given moment in time the *echekoandria* may be activating a *sepulturie* that historically has hosted lineally unrelated domestic groups. Furthermore, given the emphasis on male succession, the woman is usually an affine and therefore a person who has no blood connection with the ancestors.

Thus, the sepulture is not necessarily identified with a particular set of ancestors. When a domestic group changes residence from one *baserria* to another, it ceases to use the old *sepulturie* and activates that which corresponds to their new *baserria*. To the degree that rites are performed for a specific set of lineally related ancestors, one must pick them up and carry them along when a change of residence is made. The single *kandela* burned each Sunday on the *sepulturie* benefits all of the deceased who ever held jural rights in the *sepulturie*, whether or not they are related to members of the present-day activating domestic group.

The relationship between the living and the dead is best understood by examining the attributes of the dead. In Murélaga there is little indication that the dead are believed to play a significant role in the affairs of the living. The dead are seldom prayed to nor are they remembered as individuals beyond a brief period of time.[37] There are instances in which dead persons are said to have appeared to the living, but this is a rare event and does not suggest that the living are somehow wanting in their fulfillment of obligations to the dead, but rather that the deceased had unfinished business on earth which prevents him from resting in peace. There is no indication that the rites centering upon the *sepulturie* are designed to placate the dead in order to prevent them from harming the living.

---

[37] While the memory of the dead in general lives on through the activation of the *sepulturie*, there is nothing comparable to the ancestor tablets in the Orient as a means of remembering a deceased individual (Plath 1964:302). However, there is one Basque custom that does serve to preserve the memory of specific individuals. In the *sala,* a dining room furnished with the household's finest furniture and reserved for banquets on special occasions, the walls are covered with photographs of former and present household members. Over time a picture gallery of deceased members is established.

The significance of the *sepulturie* complex is best understood in terms of the Catholic beliefs in the Communion of Saints and Purgatory. The Communion of Saints is defined as all Catholics, living and dead, who are not damned. The living members are able (and, indeed, are expected to) render assistance to the dead who are suffering in Purgatory. The living of today receive compensation for spiritual services rendered to the living of yesterday from the living of tomorrow. In this manner there is a banking system of spiritual credit or capital. The way in which the present generation of adults guarantees that they will be assisted by their descendants after death is to impress upon the young people the importance of traditional behavior. The act of performing faithfully the prescribed rituals provides an example for the young people.

During the funerary rituals there are several occasions when the living members of the bereaved domestic group activate the *sepulturie* on behalf of the soul of the deceased. Beginning with the *bedeatziurrune,* followed by *argia* and *lutue,* and terminating with the *ogistie* service, the *sepulturie* is regularly activated in honor of a special deceased person. The purpose of the ritual is to benefit a particular, identified individual. While anniversary Masses may be offered on his behalf later, after the year of formal mourning the deceased must soon take his place among the undifferentiated ancestors.

The *echekoak* is felt to have "obligations" with respect to a set of "ancestors." The category of ancestors is determined by tracing ties of ascent from the present heir to former selected heirs of the household. Thus the reckoning may be ambilineal. The spouse of the selected heir in each generation is included within the definition but does not serve as the basis for further extension of the system of reckoning. Conversely, unmarried siblings of the selected heir are *included,* while his (or her) married siblings are *excluded.* So we find that the ancestor category is determined by projecting back in time the same structural principles which define the membership of consanguines and affines within the domestic group organization. A strong sense of ancestor "obligations" arises only if there is the continued presence of a family line on a particular farmstead over a number of generations or if a full-blown three-generation domestic group changes its *baserria* of residence. In the latter case the *echekoak* takes its "obligations" with it during the transfer of residence. When two siblings of selected heirs marry and take up neolocal residence on a *baserria*, they do not have a set of "obligations," although they may be founding an ancestral line (if their future descendants maintain residence on the *baserria*).

When the *echekoandria* activates the *sepulturie* for her domestic group's "obligations," she does so with reference to the lineally connected series of domestic groups of which hers is the last. Once she attains full jural status within her husband's *echekoak*, she assumes equal status within the *echekoak* ancestor line. Thus, at her marriage she changes allegiances not only with respect to domestic groups but also with respect to ancestral lines. The transfer of her allegiance is given formal expression during the marriage ceremony. Soon after her wedding the new *echekoandria* is likely to offer a Mass for her "obligations" (that is, on behalf of the deceased of her natal domestic group's ancestral line) and for her husband's "obligations" (that is, for the deceased of her new domestic group's ancestral line). This may be interpreted as an act of separation from her former "obligations" on the one hand and an act of incorporation or initiation with respect to her new set of "obligations." While the transfer is abrupt, it is not absolute. For the duration of her life she retains some personal sense of obligation to her former ancestors. This is given formal recognizance once annually during the All Souls' and All Saints' Day proceedings when she places a *kandela* on the *sepulturie* of her natal households and offers *responsuek*. However, when she dies she enters the ancestor category of her domestic group of postmarital residence and is not included in the "obligations" of the next generation inhabiting her natal *baserria*. Less commonly, her husband makes similar Mass offerings after the wedding, one for his "obligations" and one for her former "obligations." In this manner he compensates her domestic group's ancestral line for the loss of her allegiance and also dramatizes his new status of *echekojaun* before his own domestic group's ancestral line.[38] Once the *echekoandria* assumes full jural status within her husband's domestic group, her "obligations" are the same as his.

The degree to which obligations or ancestor remembrance is felt and expressed varies from one domestic group to another. In some *echekoak* the ancestors are remembered before every meal. Domestic groups faced with a particular crisis, such as illness to livestock or the impending departure of a member for the New World, may choose to sponsor a Mass and *responsuek* on the *sepulturie*. The latter are offered to meet the "obligations." Finally, domestic group memberships differ in the degree to which they participate in the All Souls' and All Saints' Day proceedings (although the majority take these occasions very seriously).

There is a third emphasis with regard to the relationship between the living and the dead. This is the territorial emphasis in which an offering is made by the living for the deceased individuals who at some point in time held jural rights in the *sepulturie* and performed their funerary rites on it. Inclusion in this category is determined solely by the criterion of common residence projected into the past. There need be no demonstrable blood tie between the present-day inhabitants and former residents of the farm. When activating the *sepulturie* in this capacity, the *echekoandria* is representing a number of lineally unrelated domestic groups. In this capacity she is not the "priestess" of an *ancestor cult* but of a *predecessor cult*. The major expression of this relationship is the minimal weekly activation of the *sepulturie* at the Sunday High Mass. On such occasions the *echekoandria* lights a *kandela* and makes an *olata* offering. If pressed for an explanation as to her intention, she replies that she is

---

[38] In other parts of the Basque country, the formal transferral of allegiance by the inmarrying affine is more elaborate. It may consist of a ceremony in the church in which the former *echekoandria* "gives" the *sepulturie* to the new *echekoandria* (Barandiarán 1923e:122; Echegaray 1925:113–18; Echegaray 1951:47–49).

offering them for the *ilyek* (the dead). However, further question-
ing clarifies the point that she is not offering them for a specified
individual or for her household "obligations." On the other hand,
she disclaims the suggestion that she is making the offering for all
of the deceased of the village. It comes down to the fact that she is
representing all those deceased individuals who have ever shared
jural rights in the *sepulturie*.

In summary, any decision as to what capacity and with what in-
tentions the *echekoandria* (or other female domestic group member) activates the *sepulturie* must be considered in context. On any
single occasion she may be operating as the representative of a specific departed soul, a series of domestic groups related through ties
of lineal descent (conceivably reckoned ambilineally), or a series
of domestic groups related solely on the basis of common residence
(albeit at different periods in time); and she may be acting simultaneously in more than one of these capacities.

4

The Auzoa

I̲ N Murélaga each *auzoa* is a discrete territorial unit in which the
dwellings of the constituent *baserriak* are in close physical proximity.
The dwellings therefore constitute a nucleated hamlet set apart

TABLE 1

	AUZOAK OF MURELAGA	
Auzoa	Number of Domestic Groups	Number of Inhabited *Baserriak*
Malax	20	17
Ibarrola *	32	27
Narea	18	15
Goyerria	13	12
Solaguren-Gadaur-Ibeta	14	14
San Anton	20	17
Zubero	12	9
Urriola	14	10
Total	143	121

* Ibarrola subdivides into three smaller units called Landaburu, Ceto-
quis, and Ibarlaundi.

from other rural hamlets and the village nucleus.[1] The total landholdings of the constituent *baserriak* surround the *auzoa* nucleus on
all sides. There are eight *auzoak* in Murélaga.

The historical selection of the site for the dwellings was not entirely fortuitous. The *auzoa* nucleus is roughly in the center of its
combined landholdings. To the degree that it is possible, the dwellings are also located in the center of the relatively flat, arable lands.
The arable lands are surrounded by a belt of meadowlands which,
in turn, are ringed by a zone of forest and wastelands.

The landholdings of the individual *baserria* are interspersed
among those of other *baserriak* of the same *auzoa*. Thus, each farmstead's holdings are highly fragmented and scattered throughout the
combined *auzoa* holdings. Each individual field, meadow, or forest
holding is quite small (rarely larger than one hectare).

The physical isolation of the *auzoa* with respect to the remainder
of the village and its internal nucleated settlement pattern and system of fragmentary landholdings serve to make the *auzoa* the main
stage of economic activity and social interaction beyond the domestic
group level. Face-to-face contact between *auzoa* members is constant. When the individual is in his own dwelling, he is within
earshot of most of the other dwellings in the *auzoa* nucleus. When
he is working on any of his lands, he is likely to be within a few
yards of neighbors from other households.

Conversely, contacts with persons in the society who are not members of the *auzoa* are limited to specific situations. Most persons only
leave the *auzoa* for infrequent trips to other areas and for a visit
each Sunday to the village nucleus to hear Mass.[2] However, some
individuals living in an *auzoa* may maintain greater contacts with
the outside. Male members employed in the marble quarries leave

---

[1] The degree of nucleation varies from one *auzoa* to another. In all of the
auzoak there are at least two or three dwellings set apart from the others.
The entire *auzoa* Goyerria is an exception to the nucleated hamlet settlement
pattern. In Goyerria the dwellings are scattered throughout the *auzoa*.

[2] One *auzoa* even has a Sunday Mass in its own chapel, thereby further
limiting its membership's contacts with the outside.

the *auzoa* daily and are therefore involved in a wider circle of personal relations. Each domestic group must send a member at least once weekly to the village nucleus for supplies. Children attend school in the village nucleus. However, *relative* social and physical isolation of the *auzoa* with respect to the remainder of the village is still a prominent feature of the rural society.

Within the *auzoa* the personal qualities of each member are known to all of the others, and public opinion is most effective as a means of social control at the *auzoa* level of social organization. Similarly, it is in the *auzoa* context that bonds of friendship and animosity are likely to develop between individuals and domestic groups.[3]

There is another sense in which the *auzoa* is of great significance to its membership. Each *auzoa* has a name (for example, Zubero, Malax, Narea) which distinguishes it from similar units within the village. The *auzoa* name gives the individual his secondary social identity within the wider society. There is a feeling that different personality types are characteristic of the memberships of specific *auzoak*. The members of one *auzoa* are said to be shrewd, those of another are mistrustful of outsiders, and so forth. Thus, the individual's primary social identity is taken from the name of his *baserria* of residence, and his secondary social identity derives from the name of his *auzoa*. Only at this point, and to a lesser degree, does the individual regard himself as identified with the wider village.

The *auzoa* possesses a rudimentary religious and political structure. Each has a chapel with its patron saint. The feast day of this patron saint is the occasion for an *auzoa*-wide festival. The management of the chapel is also an *auzoa* concern, and each year a different household assumes the responsibility of serving as chapel *mayor-*

[3] These ties of affectivity (whether positive or negative) between individuals are actually somewhat discouraged in Basque society. Ideally, the domestic group commands the total allegiance of its membership, and social interaction within the *auzoa* is on a household-to-household basis. Affective ties between individuals might prove inimical to the smooth functioning of this ideal system of interaction.

domo. The domestic groups of each of the member households serves according to a fixed list.[4]

To discharge the duties of *mayordomo* requires complementary participation of both the *echekojaun* and *echekoandria*. The *echekoandria* cares for the religious vestments and the image of the saint, and cleans the chapel. The *echekojaun* organizes the annual religious festival, cares for the money in the chapel treasury, and has certain duties in secular matters.[5]

The *echekojaun* who occupies the *mayordomo* post has the secular duty of organization of communal activities. He suggests what day should be set aside for *auzolan* (neighborhood communal labor). The *auzolan* may take place on the *andabidea*. It may be organized to repair other communally held property, such as the water supply, electric power line, or the chapel building. It may be used to repair the network of roads that link *auzoa* landholdings to the *auzoa* nucleus. While the *mayordomo* suggests that the work be carried out on a particular day, he has no power to implement his suggestion. He is successful only insofar as he is able to forge a consensus among the *auzoa* members. He may go from house to house enlisting support for his idea, or he may call an informal meeting to discuss the issue. The *mayordomo* is forced to abandon his plan if the majority rejects it.

Once the *mayordomo* names the day for *auzolan,* he is expected to coordinate the labor of the group. It is up to him to calculate what is needed in terms of building materials, make necessary purchases,

---

[4] The rotation is done by domestic groups and not by *baserriak.* Where there are two domestic groups residing on the same *baserria* each takes a turn as *mayordomo.*

[5] While the post of *mayordomo* requires both a female and male participant, the absence of an adult member of either sex does not absolve a domestic group from assuming the post. In some instances a widow may be required to serve as *mayordomo.* Under other circumstances a domestic group may, by the common consent of the others, be excluded from holding the office. For example, in one *auzoa* a domestic group was deemed irresponsible because the *echekojaun* and *echekoandria* were alcoholics. Their neighbors feared that they would squander the saint's money on drink.

and assess each domestic group its share of the costs. Ordinarily each domestic group must provide the labor of one adult male, but a female may be sent in his stead. A domestic group that fails to send a member is assessed a cash fine equivalent in value to the labor of one adult. This fine is applied against the expenses of the building materials. The *mayordomo* has no immediate sanctioning power enabling him to exact the fine, but fear of public criticism serves as an effective sanctioning agent. It is unheard of for a domestic group to refuse to pay the fine.

The role of the *mayordomo* as an organizer in secular matters is, therefore, that of a cajoler. He may *suggest,* but he is powerless to *impose.* The only means that he has at his disposal is that of manipulating public opinion to gain support for necessary labor projects. It is not surprising that the post of *mayordomo* is unpopular and is assumed grudgingly.

The patronal religious festival involves almost the entire membership of the *auzoa* in a common activity. The majority attend the Mass held in the chapel to initiate the festivities. The dance in the evening involves the young people of all the *auzoa echekoak.* However, the major social event of the day is the banquet which is held in the individual households. Each domestic group prepares its banquet for friends and relatives that do not reside in the *auzoa.* While there may be a banquet in all the *auzoa* households, each domestic group operates independently and activates social ties peculiar to it.

The structuring of the *rogativas* ceremony which is held annually in the *auzoa* chapel is similar to that of the patronal festival. All of the domestic groups support and attend the Mass, but any notion of cooperation ends there. Each sends its representative to receive salt and to have its wooden crosses blessed, and uses them as protective fetishes on its own fields.

The *auzoa* common residence tie may serve as the basis for other communal activities, but always on a domestic group rather than an individual basis. The majority of domestic groups may decide to construct a communal water system or an electric power line. Inclusion in these activities is strictly on a voluntary basis. The costs are prorated among the participants. Labor to carry out the project is also allocated on an *echekoak* basis, with the labor of one adult member deemed equivalent to that of any other. There is seldom a formal chain of command with respect to the subsequent adminis- tration of the resource. Each domestic group has an equal voice, and decisions are made by reaching common accord.[6]

Within the *auzoa* recreation often brings neighbors together. Sev- eral *auzoak* have a "rural tavern"—one of the domestic groups of the neighborhood opens its kitchen to the others. On Sunday after- noons neighbors gather there to play cards, drink, and chat, and the host domestic group sells alcoholic beverages and tobacco. An- other informal opportunity for recreation is the Sunday afternoon conversation group. Neighbors gather in an open area near the cen- ter of the *auzoa* nucleus. Usually there are benches, stones, or logs which serve as seats. The topics of conversation are quite varied, and persons of all ages and both sexes attend.

THE "BIZITA" NETWORK

There exists a network of social ties between all of the domestic groups in the *auzoa*. This is referred to as *bizitak* (which derives from the Spanish term *visitas* or "visits"). We considered one mani- festation of the *bizita* network when, in the description of funerary ritual, it was noted that *auzoa* members pay a visit to a dying mem-

---

[6] This system of organization is efficient with respect to initiating projects but proves to be grossly inefficient in the subsequent management of the re- sources. When a project is first proposed, it is likely to be carried out rapidly and in a spirit of enthusiasm. There is no coercion involved, and domestic groups that have misgivings about the project may abstain. However, the majority are quick to join, since it is usually a clear saving to participate in a communal electrification or domestic water-supply project instead of replicat- ing the effort on an individual basis at some later date. Once the project is completed, the lack of formal authority and the inability of the membership to act unless it can forge almost unanimous consensus fossilizes the project. It is exceedingly difficult to alter and improve the original installation. The members are seldom able to agree except on matters of minimal maintenance.

ber. Similarly, the *gauela* is itself the most intense form of *bizita*. Other life-crisis rites also occasion activation of the *bizita* ties. A week or so after the birth of a child, the women from the *auzoa* make a *bizita* to the household of the newborn infant. Some female representatives of related kindred domestic groups are present as well. They bring a gift of a chicken, a bottle of sweet wine, or a small sum of money. In return they receive refreshments. Everyone has a marvelous time admiring the baby, discussing details of the mother's labor and delivery, and catching up on village gossip. This affair serves as a presentation of the child to the *auzoa* membership and is called the *aur bazkaria* (infant's meal). Attendance at this function is normally limited to *echekoandriak* of the new mother's generation, although other female *auzoa* members may attend as well.

Weddings also serve as occasions for some *auzoa* members to make a *bizita*. Late adolescent and young adult unmarried members of the *auzoa* are likely to attend a bachelor or spinster party in the household of the future bride or groom. These same persons also attend the wedding and wedding banquet.

"AUZOA" SUBGROUPINGS

The cultural norm stipulates that the domestic group should be able to fulfill all of the labor demands placed upon it in the agricultural cycle. Nevertheless, some activities require more labor potential than is commonly available in the domestic group. In instances where cooperation offers an obvious economic advantage, it is common for the domestic group to enter into reciprocal labor exchange with two or three others. In this manner, subgroupings of *echekoak* are formed within the neighborhood.

The establishment of subgroups is wholly determined by pragmatic economic considerations. The more common activities of subgroups are the following:

1. The members rent a truck to take their apple crop or calves to market in Bilbao.

2. A number of domestic groups join together to harvest one another's wheat crop and then rent a threshing machine which they operate jointly (maximum operational efficiency of the thresher requires the labor of about fifteen persons).

3. The broken and hilly nature of the landscape causes the soil to slip downhill through the years. A number of domestic groups may unite to buy or rent a cart-and-pulley arrangement which is used to load the excess soil at the bottom of the slope and pull it to the top where it is deposited. This task is demanding and is best performed by a number of persons.

4. Formerly (until the 1950s) the plow was seldom employed in Murélaga. Rather, a type of hand tool called the *laya* was used to turn over the soil. Several domestic groups joined forces to do each other's fields.

5. The yearly task of taking organic fertilizer from the stable to the fields is a backbreaking chore. Animals can be used to reach level areas, but they are useless on the steeper slopes. Thus, several domestic groups join together to fertilize the more difficult to reach fields of each participant.

6. Until recently the major source of chemical fertilizer was powdered lime obtained through burning limestone in outdoor ovens. Often two or three domestic groups joined together to build an oven. Lime burning is extremely arduous and labor consuming. A large supply of wood must be felled and carted to the site. The stone must be extracted from a nearby quarry and transported to the oven. The preparation of the oven itself is a difficult task. Once the burning begins, it lasts for a period of days, and the fire must be maintained constantly. Then the finished product must be extracted from the oven and carted to the dwelling. Thus, it was common to combine labor forces to carry out lime burning. They would then divide the lime on the basis of equal shares.

7. In the past, the major source of protein in the diet was *cecina,* or cured veal (this is no longer true). Each year two or more

echekoak joined together to kill a one- or two-year-old calf. By dividing the meat between them they would each obtain enough to meet their needs, whereas a single domestic group killing a calf had more meat than it could use.

The rationale underlying these labor exchanges is one of mutual reciprocity. The labor-exchange debts are phrased in rather loose terms, and there is no strict accounting of the ledger. Since the subgroups are not formal entities with a fixed membership, there is a tendency on the part of those interested in preserving the tie to contribute equally. The domestic group that feels it is contributing more than its share may withdraw, and the *echekoak* that fails to assume its share of the work may be culled from the group by the other members. When viewed through time, the elements constituting the *auzoa* constantly fluctuate or rearrange themselves into a series of subgroups with differing life spans. Indeed, the same domestic group may participate in different subgroups for different economic activities.

THE "AUZURRIKOURRENA"

It was noted that during the events immediately following a death one domestic group within the *auzoa* of the deceased, termed the *auzurrikourrena,* performs several services for the bereaved domestic group. It is the *auzurrikourrena* that assumes responsibility for carrying on domestic tasks in the household of the bereaved. It also informs the village authorities of the death, advises relatives of the deceased, and makes arrangements for the funeral.

To lend assistance at the time of death is only one of the duties of the *auzurrikourrena.* It is expected to help the domestic group in any crisis situation. If a cow has difficulty in giving birth, the domestic group will call upon members of the *auzurrikourrena* to assist or to inform the veterinarian. Formerly, when it was customary for women to give birth at home, the *echekoandria* of the *auzurrikourrena* was informed when the woman went into labor.

She then assisted at the birth and in some cases served as the mid-wife. In the event that a member of the domestic group becomes ill, the *auzurrikourrena* sends someone for the doctor. If the domestic group wishes to borrow a tool or needs assistance to complete a particular task, its first reaction is to turn to the *auzurrikourrena*. In the majority of instances there is a bond of trust between the two domestic groups. This bond may be reinforced when the membership of one of the two *echekoak* selects a person from the other to serve as godparent for a newborn infant.

The definition of the *auzurrikourrena* is largely determined by the spatial disposition of the dwellings. The very term means "closest of the neighborhood." "Closest" here refers to physical proximity rather than social intimacy. Ideally, each domestic group defines the membership of the geographically most proximate household as its *auzurrikourrena*. In actual practice, there is a degree of flexibility and choice involved.[7]

Even in Murélaga, where the selection of the *auzurrikourrena* may be influenced by other than territorial considerations, there is a tendency for the domestic group to define the geographically most proximate household as its *auzurrikourrena*. It is also common for this tie to prove durable over several generations. If the *auzurrikourrena* relationship is modified, redefinition will most often result from endogamy. That is, if married siblings live in the same *auzoa,* a mutual *auzurrikourrena* dependency is likely to develop between

---

[7] I make this distinction because the *auzurrikourrena* relationship in one form or another is an important feature of social organization throughout the Basque country. In some areas, the relationship is not defined as loosely as in Murélaga. Where the *baserriak* are more widely dispersed, there is more rigid adherence to the territorial definition of the relationship. This reflects the "assistance in crisis" nature of the *auzurrikourrena* obligations. To be on poor terms with the nearest neighbor may mean that in a life-or-death emergency valuable time might be lost in finding assistance. Thus, in the majority of instances, the *auzurrikourrena* tie is activated with the geographically most proximate household regardless of the personal ties existing between the two domestic groups (Echegaray 1933:11–12; Veyrin 1055:258). The nucleated *auzoa* settlement pattern of Murélaga removes the urgency for a strict territorial reckoning of the *auzurrikourrena*. Within the *auzoa* in Murélaga the dwellings are only a few steps apart.

their respective domestic groups, even if the dwellings are at opposite ends of the *auzoa* nucleus. This situation may be labeled as
a case of dyadic reciprocity, that is, A ←→ B.

This example in which the *auzurriḳourrena* relationship is symmetrical (that is, each serves as the *auzurriḳourrena* for the other)
is not the usual pattern. More often there is no direct reciprocity
implied. Domestic group A is likely to depend on B, domestic group
B depends upon C, while C, in turn depends upon A. This situation
may be labeled serial reciprocity, that is, A → B → C → A. A further
complication is that a single domestic group may serve as *auzurriḳourrena* for several others. That is, we may have a case of asym-
metry. *Echeḳoaḳ* A receives *auzurriḳourrena* services without extending them. If a given domestic group depends upon another for
auzurriḳourrena functions, and does not in turn provide similar
services, it may reciprocate in other ways. The most common manner is to extend a great deal of respect and hospitality or even to
send food gifts to the *auzurriḳourrena* when it has performed a particular service. In this practice we detect one manifestation of the
rural Basque's strong reticence to ever become indebted to another.
That is, it is felt that the social ledger should never be permitted
to become noticeably unbalanced. Marked unbalance in social obligations would undermine seriously the valued independence of the
echea and *echeḳoaḳ* (see Chapter 3). However, there is no strict
accounting that demands repayment. Indeed, the *auzurriḳourrena*
is obligated to fulfill the demands made upon it if it wishes to remain uncensured by public opinion. One cannot expect assistance
from others if he is unwilling to extend it.[8]

On the basis of the evidence of the *auzurriḳourrena* relationship,
auzoa subgroupings, the *bizita* network of social relations, *auzoa*

[8] It should be noted that the *auzurriḳourrena* relationship is often ill-defined
in the minds of informants. Persons are able to verbalize the obligations of the
relationship and are usually able to identify the domestic group that they
regard as their *auzurriḳourrena*. However, in the context of everyday living,
the ideal behavioral pattern is sometimes altered. In the immediate crisis
occasioned by a death, the bereaved *echeḳoaḳ* may first advise a domestic
group which is not, strictly speaking, its *auzurriḳourrena*.

religous festivities, and the communal *auzolan* activities, it would
appear that the *auzoa* serves the individual as a significant context
of social interaction. Indeed, in rural Basque society the *auzoa* takes
precedence over both the kindred and the village as the most important extradomestic group context of social identification and
interaction. However, the special nature of the individual's participation in *auzoa* activities is not necessarily inimical to the strong
cultural norm that his paramount loyalties must be to his domestic
group–*baserria*. We find that while individuals interact in the *auzoa*
context, in the majority of instances they do so as representatives
of their respective domestic groups. Personal ties of friendship or
animosity between *auzoa* members as *individuals* are discouraged
because they run counter to the smooth functioning of formal *auzoa*
echekoak-to-*echekoak* interaction patterns.

This emphasis is seen quite clearly in the fact that entry to the
dwelling is reserved almost exclusively for domestic group members or relatives who come from outside the *auzoa*. Casual visiting
and hospitality between *auzoa* members are rare. With the exception of the formal *bizitak* during life-crisis situations, neighbors
rarely or never set foot in one another's dwellings.[9] Casual chatting
and recreation, as well as meetings to discuss matters of interest to
the entire *auzoa,* take place on neutral ground (for example, in the
fields, on the road to and from work, or in the centrally located
open-air meeting area of the *auzoa* nucleus). Anyone who wishes to
gain the attention of a neighbor stands outside the dwelling or in
the entranceway and shouts out his request. A domestic group member then goes to the doorway to discuss the matter, with no thought
of inviting the visitor into the dwelling. Even if the visitor is invited to enter, it is highly unlikely that he will do so:

In the summer of 1966 a world championship heavyweight boxing
match held in Germany was televised in Spain. I was invited by a domes-

[9] An exception, of course, is that of the household of the domestic group
which opens its kitchen to the neighbors for the purpose of making money
as a rural tavern.

tic group that owned a television set to watch the fight. Before the program began, the domestic group discussed the fact that two *echekojaunak* in the *auzoa* were avid boxing fans and were keenly interested in the fight. After much discussion, it was resolved to send a young boy to invite the men to attend. He returned with the news that one man had accepted but the other declined. The man who accepted did not arrive until the seventh round. He entered sheepishly and went to a far corner of the room where he made an obvious effort to remain inconspicuous. From time to time a member of the host domestic group offered him some wine or cake, which he refused with an air of embarrassment. When the fight ended, he thanked the hosts and made a beeline for the door. I followed him out of the house and found the man who had declined the invitation waiting in the entranceway. "Who won?" He anxiously asked.

THE "AUZOA" AND FUNERARY RITUAL

Auzoa participation in the death of a member may be analyzed at two levels. The first is the stance that the *auzoa* membership takes before the wider society. The second is that which it takes before the bereaved domestic group.

The *auzoa* takes a corporate stance before the wider society, reflected in the fact that it participates as a unit in the funerary proceedings. The personal attributes of the deceased and the position of his domestic group within the *auzoa* structure are held in abeyance as the *auzoa* membership goes through a traditionally prescribed set of rituals. All *auzoa echekoak* send members to the *gauela*. All send members to conduct the corpse to the church. All activate at least minimal *artu-emon* ties, assist at the burial, *argia,* and *ogistie* ceremonies; and all lend a *kandela* to be placed on the *sepulturie* of the deceased. Participation in this expression of *auzoa* solidarity is by domestic groups and without reference to the attributes of the individuals in each. That is, custom demands that each domestic group be represented but does not specify by whom.

The foregoing view of the corporate *auzoa* response before the wider society is only a partial analysis of the nuances and subtleties in meaning inherent in the *auzoa* reaction to the death in its membership. The *auzoa* members also fulfill certain obligations to the bereaved domestic group. In this latter context the internal structuring of the *auzoa* in terms of subgroupings and *auzurrikourrena* relationships becomes apparent. This may best be understood by viewing the relationship between *auzoa* members and the bereaved domestic group as two-directional. On the one hand, the *auzoa* domestic groups may, in the context of funerary proceedings, express their ties with the bereaved *echekoak;* conversely, the bereaved *echekoak* may use the occasion to reaffirm its ties within the *auzoa.*

While every domestic group in the *auzoa* must participate minimally at each stage in the funerary proceedings, each is in a position to condition the intensity of its participation according to its social and economic involvement with the bereaved *echekoak.* Therefore, whereas all domestic groups will send at least one representative to the *gauela,* representatives wishing to display a particularly close tie with the bereaved *echekoak* will remain for most of the night. Similarly, when it comes time to give *artu-emon* Masses, each *auzoa* domestic group is in a position to express its relationship with the deceased and his *echekoak.* A domestic group perceiving a special tie may give an entire Mass or series of Masses, whereas other *auzoa* members give only the minimum. When it is time to place *kandelak* on the *sepulturie,* each *auzoa* domestic group shows its relationship with the deceased. Some simply place the *kandela* for the duration of the *argia* and *ogistie* ceremonies, while others leave their candles on the *sepulturie* until they are consumed. At this point, the *auzurrikourrena* can demonstrate its special relationship and continue to replenish the *kandela* throughout the year of formal *lutue.* Another occasion in the funerary cycle which may reflect differential *auzoa* relationships is the anniversary Mass given for the deceased by his domestic group. *Auzoa* domestic groups that feel a particular tie with the bereaved *echekoak* may attend these functions (the *auzurrikourrena* will almost certainly send a representative).

In the context of the funerary proceedings, the bereaved *echekoak* may affirm relationships that it values with individual *auzoa* domestic groups. Its dependence upon the *auzurrikourrena* throughout the proceedings is in itself an affirmation of the close tie existing between these two domestic groups. The selection of the *anderuek* provides an opportunity to reaffirm a particularly close tie between *echekoak*. The bereaved domestic group makes its choice from among the young unmarried men of the *auzoa,* favoring those young men from domestic groups with which it has a close bond.[10]

A former opportunity for differentiating among *auzoa* members was the selection of the *ogidune* and *estipendiyue* functionaries. Informants are explicit on this point and state that the selection was made on the basis of perceived close ties between the domestic groups. Another source of differentiation open to the bereaved domestic group is the possibility of inviting certain individuals in the *auzoa* to attend the funerary meal while excluding others.

Whereas the funerary proceedings serve as a context in which existing social ties between domestic groups may be expressed and reaffirmed, the death of an individual may also serve to reorder the existing relationship between them:

Echekoak A and *echekoak* B were on bad terms. For a period of approximately twenty years the two domestic groups bordered on feuding. From time to time small incidents occurred between the two domestic groups, and these were sufficient to nurture the ill will existing between them. Then the *echekojaun* of A was killed in a sudden and tragic accident. That night the *echekojaun* and *echekoandria* of B attended the *gauela.* Their presence and support at this trying and emotional time was sufficient to mend the breech between the two families.

In summary, *auzoa* participation in funerary ritual includes two major emphases which are played out simultaneously: all *auzoa echekoak* participate in an expression of *auzoa* solidarity before the wider village society; and the occasion provides an opportunity for an affirmation of perceived ties between individual domestic groups within the *auzoa.* Significantly, the expression of concern at this

---

[10] The selection is normally made from domestic groups which participate with the bereaved *echekoak* in *auzoa* subgroupings. However, selection of the *anderuek* is seldom entirely free. The small size of the average *auzoa* and present tendency for young bachelors to leave at an early age for the New World or for jobs in nearby urban centers reduces the number of men who are available to serve as *anderuek.*

level is between domestic groups and without reference to the personal attributes of the deceased.

There is yet another aspect to participation in the funerary proceedings of a deceased member. Individuals attending the services as *echekoak* representatives may also be acting in a personal capacity. *Auzoa* participation in funerary ritual, like *echekoak* participation, requires an adult representative of each sex. Everything else being equal, the *echekojaun* and *echekoandria* are expected to meet this obligation; however, other considerations may modify this ideal pattern of representation.

Generational distinctions in the *auzoa* membership are significant conditioners of social interaction. Individuals of a given generation are likely to identify with and maintain more intensive relationships with members of their own generation than with those of another. All former *echekojaunak* and *echekoandriak* occupy a similar status within their domestic groups. Furthermore, they have known and worked with one another in common *auzoa* activities for many years. The generation of actual *echekojaunak* and *echekoandriak* occupy similar positions within their respective *echekoak*. They are the decision makers and the activators of the communal efforts that affect their individual households. Dependent, unmarried adult members of the *auzoa* occupy a subordinate position within their respective domestic groups as well as in the wider village society. More than one generation may be represented among the unmarried, dependent domestic group members present in the *auzoa*. Even here, the generational distinction is apparent. The elderly subordinated members are likely to interact more frequently with one another than with younger subordinated members. Children are also aware of the generational distinctions.[11]

---

[11] It is my impression that age-grading in Basque society, while a salient and identifiable feature of social organization, plays a less important role in the total picture than is the case in some other European peasant groups (see Arensberg 1938:107–45). In Basque society, interaction across generational lines is frequent, carried out with relative ease, and deemed to be scarcely worthy of comment by the actors themselves.

Generational differences are often reflected in the selection of
the domestic group representative for the funeral of a deceased
auzoa member. If the deceased was a former *echekojaun* or *echekoandria,* the former *echekojaunak* and *echekoandriak* of the *auzoa*
will probably serve as the representatives for their respective domestic groups. This is recognition of the fact that the bond between the
elderly is stronger than that between the young and the old.[12] The
practice of selecting children to serve as *anderuek* at the death of a
child is another affirmation of the generational distinction.

One final distinction in funerary ritual that is made with reference to the personal attributes of the deceased is the selection of
the *ogidune* and *estipendiyue.* These representatives must have the
same marital status as the deceased.

IMPACT OF DEATH ON THE INTERNAL STRUCTURING OF THE "AUZOA"

At one level, the impact of the death of a member upon the *auzoa*
is indirect. Communal projects and *auzoa* subgroupings operate on
a domestic group basis in which the labor of one individual is
equivalent to that of another. Thus, the network of cooperation between *echekoak* is not seriously affected by the death of a single
person. However, at another level, death may be a significant factor
which effects a rearrangement of *auzoa* patterns of authority and
influence. I am referring to the fact that death may remove charismatic individuals who play significant roles in the *auzoa* framework.

We have seen that there is no formal authority structure within
the *auzoa.* Even the *mayordomo* role lacks direct sanctioning power.
Still, there are many activities in the *auzoa* which are critical to the
well-being of the member households. Roads must be maintained to
ensure access to individual fields and the village nucleus, an ade-

---

[12] This does not mean that the actual *echekojaun* and *echekoandria* are excluded from the funeral. However, the elder members are almost certain to
attend. If the funeral is for a young *echekojaun* or *echekoandria,* it is less
common for retired elderly persons from the *auzoa* to attend.

quate domestic water supply must be guaranteed, electric power is
now deemed to be a necessity, and pride and deep religious senti-
ment demand that the *auzoa* chapel be maintained.

Given the lack of an effective formal authority structure and the
practice whereby *auzoa* decisions are made through public discussion of the issues, it is not surprising that those individuals who
display an inordinate amount of personal charisma are in a position
to influence *auzoa* affairs. In each *auzoa* there are one or two persons (usually males, but not necessarily so) who determine *auzoa*
policy. These individuals are skilled at presenting the issues, enlisting support for their ideas, and articulating public opinion against
those who oppose them. The death of one of these individuals becomes a matter of importance for the *auzoa* as well as the domestic
group:

"Sakoneta" was a charismatic person. He was not a native of Murélaga;
rather, he came from a *baserria* in Marquina. The name of his natal
baserria was "Sakoneta." Before he married he was a professional weight
lifter, and his reputation, both as an athlete and a gambler, was widespread. When he finally settled in Murélaga, his personal fame was of
such magnitude that he never assumed the name of his *baserria* of residence. Until the day he died the villagers referred to him as "Juan
Sakoneta" or simply "Sakoneta." His influence upon *auzoa* affairs was
great. Informants describe him as being alternately bullish and foxy. If
he was crossed, he would fly into a rage, which would usually have the
effect of cowing the dissenter. Although it was felt that Sakoneta tried to
manipulate *auzoa* projects in such a manner as to benefit his own household, his suggestions were rarely rejected.

Sakoneta's domestic group became the most influential in the *auzoa*.
This was partly due to the fact that he was the natural leader (and on
very good terms with the local parish priest) and partly to the large number of offspring that he fathered. However, with the passing years his
wife died and his children married into other households or emigrated.
Finally he named a daughter as heir to the household, and soon after her
marriage he died. His domestic group's former influence on *auzoa* affairs
ceased immediately. Instead of the charismatic figure who was the *echekojaun* of the numerically largest domestic group in the *auzoa*, the *baserria* now hosted a young couple living alone. Not only did Sakoneta's son-

in-law occupy a relatively unimportant position because of his age and short-term residence, he also had to labor under the shadow of his deceased father-in-law. Instead of being identified with the *baserria* on which he was residing, the young man was often referred to as "Sakoneta'n Juan" (Sakoneta's Juan). Some members of the *auzoa* directed their resentment of the deceased Sakoneta toward the young *echekojaun*.

INTER-"AUZOA" TIES

The memberships of contiguous *auzoak* were seen to have reciprocal obligations with respect to funeral attendance and *artu-emon*. The latter is played out at the level of minimal *artu-emon* exchange between all of the domestic groups of the two *auzoak*. This practice results partially from the fact that the majority of face-to-face contacts beyond the *auzoa* are likely to be with members of contiguous *auzoak*. At their peripheries, the landholdings of the two *auzoak* have a common border. Furthermore, there may be a basis for some formal cooperation between contiguous *auzoak*. Both *auzoak* may have forest reserves in the same region and may unite to perform common *auzolan* to ensure that the access roads are maintained. Specific economic ties between domestic groups of two contiguous *auzoak,* while not common, do develop. A handicapped or weakened domestic group may rent a meadow or field to a domestic group from another *auzoa* (the property in question is normally located near the periphery of the *auzoa* and therefore roughly equidistant from the two households).

Significant ties between *auzoak* are established through marriage. There is no stated preference for *auzoa* endogamy, although there is a fairly high statistical incidence of such marriages (see Table 2). If the individual does marry outside the *auzoa,* he is more likely to marry into a nearby *auzoa* than into a more distant one. Proximity affords greater opportunity for initial contacts and later courting, and as a result the individual domestic group is more likely to have kindred members and ties of filiation with domestic groups in a neaby *auzoa* than in more distant ones. Table 2 illustrates the distribution of residence origins of the spouses of 115 heirs to *baserriak*.

TABLE 2

RESIDENCE ORIGIN OF THE AFFINES OF 115 MARRIAGES
INVOLVING HEIRS TO BASERRIAK

Origin of Affine	Number
Same *auzoa* as the heir	23
Auzoa contiguous to that of the heir	25
Other *baserria* in Murélaga	28
Village nucleus	6
Baserria from nearby town	24
Baserria from rest of Vizcaya	9

Of the 115 marriages in the sample, 48 (or 41.7 per cent) involve two persons from the same or contiguous *auzoak*. In 76 cases (or 66 per cent of the total) both partners are from a *baserria* in Murélaga, while in 109 instances (or 94.8 per cent of the total) both partners were raised on *baserriak*. If we examine the problem more closely, we find that certain contiguous *auzoak* are in a dyadic relationship with respect to total *artu-emon* exchange, whereas the domestic groups of other similarly contiguous *auzoak* do not share total reciprocity. The *auzoa* Zubero is a case in point. There is *artu-emon* reciprocity between all of the domestic groups of Zubero and those of the contiguous *auzoa* Malax. However, Zubero *eche-koak* do not entertain the same degree of reciprocity with those of the *auzoa* Urriola (which is also contiguous to Zubero). The significant factor seems to be that Malax and Zubero share a common funerary road or *andabidea,* whereas Urriola is on another road system.

In the foregoing statistics, at least two trends are apparent. First, as physical distance between the *baserriak* of two prospective marriage partners increases, the likelihood of their marrying decreases. This suggests that face-to-face contact in the context of agriculture and everyday activities is a stronger basis for forming lasting ties than the periodic and sporadic contacts made in the village nucleus through attendance at church, village fiestas, and the village schools.[13] Second, few persons from the village nucleus ever marry into farming domestic groups. The reason lies partly in the fact that one of the qualifications for being named heir to the farm is for the candidate to contract marriage with a "suitable" affine (see page 107). "Suitable" for the farming domestic group means that the prospective affine has experience and demonstrated ability in agriculture. Few persons from the nucleus are as qualified in this area as persons raised on a *baserria*.[14] While marriages between persons from contiguous *auzoak* are frequent, this alone is insufficient to account for the presence of *artu-emon* reciprocity between the total memberships of contiguous *auzoak*.

[13] While school attendance brings young people into daily contact, children leave school at the age of fourteen. This means that they cease to have daily contact before they might entertain the idea of entering into a relationship which could lead to marriage. A factor which further reduces the likelihood that an acquaintanceship made during one's school days might lead to marriage is the fact that the schools themselves are segregated along sexual lines. Boys and girls attend separate classes, and they seldom mingle, even during recreation periods.

[14] Conversely, it is quite common for persons from *baserriak* to marry into households in the village nucleus. It is also quite common for two persons who are excluded from the heirship in their respective rural household to contract marriage and move to the nucleus. In fact, the majority of adults in the nucleus today were raised on *baserriak*.

5

The Kindred and Ritual Kinship

𝒯HE Basque kinship system is bilateral in that ego traces his kinsmen to an equal degree through both his father and mother. The reckoning is rather shallow from both the lineal and the lateral viewpoints. Informants are often hard-pressed to provide accurate genealogical data on their grandparents—particularly if they did not know them personally. Traced laterally, kinship ties are deemed important to the second-cousin degree of relatedness, although there exists a blurred perception of third cousins as being related.[1]

When discussing their kinship relationships, informants distinguish between the categories of *familizhe* and *familizhekue*. In Chapter 3, we examined the *familizhe,* which includes ego's parents, spouse, siblings, and offspring. The present chapter is concerned with the *familizhekue.*

---

[1] An area of suggested research is the degree to which ego's perception of his kindred relations is conditioned by his age and position within the domestic group. Interviews with Basque informants indicate that within the course of his lifetime, the individual changes from being "ascent-oriented" to "descent-oriented." Elderly informants who can produce a wealth of information on far-removed nephews and nieces often find it difficult to provide data on their own deceased parents or siblings of their deceased parents. This may be a common feature in other bilateral kinship systems.

The *familizhekue* includes both affinally and consanguineally reckoned relatives. Included in ego's *familizhekue* are all of his consanguineal relatives reckoned bilineally to the grandparental generation and bilaterally to the degree of second cousins. In addition, a corresponding affine is appended to each consanguineally determined position within the *familizhekue*. The kinship terminology is totally consistent with the fact that a position in the *familizhekue* structure may be occupied by either a consanguine or an affine, and the attendant behavior is the same in either case (see Figure 4). FaBro is called *osabie* and FaSi *izekue*, and FaBroWi is *izekue* while FaSiHu is *osabie*. Similarly, FaBroSo is termed *lengosue* and FaBroDa *lengosinie*, while FaBroSoWi is also *lengosinie* and FaBroDaHu is *lengosue*. Thus, blood and marriage are equally significant as criteria for membership in the *familizhekue*.

I consider the *familizhekue* to be an example of a *kindred*. Freeman states: "...a kindred—is not a group in the sociological sense of the term, but rather a category of cognates, a set of persons who have in common the characteristic that they are all related cognatically in varying degrees to the same person" (Freeman 1961:202). He expressly rejects the notion that affines may be included (*ibid.:* 201). Thus the Basque *familizhekue*, which includes affines, fails to fit the definition. However, Goodenough believes it may be a mistake to assume that the kindred is necessarily composed of individuals; rather, we may have to consider it as being constituted of nuclear families (Goodenough 1961:1345). Goodenough supports his contention by employing Freeman's own data on the Iban of Borneo to demonstrate that the Iban kindred is made up of *bilek* families rather than individuals (*ibid.*).

The crux of the matter lies in distinguishing between the kindred, treated as a social category, and the category as a pool for the formation of action groups. As a social category, the Basque *familizhekue* is defined by the network of consanguineal ties traced cognatically from a single ego. Activation of these ties for the purpose of forming common activity groups is done on a domestic

group basis. Therefore, in spite of the fact that the structural definition of the kindred is contingent upon the grid of biological ties,
translation of these relationships into organizational terms entails the
participation of *echekoak* memberships rather than individuals.[2]
The kindred obligations of the domestic group are defined by tracing the cognatic ties of the active selected heir. At marriage the
affine assumes jural status in a new kindred and relinquishes membership in a former one. While affines are appended on to the *familizhekue* at each of the structural positions, they do not serve as
links for further extension of the network. FaBroWi is an *izekue*
for ego, but FaBroWiBro is not a relative.

Inclusion of the affine into the domestic group network of kindred
obligations outlasts the death of the blood relative through whom
the tie was originally established. That is, a woman who marries
ego's *osabie* and thereby becomes his *izekue* remains an *izekue* even
after death of *osabie*. This widowed *izekue* is then capable through
remarriage of extending ego's definition of his kindred obligations.
The second husband of the *izekue* become an *osabie* for ego. This is
in accordance with the principle that the spouses of relatives are
relatives.

One of the structural features of the kindred is that it is not a discrete social unit. The kindred is defined by tracing the bilateral kinship ties of a particular ego. For each ego (excepting full siblings),
the kindred boundaries are different. The kindred defined by ego,
while discrete from his point of view, is abstracted from a con-
tinuum of overlapping social categories (that is, the kindred definitions of other actors). In Basque society the kindred tie between
two individuals (which translates into a tie between their respective
domestic groups) is reciprocal and symmetrical. No individual defines another as a part of his *familizhekue* without in turn being

---

[2] When providing genealogical information, informants use house names
rather than personal names to identify their relatives. Thus, the informant
identifies the entire *echekoak* membership of another household as "first
cousin."

defined as a member of the other's *familizheḳue*—and at the same degree of intimacy.

The organization of kindred-based action groups involves an extension of the same logic that underlies the domestic group structure in that there is full equivalence between the sexes and between affines and consanguines. Both the *echeḳojaun* and *echeḳoandria* discharge the kindred obligations of their domestic group. This is true whether they are participating in economic activities or providing moral support at a death in the kindred membership. Just as the affinally residing *echeḳoandria* activates the *sepulturie* of her spouse's natal household, it is she who represents the domestic group in the female sections of the church and procession during the funerary proceedings of a deceased kindred member.

If at marriage, or after producing offspring, affines are incorporated into the domestic group and *familizhe* of the heir, theoretically there are four lineal ties which could be reckoned and activated to define the kindred of each *echeḳoaḳ*. The kindred for a given domestic group could consist of the bilineally and bilaterally reckoned ties of both the *echeḳojaun* and *echeḳoandria*. In this case the kindred definition on a given generational level would consist of all domestic groups with which at least a second-cousin tie—reckoned from both the *echeḳojaun* and *echeḳoandria*—could be demonstrated.

To a degree, this is precisely what happens. The marriage between the *echeḳojaun* and *echeḳoandria* creates a special tie between the heir's *echeḳoaḳ* and the affine's former domestic group's kindred. Just as ego has special terms for the members of his *familizhe*, so he assumes a similar set of terms for spouse's *familizhe*. With respect to spouse's *familizheḳue*, both ego and spouse employ the same kinship terms. Ego employs the same terminology for members of spouse's former *familizheḳue* that he employs for members of his own. WiMoBro is *osabie* for both ego and his spouse, and *osabie* reciprocates with the term *lobie* for both of them. Ego and his wife use the term *lengosue* for WiMoBroSo and *lengosinie* for WiMoBro-

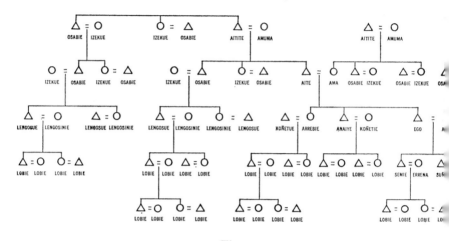

Figure 4

SoWi. They reciprocate with *lengosue* for the male ego and *lengosinie* for his spouse (see Figure 4).

While, theoretically, the operational kindred of a given *echekoak* might include all domestic groups with which cognatic ties of both the *echekojaun* and *echekoandria* could be demonstrated, in actual practice there is differential reckoning. This restriction is partially dictated by the need for parsimony. Total activation of the full range of potential relationships would make the system unmanageable. On any one generational level, emphasis is upon the relationships established by reckoning the consanguineal ties of the heir to the household. The ties established by the inclusion of the ego-heir into his spouse's kindred are, for the time being, held in abeyance. A bilineal reckoning of the heir's consanguineal ties, extended bilaterally to include second cousins, defines the parameters of the domestic group's kindred obligations.

However, at this point there is further operational limitation of the network of relationships out of which action groups are likely to arise. Ego's domestic group (that is, the definer) is likely to enter into economic activities only with those *echekoak* with which it can trace a consanguineal tie with the *active selected heir*. This re-

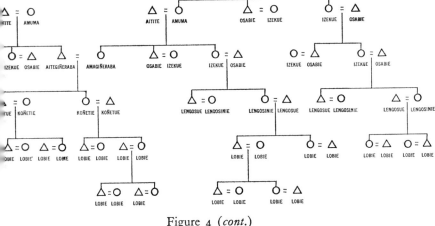

Figure 4 (*cont.*)

stricted group of *echekoak* may be referred to as ego's kindred core.[3]

Figure 5 is a diagrammatic view of the kindred core of ego's domestic group. The letter H designates first cousins of ego who occupy the heirship in their respective households, which form ego's kindred core.[4]

The discharge of obligations within the kindred core is done on a domestic group basis, entails the equal participation of the affines, and is reciprocal. No domestic group defines another as a part of its kindred core without in turn being included as a member of the other's kindred core.

For ego's *echekoak* there is a great deal of similarity between its kindred core and its *auzoa* subgroupings. Both are abstracted from a wider social category (the kindred category and the *auzoa*, respectively) for the purpose of forming action groups which engage

---

[3] While informants are aware of and able to verbalize this distinction, there is not a single corresponding Basque term to designate it.

[4] In this particular instance the tie is seen as obtaining between first-cousin *echekoak*. Indeed, the relationship is viewed as being most intense at that level. However, it may also be extended in a more muted manner to second-cousin *echekoak* where ego can trace a consanguineal tie to the heir.

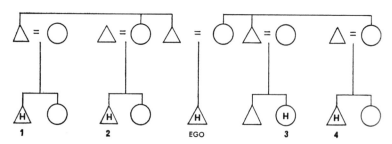

Figure 5. The Kindred Core

in economic cooperation. In fact, it is common for the defining domestic group to activate both simultaneously, particularly in the
formation of wheat threshing groups. The notable difference between the *auzoa* subgroupings and the kindred core is that each
echekoak has the potential of entering into several of the former,
whereas each has but one of the latter.

In Chapter 4 we noted the importance of the spatial arrangement of the dwellings within the *auzoa* as a conditioner of social
relations between their memberships. The *auzurrikourrena* is
usually the nearest—in a geographical sense—to the definer. *Auzoa*
subgroupings are most likely to arise between the memberships of
three or four contiguous dwellings. Activation of kindred-core ties
is similarly influenced by the spatial arrangement of the constituent
households. If a domestic group has a kindred-core tie with another
in a different village, it is unlikely that this tie will be activated
for the purpose of labor exchange. Kindred-core ties only serve as
the basis for economic cooperation between domestic groups of
the same village. Whereas all of the *echekoak* in Murélaga with a
kindred-core tie could enter into labor exchange, this rarely happens.
The domestic group is not likely to activate all of its kindred-core
ties to carry out a particular economic task.[5] Rather, it activates
those ties that it maintains with *echekoak* in the same or contiguous

---

[5] This is not to say that the total kindred core is not activated at social
events. All kindred-core *echekoak* participate in the funerary proceedings of a
deceased member.

auzoak. Kindred-core ties with *echekoak* in more distant sectors of the municipality are seldom activated.[6] Thus, the kindred core serves as a social category within which the domestic group activates ties of reciprocal labor exchange with a limited circle of *echekoak*. Everything else being equal, the definer activates ties with kindred-core *echekoak* that are close by and neglects its more distant kindred-core *echekoak*.

Further spatial conditioning of social relations is seen in the fact that when it comes to interacting with kinsmen, geographical proximity may override genealogical considerations. Strictly speaking, informants are on a more intimate basis with first-cousin *echekoak* than with second cousins.[7] However, in actual practice the domestic group is more likely to interact with a second-cousin domestic group living in the same or a proximate *auzoa* than with a first-cousin domestic group located in a more distant sector of the municipality. Therefore, as a rule of thumb in rural Basque society, when dealing with interaction based either on bonds of kinship or on common residence, the greater the physical distance between two *baserriak,* the greater the social distance between their *echekoak* memberships.[8]

---

[6] Where the defining and the defined *echekoak* are members of the same *auzoa*, the relationship between them is particularly intense. They will almost certainly participate jointly in one (or more) *auzoa* subgrouping(s). Furthermore, they may have an *auzurrikourrena* tie. This is not surprising since a kindred-core relationship between two domestic groups in the present generation is likely the result of a sibling tie between one of their respective heads in the last generation.

[7] This is true in spite of the fact that the differentiation between first and second cousins is not reflected in the kinship terminology (see Figure 4). However, if pressed to make the distinction, informants can interject the Basque equivalents of the words "first" and "second" before the terms *lengosue* and *lengosinie.*

[8] I am here concerned with a conditioning factor at the conceptual level and not with considerations of actual physical scale. The definition of distance is specific to the individual social setting and differs as one moves from village to village. In the nucleated *auzoa* settlement of Murélaga, distance between dwellings is on an entirely different scale than in some parts of the Basque country, where the closest neighbor may live more than a kilometer away.

Common activities based upon the perception of a kindred tie between domestic groups include some labor exchange and participation in significant rites of passage. We have seen that labor exchange is restricted to three or four kindred domestic groups in close physical proximity to one another. The forms of labor exchange are the same as those described for the *auzoa* subgroupings. In fact, it is common for kindred-core and *auzoa* subgrouping members to work side by side on the particular project. In either event the recipient domestic group has the obligation to reciprocate.

Financial assistance offers a further example of economic interaction between kindred-core domestic groups. If the domestic group is in need of money, it will most likely request it from a kindred domestic group with which it maintains a degree of intimacy and mutual trust. The most common reasons for borrowing money are to make a down payment on a farm as part of a contract of purchase or to provide a domestic group member with passage money to the New World.

Kindred members are asked to participate in the rites of passage of members of the defining domestic group. Kindred participation in funerary ritual is the subject of a subsequent section. However, the funeral is not the only ritual context in which kinsmen participate. Whenever there is a newborn child in the domestic group, female representative of kindred-core *echekoak* are expected to attend the *aur bazkaria*. This is also the occasion at which the child is presented to the *auzoa*. Usually only those kindred domestic groups residing in Murélaga send a representative. At a child's First Communion[9] a number of kindred members from physically proximate households are invited to a banquet. A wedding serves to activate kindred ties. Generally, all domestic groups within the kindred core whose memberships reside in Murélaga will be represented at the wedding banquet. Some kindred members from outside of the village may attend as well.

---

[9] The custom of hosting a large fiesta on the occasion of a child's First Communion is relatively recent in Murélaga (dating from the Spanish Civil War).

Patterns of hospitality between kindred members are defined quite rigidly. It is not customary for kindred members residing in the same village to make informal visits to one another's *baserria*. However, if such a visit does occur, the host domestic group feels obligated to treat the guest with a great deal of respect and attention.

The banquet given yearly by the domestic group on the feast day of the *auzoa* patron saint provides an important opportunity to affirm kindred ties. Each *echekoak* in the *auzoa* invites those members of the kindred with whom it perceives a special tie. Two categories of relatives attend such affairs. Members of the kindred core and married siblings of both the *echekojaun* and *echekoandria* form one of the categories. These are persons who are residing on other *baserriak* in Murélaga, on *baserriak* in nearby villages, or in the village nucleus. These guests later reciprocate by playing host at a banquet on the feast day of the patron saint of their *auzoa*. The second category of kinsmen likely to attend the banquet are relatives residing in urban areas like Eibar, Guernica, or Bilbao. These relatives may be genealogically close to members of the host domestic group, but they may also be as distant as second or third cousins. Their presence is indicative of the modifications that kinship ties may undergo when they are between an urban and a rural domestic group. This urban-rural kinship relationship turns upon a symbiotic exchange of goods and services. While the relationship is played out along kinship lines, it is as much a relationship between the agriculturalist and urbanite as between kinsmen. When members of the rural *echekoak* visit the city, they depend upon their urban relatives for meals, advice, directions, a place of refuge in a generally unfriendly atmosphere, and a possible place to spend the night. If a young man or woman leaves the village to study or serve an apprenticeship in an urban area, he or she is likely to seek room and board with a kinsman. These rural visitors are normally quite welcome since they bring with them gifts of fresh garden produce, eggs, poultry, and milk products. If the visit lasts for a long period of time, the rural guest pays cash for his room and board, and his *echekoak* sends a steady stream of farm produce to the host domestic group. It is quite common for urban kinsmen to visit their rural relations on a Sunday outing. In some instances, an urban family will spend its annual vacation time on the *baserria* of a kinsman. During the annual fiesta (which lasts for a number of days), many *echekoak* in Murélaga extend such hospitality to visiting urban kinsmen.[10]

Therefore, a relationship of mutual convenience exists between urban and rural relatives which is often out of proportion to the degree of their genealogical relatedness. If both domestic groups resided in rural areas, their kinship tie would be insufficient grounds to interact beyond a minimal level.

The manner of attending the *auzoa* fiesta day banquet differs for the two categories of kinsmen. The urban relatives attend as *echekoak* units in the spirit of an outing. Fewer members of local kindred-core domestic groups attend—the *echekojaun* or the *echeko-andria,* or possibly both. However, not uncommonly a local kindred-core *echekoak* will be represented by a single young child or old person.

Within the *auzoa* framework, each domestic group is likely to entertain one dyadic relationship with another (*auzurrikourrena*). Within the kindred there is also the possibility of forming a dyadic tie between two *echekoak*. The relationship is based upon the mutual convenience of both. In some instances, they may interact on equal terms, as when the domestic group shops at a store in the

---

[10] The kinship ties that the urbanite maintains with rural relatives may be important to him for reasons of personal identity. The *baserria* and rural way of life are deemed to be symbols of the "Basque" way of life. In the rural areas the Basque language is best preserved, and Basque cultural and ethnic features predominate. In the cities, the Basque population is in the minority, and the Basque ethnic identity under attack. Finally, the notions that agriculture is a more honorable and moral way of life and that the peasant is more representative of "natural man" possessed of a straightforward manner of dealing with his fellows permeates the thinking of many urbanites. The urbanite of rural origins is often proud of the fact. He jealously conserves his ties with kinsmen in the rural areas, although he is not about to return or change places with the farmer.

nucleus owned by a kindred member. It receives special treatment in return for the guarantee of its continued patronage. However, the dyadic relationship between two domestic groups may be more that of patron and client:

V.C. is an erudite individual. He is an ex-village secretary, a layman's lawyer, and a civil engineer. Since he is from Murélaga, he enjoys the trust of the villagers. Many prefer to call upon him rather than the village secretary when in need of legal advice. He is constantly employed framing legal documents, interpreting contracts, settling boundary disputes, and mapping landholdings. The majority of *echekoak* that have a kindred tie with V.C. are careful to maintain and reinforce it. When he became seriously ill and was taken to Bilbao, there was a continual procession of relatives to visit him.

Kinship ties are often activated with a relative in the New World or Australia who is in a position to assist a domestic group member to emigrate to these areas:

Enrique wished to go to the United States, but he was not interested in working as a sheepherder. He requested the aid of his older brother in Idaho (a United States citizen). The brother made the necessary arrangements for Enrique to enter the United States as a regular immigrant.

Conversely, a relative in a foreign land may desire to have a member of his kindred with him.

Matilde's uncle and aunt from Argentina were childless. While on a trip to the Basque country, they visited her domestic group. After returning to Argentina, they petitioned the parents to allow Matilde to live with them as a daughter. Matilde went and stayed for two years. She would have stayed longer, but she disliked Argentina.

Presently, the majority of villagers who emigrate to foreign areas do so with the assistance of a relative who preceded them.

Thus far kindred relations have been treated as a network of ties existing between *echekoak*. Individual actors activate the ties, but in the capacity of domestic group representatives. However, personal ties between individual kindred members are also present.

Generational and sexual distinctions condition activation of personal ties with other kindred members. A young male is likely to be on particularly friendly terms with a male cousin of the same age. After Sunday Mass, the two young men may seek out one another's company. They go to the tavern to play cards or challenge one another to a *pelota* match in the *frontón*. Similarly, it is common to find *echekojaunak* who are cousins and of comparable age seated together in one of the taverns. Young women may entertain a particularly close friendship relationship with one or more of their female cousins. The girls may attend a dance in the nucleus together or plan an excursion to the mountains.

Marriage between kindred members is a possibility. Of the 115 marriages sampled in Table 2, eight (or 6.95 per cent) involve second cousins, three (or 2.60 per cent) involve first cousins, and there is one marriage between a woman and mother's brother.[11] The occurrence of such marriages is not surprising. In a situation where cousin marriage is neither prohibited nor discouraged, where there is a tendency toward village endogamy,[12] and where the total population is a little over one thousand persons, random selection of mates would produce an incidence of cousin marriage. Nor is the selection of a kinsman as spouse always the result of chance. If the selected heir to the *baserria* is particularly shy or unsuccessful in his relationships with members of the opposite sex, his parents may arrange a marriage with one of his cousins. In this way they ensure succession on the farm.

We have seen that each *echekoak* is at the center of a kindred category which is defined by tracing the consanguineal ties of the selected heir. It was noted that the spouse of the selected heir is also integrated into the domestic group's kindred category. The affine

---

[11] In these instances, a special dispensation must be obtained from the religious authorities. However, even in the case of first-cousin marriage, this is treated as a formality, and the priests make no effort to discourage the couple.

[12] Of the 115 marriages of heirs to *baserriak* that were sampled in Table 2, some 82 (or 71.3 per cent) are village endogamous.

and heir then play equal and complementary roles in meeting their domestic group's kindred obligations. It was also noted that the selected heir is incorporated, at least as reflected in kinship terminology, into the kindred category of the affine's natal *echekoak*. Thus, after his marriage, ego applies the same kinship term *osabie* for both his FaBro and his WiFaBro and, in turn, is referred to as *lobie* by both of them. He maintains a similar respect relationship with both. However, from ego's point of view, this kinship obligation to spouse's kindred members is defined on a personal rather than a domestic group basis. His *echekoak* has no special relationship with *echekoak* in spouse's natal kindred category or kindred core.

The significant fact is that the selected heir treats affinal relatives with the same respect accorded to consanguines, not because he interacts with them personally, but rather because his marriage is the basis for the formation of an *echekoak* obligation in the next generation. Ego's heir will define his own kindred category as consisting partly of relationships traced through ego's own family line and partly by tracing ego's spouse's family line. Thus, the affinal link existing between *echekoak* in one generation is transformed into a consanguineal tie once offspring are present. To the degree that ego's behavior toward spouse's kinsmen suggests that he identifies with them, we are presented with a reverse usage of the principle of filiation as it is commonly understood. Rather than "the relationship created by the fact of being the legitimate child of one's parents" (Fortes 1959:206), ego is activating the relationship established by being the legitimate parent of one's child.

Ego's behavior is not the same toward all of spouse's kinsmen. Marriage is felt to create a particularly close bond between ego and spouse's siblings (who are referred to generically as *koñatiek*). Just as ego maintains strong ties of sibling solidarity even after marriage, he recognizes that his spouse has a similar set of loyalties. These loyalties are so strong as to suggest that they are converted into an *echekoak* obligation between ego and his *koñatiek* domestic groups.

We may therefore refer to an *echekoak* sibling core of kinship obligations. The sibling core is made up of the siblings of the selected
heir *and* the siblings of the heir's spouse.

Figure 6 is a diagrammatic view of the sibling core for the *eche-*

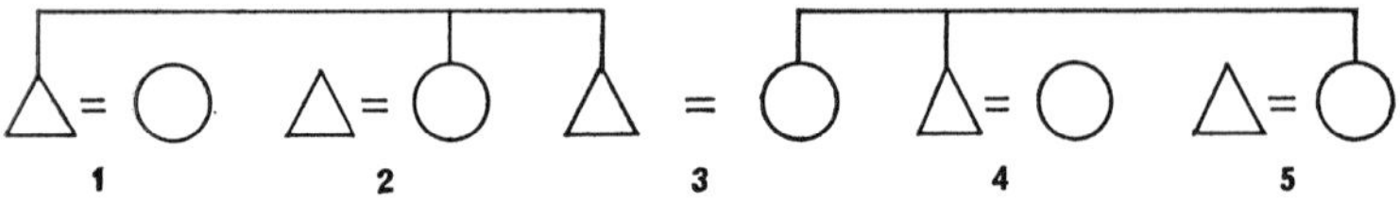

Figure 6. The Sibling Core

koak of the *echekojaun-echekoandria* couple designated by the number 3. The domestic groups of married couples 1, 2, 4, and 5 constitute the sibling core of 3. However, in accordance with the
principle that, with the exception of one's own spouse, affinal links
do not serve as the basis for a further extension of one's kinship ties,
domestic groups 1 and 2 are not felt to be related to domestic groups
4 and 5.

Action groups are likely to arise out of the sibling core. However,
with the sole exception of participation in funerary ritual, it is
unlikely that the entire sibling core of a particular *echekoak* will be
mobilized at any one time. The defining domestic group treats the
sibling core as a category in which it may activate one or several
ties for labor assistance. It is therefore not unusual to find that the
wheat-threshing team of a particular *echekoak* includes one or more
of the siblings of the selected heir's spouse. Here again spatial considerations partially determine which relationships will be activated.
Sibling-core ties serve as the basis for labor exchange only between
domestic groups residing in the same village. Similarly, sibling-core
ties are more likely to be activated with *echekoak* in the same or
proximate *auzoa* than with those in more distant sectors of the
municipality. Also sibling-core ties with spouse's siblings who reside
in urban areas are a frequent source of the same kind of rural-urban
kinship behavior as described for kindred members. In summary,

we have considered the following categories of kinship organization:

1. Kindred category. A pool of related *echekoak* with which the present heir of the defining *echekoak* may trace a consanguineal tie within the second-cousin degree of relatedness.

2. Kindred core. Those *echekoak*, normally within the first-cousin degree of relatedness, with which the household heir may trace a consanguineal kinship tie with the active household heir.

3. Kindred dyadic relations. The special relationship that develops between two kindred *echekoak* either because each provides the other with a comparable service or one provides the other with an extraordinary service (patron-client relationship).

4. Kindred personal ties. The relationship between two relatives of the same sex and generation.

5. Sibling core. A category which includes the *echekoak* of the married siblings of *both* the active *echekojaun* and *echekoandria*.

DEATH AND THE KINDRED

Kindred ties do not constitute a very significant basis for social interaction among the individual members of Basque society. Only rarely do common activity groups arise out of kindred relations. Given the dispersed nature of the settlement pattern and the fact that so many individuals are mobile and move to other parts of the Basque country and the world, the individual is in a position to activate only a few of his kindred ties. Months and even years go by without any contact between certain kindred members.

Participation in the kindred structure is largely on a domestic group rather than an individual basis. When an individual engages in a particular activity, he does so as a representative of his *echekoak*. We found this to be true of the majority of *auzoa* interaction as well. However, there is one significant difference. Since the *auzoa* is a common residential unit with corporate property, it must make decisions about common economic problems. Within the *auzoa* membership there is some structuring according to differential distribution of power and influence. The personal charisma of an individual is an important factor, and his removal by death leads to the redistribution of influence and authority. There is no analogous power structure within the kindred. Activation of kindred ties for the purpose of forming a common activity group involves the needs of only one of the participant *echekoak* (the domestic group which defines and activates the ties in the first place). The others attend and lend assistance, but they are not affected directly by any decisions that might be made. The participants hold no common property, have no common economic destiny, and need not make decisions in common. There is no internal kindred power structure, and personal charisma is an unimportant feature of kindred social organization.

The death of a member is not as significant for the kindred as it is for the domestic group or even the *auzoa*. The individual per se plays an unimportant role within the kindred. However, in another sense the death of a single individual may alter the very nature of the kindred structure. While participation in kindred relationships is by domestic groups, the definition of the kindred is always with respect to ties of blood or marriage traceable through specific individuals. We have noted that definition of the *echekoak* kindred in any one generation is derived by tracing the consanguineal ties of the selected heir. This means that over time there is attrition of some former kindred members (the new heir is genealogically one degree further removed from kindred members as defined through the former heir) and accretion of new kindred members (since the new heir includes in his definition *echekoak* with which he is related by reckoning ties through the parent who was residing in the household as the affinal spouse in the last generation). However, given the fact that the domestic group is ideally three-generational, it is possible that two selected heirs will be in residence simultaneously (the one active and the other retired). While, strictly speaking, the domestic group's kindred definition is traced through the active heir, in actual practice kindred ties as defined through the former heir are retained and activated insofar as the former heir (*or* spouse) is alive and present on the farm.[13] Therefore, to the extent that death removes a key individual in the system of reckoning, it causes the defining *echekoak* to redefine the parameters of its kindred. From the bereaved domestic group's viewpoint, the death of the former heir or spouse forces a reassessment of kindred ties with the most distantly related kindred members (as defined through the old couple). Similarly, these distant *echekoak* reassess their status with respect to the bereaved domestic group. The perception of the kinship relationship between the domestic groups is now so weak that it provides little basis for kindred interaction.

Death also forces internal restructuring of personal ties between kindred members and ties between domestic groups which are in a dyadic patron-client relationship. In the latter instance, the degree to which the client interacts with the patron because of the service provided by a specific individual of the patron domestic group will, of course, be altered if that individual dies. Thus, in the case of the erudite V.C. (see page 177), one can be certain that after his death few kindred members will continue to interact intensively with his domestic group.

PARTICIPATION OF THE KINDRED
IN FUNERARY PROCEEDINGS

A death in a member domestic group initiates the widest activation of kindred ties. All *echekoak* within the kindred category are advised immediately insofar as this is possible. Members of the

---

[13] As a corollary, even after both the former *echekojaun* and *echekoandria* are deceased, the domestic group will continue to activate kindred ties with distant kindred members (that is, "distant" as defined through the former heir and nonexistent as defined through the present heir) as long as the distantly related *echekoak* still contain members from the former generation. Thus, informants make statements like, "*Baserria* X is still a part of the *familizhekue* because old Maria, who was my deceased father's second cousin, is still living there. However, once she dies, they will no longer be relatives."

kindred core and sibling core who are residents of Murélaga are expected to send representatives to the *gauela*. Those members who live some distance from the village (but in the Basque country), while exempted from the *gauela,* are expected to attend the burial, *argia,* and *ogistie* services. The kindred-core and sibling-core *echekoak* are felt to have a particularly intensive obligation to the bereaved domestic group. They make a special effort to send both a male and female representative to the various funerary functions. They are likely to make a larger than minimal *artu-emon* donation (in some instances an *arimen onrak*). They also place a *kandela* on the *sepulturie* of the deceased during the *argia* service. Relatives of the deceased who stand in a close genealogical relationship to him, but who are not part of the sibling and kindred cores of the bereaved *echekoak* (that is, first cousin of the deceased, residing affinally in his or her household of postmarital residence), are likely to participate in the proceedings, but on an individual basis rather than as *echekoak* representatives. That is, the actual relative of the deceased attends the burial service and makes an *artu-emon* offering but does not place a *kandela* on the *sepulturie.*

While the social obligation of the kindred-core and sibling-core domestic groups is to send one representative of each sex to the services, custom does not dictate who must serve as *echekoak* representatives. The normal practice is for the *echekojaun* and *echekoandria* to meet this obligation, although there are exceptions. If the deceased, at the time of death, was residing in the household as a retired *echekojaun* or *echekoandria,* at least some of the representatives from kindred-core domestic groups will be former *echekojaunak* and *echekoandriak.*

All sibling-core and kindred-core *echekoak* have the obligation to send representatives to a funeral. This obligation holds true regardless of the personal attributes of the deceased or the position that he occupied within his domestic group prior to his death. Throughout the chapters on the domestic group and the *auzoa* we noted the full equivalence between affines and consanguines in the discharge of household obligations. This is also reflected clearly in the ways in which *echekoak* meet their funerary obligations to kinsmen. In the kindred section of the funerary procession, *echekojaunak* who are affines in their respective households walk alongside *echekojaunak* who are the heirs. There is no preference shown to the latter. The same is true in the ordering of the women's section. The following examples illustrate the equivalence between affines and consanguines in meeting *echekoak* funerary obligations:

1. A former *echekoandria* died in *baserria* X. Three of her grandsons were residing in the household so it was resolved to appoint them *anderuek* (in lieu of neighbors). The fourth person selected by the domestic group was the husband of one of the granddaughters of the deceased. In this instance all four men were felt to stand in the same kinship relation to the deceased.

2. J. was working in the fields when word arrived that the wife of her husband's first cousin had just died. She returned to her dwelling to inform her family. It was resolved that someone should set out immediately for the *baserria* of the deceased to attend the *gauela*. J. decided to go and left her husband at home to care for the livestock.[14]

3. J. received news that her husband's married brother had died in the New World. Since the man was married, and since in this case he was not even from J.'s natal household (her husband was the affine and she the heir), there was no formal obligation. However, J. chose to activate her sibling-core tie, offered a *memorizhe* for the deceased, and went into personal mourning.

In the chapter on the *auzoa* we noted that *auzoa* members are able to express, through differences in degree of participation in funerary proceedings, their perception of the tie they have with the bereaved domestic group. The domestic group may pattern its participation at the minimal level of traditionally sanctioned practice (that is, simply send representatives to the burial, *argia,* and *ogistie* services, make a minimal *artu-emon* donation, and provide a *kandela* for the *sepulturie* of the deceased for the duration of the

---

[14] An affine fulfills her *echekoak* obligation to the bereaved domestic group. The deceased in this instance was also residing as an affine.

argia and *ogistie* services). At the same time, the *auzoa* member is in a position to intensify his expression of involvement by making a more elaborate *artu-emon* donation (sometimes even an *arimen onrak*), by leaving a *kandela* on the *sepulturie* until the candle is consumed, and by attending services at which attendance is optional, such as anniversary Masses offered for the deceased. These same alternatives of intensified participation are also open to kindred members.[15] Kindred domestic groups that perceive no special tie with the bereaved domestic group participate at the level of minimal standard of accepted behavior.

Kinship serves as the basis for one other important source of assistance in funerary proceedings. A domestic group residing on a *baserria* that lacks a *sepulturie* depends upon an *echekoak* in its sibling core (most probably the domestic group of a married sibling of the selected heir) or its kindred core for the loan of a *sepulturie*. It uses this borrowed *sepulturie* throughout the year of formal mourning. Similarly, if the bereaved domestic group lacks an appropriate adult member to represent it in the *luto bankue* or *sepulturie,* it may arrange for a kinsman substitute. For instance, if there are no adult males in the bereaved domestic group, it may call upon a male sibling, sibling-in-law, or even first cousin to accept the obligation of representing the domestic group each Sunday in the *luto bankue*. An extreme case illustrates how both a substitute *sepulturie* and substitute representatives may be arranged for:

A. was an unmarried woman in her late seventies. She resided in the village nucleus and outlived all of her *familizhe* with the exception of a

---

[15] It should be mentioned that differential involvement in funerary proceedings, whether by kindred or *auzoa* members, is not always an indication that a special tie exists between the donor and the bereaved domestic groups. Individuals and domestic groups differ in their interpretations of acceptable funerary procedure. Some domestic groups may be said to overreact while others underreact. There are *echekoak* that are represented at every funeral that takes place in Murélaga, whereas there are others that are not represented at funerals where they have a kindred or *auzoa* obligation to participate, although the latter behavior is quite rare. The most socially withdrawn domestic groups tend to meet their funerary obligations, even if they reject social obligations in other contexts.

married brother residing near Bilbao. A. died and her brother came to the village to make the funerary arrangements. He was at a loss as to how to provide *sepulturie* and *luto banƙue* representation for his dead sister. The household where she resided lacked a *sepulturie*. The solution was found when a first cousin of the deceased agreed to activate his household *sepulturie* in her honor and attend the *luto banƙue*. In effect, the deceased was transferred to another *echeƙoaƙ* after death.

In summary, funerary ritual is the only occasion on which total membership of the kindred category is mobilized and participates in a common activity.[16] The distinction between the kindred category and members of the kindred core is reflected in gradations of the degree to which *echeƙoaƙ* participate in the proceedings.

RITUAL KINSHIP

Ritual kinship, as expressed in baptismal godparenthood, may or may not parallel existing blood ties. It is common for the parents of a newborn infant to select its godparents from members of their respective *familizheƙ*. This is especially true for the first few children. In the case of the first-born, it is common to name the father of one parent as *aite bezuetaƙo* (godfather) and the mother of the other as *ama bezuetaƙo* (godmother). At the birth of the next child, the order is reversed. Subsequent selections of godparents are made from *osabieƙ* and *izeƙueƙ* (uncles and aunts), either on the child's parental or grandparental generations. A further source of godparents is the child's older siblings, and members of the wider kindred, the *auzoa,* or simply friends are also possible candidates.

The godparents pay the expenses of the baptism. They alone take the infant to the church (the parents do not attend the ceremony). Afterward the parents treat them to a light meal.

In the eyes of the Church a relationship of spiritual affinity is established between individuals who serve as godmother and god-

---

[16] Kindred members residing elsewhere in Spain or in foreign areas participate as well. Distance prevents them from attending the actual burial, but once news of the death reaches them, they are quick to send condolences and *artu-emon* offerings.

father of a child. This affinity is expressed in the fact that an incest taboo is imposed between them. However, in Basque society there is little indication that this formal religious interpretation serves as the basis for a deeper and more intensive relationship between the two godparents. Similarly, there is little emphasis placed upon the tie established between the godparents and the natural parents of the child. The elaborate godparenthood relationship, which exists in other parts of Spain (Pitt-Rivers 1958), is not a feature of the social organization of Murélaga.

The one significant relationship created through godparenthood is that between the godparent and the godchild. This tie is deemed to be particularly important for any individual. The godparent provides the godchild with gifts and guidance throughout his lifetime. Each year at Easter the godmother bakes a special pastry for her godchild. The godfather gives the child a small sum of money. A little girl's first dress and first pair of earrings are often gifts from her godmother. A boy's first pair of long pants is likely to be a gift from one or both of his godparents.[17] Godparents are invited to most of the significant events in the life of the godchild. Both attend his First Communion and give him a present. Both are present at his Confirmation and wedding and give gifts on these occasions.

The godchild is expected to treat his godparents with a great deal of respect. Ideally, they should be accorded the same respect extended to natural parents. If the godparent is in need of assistance, the godchild feels obligated to help. Thus, a godchild may contribute to the economic well-being of the godparent's household. The godchild frequently gives presents to his godparents, particularly when he returns from a foreign land. He brings back small gifts for *familizhe* and *echekoak* members, but almost certainly includes gifts for his godparents as well.

The godparental relationship is overlain with emotion in the

---

[17] A description of the gifts commonly given to godchildren by godparents may be found in Azkue 1959:189.

event of death. If the godparent dies, the godchild will mourn as if the deceased were a natural parent. This mourning is at a personal level and does not necessarily involve the *echekoak* of the bereaved. The death of a godchild touches the godparent as if one of his own children had died. If the godchild dies in infancy or early child-hood, the godmother purchases a suit of clothing for the corpse, and the godfather purchases the coffin. Throughout the Basque country there is a high degree of intimacy and affect in the god-parent-godchild bond. Some say that "When godchildren die and go to heaven, they greet their godparents there before greeting their natural parents," or that "When a godmother dies, her godchild [who died as an infant] will come forward to welcome her to heaven" (Azkue 1959:188). The structuring of the funerary proces-sion reflects the special nature of the godparent-godchild relation-ship. The survivor of the relationship takes his or her place among the bereaved domestic group members throughout the funerary proceedings.

An example of the manner in which the godparent tie may over-ride other considerations is seen in the following:

F. was the *echekojaun* of *baserria* X. The only other adult male present in his domestic group was the former *echekojaun*. F. fought on the side of the Basque Nationalists during the Spanish Civil War. When his side lost, he was sent to prison for three years. While F. was in prison, the former *echekojaun* died. The bereaved *echekoak* lacked a male repre-sentative for the *luto bankue*. Normally, a substitute would have been selected from among kinsmen, but the *echekojaun* of the *auzurrikourrena* volunteered his services. The bereaved domestic group accepted on the grounds that the man was the godson of the deceased.

In summary, godparenthood creates a special relationship between two individuals. This is a personal tie and is not expressed in terms of *echekoak* obligations. The importance of the relationship is re-flected in the course of funerary proceedings when the surviving godparents or godchildren of the deceased are included in the be-reaved domestic group.

6

The Village

VILLAGE-WIDE levels of social organization that are activated in funerary proceedings include voluntary associations and the network of *artu-emon* donations made at the minimal level of intensity.

VOLUNTARY ASSOCIATIONS

In Murélaga there are a number of voluntary associations, membership in which provides the basis for social interaction between individuals. The total number of associations may be subdivided into those with a secular purpose and those that are religious in nature. Secular voluntary associations do not enter into funerary proceedings; they are normally organized by domestic groups and have a specific economic purpose.

1. The Hermandad de Labradores (Brotherhood of Farmers) is, in spite of its title, more concerned with fire insurance than with agricultural matters. The majority of domestic groups in the village belong to the association, which also includes a number of *echekoak* from nearby villages. The *echekojaun* of each member domestic group must attend the annual meeting, which consists solely of reading the annual financial report and election of officers. A fine is levied against any member failing to send a representative. Each

year the membership names three or four persons to serve as assessors. They receive a salary for the few days that they work for the association. They visit the domestic groups that petition for membership in order to determine the worth of the household dwelling. If there is a fire, the assessors calculate the damages, and the association indemnifies the owner to a maximum amount of one-third of the assessed value of the structure. The costs of this payment are prorated among the membership by calculating the amount of coverage that each member domestic group enjoys on its own dwelling. If there are no fires during the year, no economic demands are made upon the membership.[1]

2. Another type of voluntary association was the livestock insurance group. Designed to insure the cows and calves of the member domestic groups against sickness and accidental death, these associations were generally restricted in membership to the households of one *auzoa,* although some associations counted members from two or more contiguous *auzoak.* Each association had a bookkeeper, whose small salary was prorated among the membership. In addition to the bookkeeper, the *echekojaunak* of two member domestic groups served one-year terms as assessors. The posts rotated among the membership according to a fixed list, so that every member was required to give service. The assessors were obliged to make periodic visits to each member *echekoak* in order to place a value upon its cows and calves. If an animal died, the owner was compensated up to three-fourths of its assessed value.[2] This cost was prorated among the members according to the coverage enjoyed by each. If an animal insured by the association became ill, its owner had an obligation to inform the assessors. The assessors would then decide whether to sell the animal for meat or to consult the veterinarian. In either event, the owner had to abide by their

---

[1] According to one authority, fire insurance associations have been common on the Basque rural scene since at least the nineteenth century (Vicario de la Peña 1901:234–45).

[2] The schedule of payments and the extent of the association's liability varied somewhat from one group to another.

decision. Until about ten years ago these associations were general throughout the province (see Unamuno 1902:57–60; Vicario de la Peña 1901:247–59).

3. Road maintenance associations are a comparatively recent phenomenon in the village. Their growth parallels a shift in the village economy away from agriculture in favor of privately owned commercial pine plantations. Most of these stands are located in rather isolated mountain areas. Under the traditional form of exploitation (sheep grazing), there was little need to provide access roads to the mountainous sectors of the municipality. In the few instances where there are long-standing roadways to mountainous areas, the roads were designed for cart traffic and are incapable of carrying the large trucks presently used to transport pines. Thus, the pine owners have created two large road maintenance associations. Each association financed initial construction of an all-weather road into that sector of the municipality where its members have their pine plantations, prorating the cost of building the roads on an *echekoak* basis among the membership. Maintenance is financed by charging those who use the road for each truckload of pines.[3] Each association has one salaried functionary who keeps an accounting of the number of trucks utilizing the road and collects the revenue. Members are assessed a much lower rate per truckload than nonmembers.

4. In 1963 a new marble quarry was discovered in the village, and the village council resolved to grant a long-term lease to commercial interests engaged in quarrying. The offers from several companies were deemed unsatisfactory, however, and the bidders were suspected of bid fixing. So a group of local villagers formed a corporation to work the deposits. Approximately 240 domestic groups each invested 25,000 *pesetas* (a little over four hundred dollars) into the enterprise. Membership in the corporation was

---

[3] On occasion the membership may resolve to organize a work project on the road system (analogous to *auzolan* on the *auzoa* roadways). Each member *echekoak* must send a representative or pay a fine equivalent to one day's wages.

restricted to residents of Murélaga. Officers were elected, buildings constructed, outlets for the marble developed, and a number of local men employed to work the deposits. By 1966 the operation was in full swing, and the prospects of success were favorable.

5. In recent years, a farmers' cooperative has been organized in the nearby town of Marquina to furnish the farmers with seed, fertilizer, prepared animal feeds, tools, and even livestock at wholesale prices. The cooperative, which markets calves and dairy products for its members, also operates a grocery store. The members share in the annual profits to the degree that they shop through the cooperative system. Several domestic groups in Murélaga (particularly those whose *baserriak* are located on the road to Marquina) have joined.

While secular voluntary associations are concerned with economic activities and membership is by *echekoak,* the religious associations have direct bearing on the death theme, and membership is on an individual basis.

1. Hijas de María (Daughters of Mary) is a religious association whose membership includes the majority of unmarried girls and women in the village. Girls who have been confirmed and who have left school (usually at fourteen years) are eligible for membership. Each year on the day of the Immaculate Conception of the Virgin Mary (December 8) these girls are initiated into the group. Most girls who qualify are members. Affiliation terminates with marriage or, in rare cases, through expulsion for conduct unbecoming a member (usually sexual delicts). Ostensibly the association is dedicated to Catholic action. One Sunday each month the members attend Mass together, and the majority take the sacrament of Holy Communion. That same afternoon the group meets for spiritual exercises and a religious retreat.

The total membership of the Hijas de María participates in the funerary proceedings held for a deceased member. They gather in the village nucleus to await the arrival of the burial procession. The president of the association enters the procession immediately in front of the coffin. She carries the banner of the group. Four members attach blue ribbons to the coffin and walk beside it. The remaining members, each wearing a distinguishing scapular medal, walk immediately behind the coffin. Thus, during the final stages of the funerary procession the Hijas take precedence over all other participants (even displacing the bereaved domestic group). Once the church service is over the Hijas accompany the corpse to the cemetery. Each carries a lighted candle, and all enter within the confines of the *il erria*.

After the burial the president of the association makes arrangements with the parish priest for a special Mass offered on behalf of the soul of the departed member. The association pays for the Mass out of its treasury, and all members are expected to attend.

2. The Luises (*Cofradía* of San Luis) is a group for male adolescents and unmarried men that is analogous in every way to the Hijas de María. It, too, is a Catholic action group with its monthly Communion Sunday and afternoon religious retreat. Membership is gained once a boy leaves school and is maintained until he marries or is expelled for moral delicts (again, usually sexual).

The role of the Luises in the burial proceedings for a deceased member is similar to that of the Hijas. The president of the Luises precedes the corpse, carrying the association's banner. The membership follows immediately behind the coffin. The Luises also have a Mass said for a deceased member. This Mass is paid for out of the treasury of the association, and it is felt that the total membership should be in attendance.

For both the Hijas de María and the Luises, membership is not contingent upon continued residence in the village. If a member emigrates or moves up to a nearby city, he (or she) is still felt to retain membership (insofar as the individual does not marry). If a member dies while residing outside the village, the relevant association participates fully in the funerary proceedings that are held in Murélaga. The association sponsors a Mass on behalf of the soul of the departed member.

Both the Hijas and the Luises are relatively recent organizations in the village dating from the late 1950s in their present active forms. Both are local versions of international Catholic groups. What is of interest is the degree to which these associations have been integrated into the cycle of funerary proceedings, particularly since such activities are not included in the charters of the parent organizations.

3. Aspirants to the Hijas and Luises are two rather informal organizations of school-age children in training to take their places in the Hijas and Luises. These aspirants hold a monthly Communion Sunday and religious retreat. However, they have no formal organizational structure and no banner. They do not participate as a group in the funerary proceedings of a deceased member.

4. In 1967 in Murélaga there were four religious *cofradías* (brotherhoods). They are the *cofradías of Ánimas* (Souls), *Santísimo* (Holiest), *Vera Cruz* (True Crucifix), and *Rosario* (Rosary). These *cofradías* date from the eighteenth century. Their sole function is to provide spiritual support at death for members. Each *cofradía* has a *mayordomo,* who is selected from a list of the membership on the basis of strict rotation. This person must stand at the back of the church during the Sunday High Mass to collect alms for the association. The money is turned over to the priests, who calculate how many Masses can be said with the amount collected during the year. These Masses are offered for the departed souls of all persons who ever belonged to the *cofradía.*[4]

Membership in the *cofradías* is generally restricted to married persons. The individual inscribes his name at the time of his (or her) wedding, and he may join more than one of the *cofradías.* Membership entails nothing more than the collection of alms with the promise of ultimate participation in Masses for deceased members The spiritual support offered by the *cofradías* for their deceased members is durable for many years, even centuries.

---

[4] The collection of the offerings has been a problem in recent years. Many members either reject their obligation to perform the *mayordomo* role or hire a substitute.

5. The Apostolado de la Oración (the Apostleship of Prayer) is the largest married person's religious voluntary association. About three-fourths of all married persons in the village are members. Membership is normally assumed immediately after the wedding ceremony.[5] Members of this association do not beg for the Church as do the *mayordomos* of the *cofradías*. However, the membership of the Apostolado engages in other activities not characteristic of the *cofradías*. The Apostolado, like the Hijas and Luises, has a monthly Communion Sunday and religious retreat.

The total Apostolado membership is divided into subgroups, which tend to be ordered by *auzoak*. The subgroups also tend to be sexually divided, although there are exceptions. The parish priest appoints a leader for each subgroup, and this leadership post usually is transmitted from generation to generation within the household. The leader has few duties. His (or her) major obligation is to keep a record of the membership and inform the priests whenever a member dies (even if the deceased no longer resides in Murélaga at the time of death). Whenever the priests are informed of a death, they automatically offer a Mass for the departed soul. The Mass is given in the name of the Apostolado, and members are expected to attend. At the end of the year the priests calculate the number of Masses said at the request of the Apostolado. The individual subgroup leaders are informed, and the cost is prorated on the basis of equal shares among the membership. It is then the leader's obligation to collect this stipend from each member of his group and turn it over to the religious authorities.

In sum, through participation in the Hijas (unmarried women), Luises (unmarried men), or the Apostolado (married persons of both sexes), the individual is guaranteed spiritual support at his death from a significant number of otherwise disinterested villagers. Through participation in one of the four *cofradías*, he is ensured of

---

[5] Again, there are exceptions, since some persons are enrolled by their parents at baptism. Some of these persons enrolled as children fail to marry, but they remain members of the Apostolado.

ongoing participation in Mass offerings for an indefinite period of time after his death.

THE NETWORK OF MINIMAL "ARTU-EMON" RECIPROCITY

At the village-wide level of social organization, there are few common activities and expressions of unity. There are no economic activities in which the entire village membership is mobilized simultaneously.[6] Every domestic group in the village depends upon the local town hall for registering vital statistics, recording transfers of property, paying taxes, and the like; however, each deals with the town officials on an individual basis. Political organization scarcely serves to produce a sense of village social solidarity either. In that local officials are largely chosen by outside political agencies, there is marked apathy toward local village politics.

The two contexts in which there is an expression of village social solidarity and common activity are religion and recreation. There is scarcely a villager (excluding the infirm) who fails to attend Mass on Sundays and holy days. The church is crowded for most religious services, and afterward the plaza and the local taverns are the settings for a great deal of socializing. Athletic events provide an excuse for many villagers to gather together. Handball matches held in the local *frontón* are well attended. If the match pairs a local team against a team from a nearby village, the interest and local loyalties of the spectators are quite apparent.

The major annual event that occasions common activity for all villagers, while at the same time underlining their identification with the village, is the four-day fiesta (June 20–23) of the patron saint, John. During the course of the festivities there are many religious services, athletic events, and public dances. At this time, the local loyalties and pride of the villagers are put to a test; many outsiders attend the festivities, and honor demands that they not be disappointed.

---

[6] The recently organized marble quarry corporation approximates an exception, since about 90 per cent of the *echekoak* in the village are members.

With the exception of the foregoing, contacts between members of one *auzoa* and persons of other *auzoak* and the village nucleus are almost nonexistent (unless there is a kinship tie between them, or they are both members of the same voluntary association). However, in the context of funerary ritual there is a network of reciprocity linking otherwise unrelated domestic groups. This is the system of minimal *artu-emon* donations.

Minimal *artu-emon* presently consists of a five-*peseta* donation at the burial, *argia,* and *ogistie* services. In addition, the donor *eche-koak* should be represented at each of these functions by a single representative. The donor also places a *kandela* on the *sepulturie* of the deceased for the duration of the *argia* and *ogistie* services. Formerly, it would also contribute a single *olata* on both of these occasions.

The network of *artu-emon* relations is specific to each individual domestic group. This network of minimal *artu-emon* reciprocity is the residue of former intensive *artu-emon* relationships (as based upon bonds of common residence, kinship, or friendship ties). To understand why the residual ties are still activated, it is necessary to examine the ways in which *artu-emon* is defined and recorded.

During the funerary proceedings the sacristan serves as a representative of the bereaved domestic group. He receives *artu-emon* donations and records the name of the donor and amount of his donation in a notebook. He then gives this list to the bereaved domestic group. Whenever there is a death in the village, the membership of each *echekoak* consults its notebooks (usually the two or three most recent ones) to determine if it has an obligation to make a donation. The act of making the donation places the donor's name in the book prepared for the newly bereaved domestic group. Thus, the relationship between them is perpetuated over time. Once an *artu-emon* tie is established between two *echekoak,* it is almost impossible to terminate it.

An important feature of the *artu-emon* system is that it is not defined on the basis of a fixed charter of domestic group obligations.

The list is modified over time as new names are added and old ones dropped (although it is easier to add names than to drop them). The notebooks are specific to the domestic group and are not identified with a particular *baserria*. When a domestic group changes residence, it takes its notebooks with it.

The redefinition of the domestic group's kindred in each generation provides the major source of minimal *artu-emon* ties. A new heir defines the kindred differently than did the former heir—adding some domestic groups and dropping others. In each generation, *echekoak* that were defined as being in the periphery of the kindred are dropped from the category altogether. However, the names of these *echekoak* exist in the *artu-emon* books, and it is difficult to drop them without giving offense. Thus the domestic group continues to maintain its former kindred *artu-emon* ties, but at the minimal level of intensity.

A second source of minimal *artu-emon* results from a change in residence. If the domestic group moves from one *auzoa* to another, it takes its *artu-emon* books with it. All members of the former *auzoa* are inscribed in the books (some at the intensive level of *arimen onrak* donations). When a death occurs in one of these *echekoak* of the *auzoa* of former residence, the domestic group is certain to make an *artu-emon* donation (possibly at the more intensive level). With time, this tie diminishes, but it is retained at the level of minimal *artu-emon* donations.

Artu-emon reciprocity may be established between two *echekoak* on the basis of a friendship tie between a member in each. It may be that the two individuals worked together in the same marble quarry or belonged to the same Sunday afternoon card-playing clique. They may have emigrated to the New World together. At the death of one of the friends, the other is likely to make an *artu-emon* donation, and this is entered in the notebook. If both are from Murélaga, the basis is established for continued minimal *artu-emon* reciprocity between the respective domestic groups.

In light of the above, it is not surprising that the majority of *echekoak* in Murélaga have extensive lists of minimal *artu-emon* obligations. In fact, there are a few *echekoak* which automatically make at least a minimal donation at *every* death. However, while it is difficult to terminate an *artu-emon* relationship, there are certain limitations on the extension of the system. For the relationship to endure, it is necessary that both the donor and recipient domestic groups reside in Murélaga. Once a domestic group moves away from the village, it relinquishes the majority of its *artu-emon* ties. The first to go are the minimal *artu-emon* ties and those intensive ties based on common *auzoa* residence. In succeeding generations, kindred-based ties are also relinquished. The break need not be abrupt. Indeed, many former residents of Murélaga try their best to meet *artu-emon* obligations from Bilbao or some other distant urban area. However, the problem of communications makes this extremely difficult. A former resident may not learn of a death until after the funeral.

Artu-emon may be established between a domestic group in Murélaga and one residing elsewhere, but such relationships prove to be particularly brittle over time. The two common sources of extra-village *artu-emon* are kinship ties between *echekoak* members and friendship ties between individuals. In the case of the former, a marriage between a person from Murélaga and one from elsewhere establishes a sibling-core tie between the two *echekoak*. This is fully expressed in intensified *artu-emon* reciprocity between the two domestic groups. In the next generation, this is converted into a kindred tie which may or may not be expressed at an intensive level of *artu-emon* (but which will certainly entail minimal *artu-emon* reciprocity). The kindred tie lasts for a couple of generations, at which point the two *echekoak* are no longer related. Once the blood relationship between the two domestic groups is weakened to the point where they are no longer a part of one another's *familizhekue,* all trace of the former tie is lost. The two *echekoak* will not engage in indefinite minimal *artu-emon* reciprocity (as might be the case if both resided in Murélaga).

Artu-emon based upon extravillage friendships is particularly tenuous. If the friend of the deceased comes to the village to attend the funeral and makes an *artu-emon* donation, this fact is recorded in the notebook. However, the recipient domestic group defines its future obligation as being to the individual and *not* to his domestic group. If they learn of his death, they reciprocate with a comparable offering, and the relationship is dropped.[7]

In sum, at the village-wide level of social organization, two networks of social relationships—religious voluntary associations and minimal *artu-emon*—are activated within the context of the death theme. Each represents a different axis of social organization along which otherwise unrelated individuals (in the case of religious associations) and *echekoak* (in the case of minimal *artu-emon*) are united in the face of the crisis occasioned by a death in the village.

The participation of "fellow villagers" (that is, those who have no other tie with the bereaved domestic group than that of common residence in the village) is less pronounced than that of the dead person's *echekoak, familizhe, familizhekue,* and *auzoa* members. The less intensive involvement in funerary proceedings of fellow villagers is one reflection of the atomistic nature of rural Basque social organization. That is, ideally each Basque domestic group, leading an independent existence on its *baserria,* is a society unto itself. To the degree that this is impossible, rural Basques interact with close kinsmen and fellow *auzoa* members. Village loyalties are weak and infrequently activated or expressed. In terms of his social identity, the actor is first a resident of a particular household (*echea*) and second a resident of a particular neighborhood (*auzoa*). Residence in Murélaga provides the actor with but a tertiary social identity.

---

[7] Cross-village friendships are rare in the Basque country. The most common sources of such friendships are the acquaintanceships between persons who meet while in a foreign area. If both return to the Basque country, they may continue to visit one another.

7

Conclusion

In rural Basque society, the cultural norms underlying the ways in which the individual patterns his behavior as a participant in the several levels of social organization are reaffirmed in the course of funerary proceedings. The primary loyalties of the individual are to his domestic group (*echekoak*) and household (*echea*). The complexity of roles that he plays within this context take precedence over all others. The domestic group, identified with a territorial unit or *baserria*, is the basic unit of the society. Death has its greatest impact at this level of social organization. It initiates or finalizes the transferral of control over the household's economic resources. It may, by removing a key member, alter the authority structure within the domestic group and seriously undermine its ability to meet the labor demands of agriculture. Consequently, a death in the *echekoak* membership may radically change the relative economic strength of the household and, by implication, its standing within the village.

In the structuring of the domestic group's participation in funerary proceedings,[1] there is clear affirmation of two cultural norms basic to rural Basque society: (1) egalitarianism between the sexes; and (2) equality between affines and consanguines. Throughout the proceedings there is strict complementarity of male and female roles, with no indication that one is emphasized at the other's expense. Similarly, the description of a funeral in Murélaga fails to provide ready indicators as to the sex of the deceased.[2] The same funeral serves for both a male and female.

In this vein, it is impossible to distinguish from context whether a particular *echekoak* representative in the proceedings, or the deceased person for whom they are held, is present in his (or her) household of adult residence by virtue of birth, of marriage, of fictive kinship ties, or of consent. Affines play the same roles as consanguines in discharging domestic group obligations, and they enjoy an equal right to burial. This egalitarianism between the sexes and between affines and consanguines is but one manifestation of the complementarity of role playing that is characteristic of the *echeko-jaun-echekoandria* dyad. Adopted members enjoy the same privileges as "natural" members.

The strongest emotional bonds in Basque society are between *familizhe* members. The husband-wife, parent-offspring, and sibling-sibling social relationships are all idealized in Basque world view as intensive "love" relationships. At the death of an individual, his *familizhe* members, whether or not they are residing in the household of the deceased, play a prominent role in the funerary proceedings and are entitled to the most extensive expressions of personal grief. That *familizhe* members act in a personal capacity is seen in the fact that married siblings and offspring of the deceased

---

[1] I am here referring to participation of *both* the bereaved domestic group and domestic groups sending representatives because of a kindred, *auzoa*, or minimal *artu-emon* obligation.

[2] The exceptions are the differential ringing of the church bells when the death is first announced, and the presence of the Hijas or Luises (assuming that he or she was a member).

do not, by their participation, involve their respective *echekoak* in the proceedings. The same may be said for godparents and godchildren of the deceased who are in a ritual *familizhe* relationship with him. These ritual kinsmen also occupy a prominent place in the structuring of the funerary procession, the seating arrangements in the church during the burial, and the funerary banquet(s).

The intense participation in the funerary proceedings by members of the neighborhood of the deceased underlines the importance of the *auzoa* as the major extradomestic group context of social interaction. It is within the territorial bounds of the *auzoa* that the domestic group carries out the majority of its economic activities. Face-to-face interaction with neighbors is a daily occurrence.

The kindred is another significant level of social organization where members interact both on an individual and a domestic group basis. Labor exchange, common recreational activities, and mutual trust in crisis situations are based upon the kindred tie. Whereas face-to-face interaction between *auzoa* members is common and casual, interaction between kindred members is less frequent and more formalized.

The kindred and *auzoa* appear to have equal if somewhat different significance for the domestic group membership. During the funerary proceedings, kindred and *auzoa* households have comparable obligations toward the bereaved domestic group. Members of both are expected to visit the dying person before death. Both attend the *gauela,* although it is primarily an *auzoa* affair. Both attend the funerary banquet, although it is primarily a kindred affair. Either may serve as the source for *anderuek,* although custom favors a selection from the *auzoa* membership. Both kindred and *auzoa echekoak* are expected to give more than minimal *artu-emon* Mass donations, provide *kandelak* for the *sepulturie* of the deceased, and send both a male and female representative to the burial, *argia,* and *ogistie* services. Informants are able to verbalize this relative equivalence between the kindred and *auzoa.* They emphasize that it is important to maintain good relations with both, and to about the same degree.

One woman stated, "Neighbors are like first cousins and first cousins are like neighbors." In times of crisis, the domestic group may depend upon neighbors, relatives, or both simultaneously.

In both the kindred and *auzoa* memberships there is ranking of social obligations which is, in turn, reflected in differential involvement in funerary proceedings. At a death, the *auzurrikourrena echekoak* has several specified duties to perform, and it is likely to make an *arimen onrak* rather than a lesser *artu-emon* Mass donation. Similarly, members of the sibling core of the deceased participate with greater intensity than do more distantly related *echekoak*, and, therefore, make *arimen onrak* donations. The *auzoa* subgrouping *echekoak* are likely to participate to a greater degree than the remaining *auzoa* domestic groups (for example, by providing *kandelak* for longer than the traditionally prescribed period of time and by attending anniversary Masses). The same is true of kindred-core *echekoak* as contrasted to more distantly related members of the kindred of the deceased.

Participation in funerary proceedings by the kindred and *auzoa* members is on a strict *echekoak*-to-*echekoak* basis. That is, the membership of *echekoak* A participates at the death of a member of *echekoak* B because a kinship tie or a bond of common residence exists between them. However, there is another sense in which the entire memberships of the kindred and *auzoa* take a corporate stance before both the bereaved domestic group and the wider society. It is felt that *the* relatives and *the* neighbors should be represented. During the burial procession and in the seating arrangements in the church, the relatives and the neighbors form discrete groups.

In order for the kindred and *auzoa* to function as corporate groups during the crisis occasioned by death, the social relationships that they normally entertain with the bereaved domestic group are altered. In the case of the kindred, this entails actualizing theoretical ties. In effect, the kindred members are faced with this problem: "We are relatives and should interact but in fact seldom do." Thus, participation by kindred members (particularly those who are not in the kindred core and sibling core) entails activation of what are essentially dormant social ties. It is only in the context of funerary proceedings that kindred ties translate into the formation of an action group. Thus, the very definition of the kindred at the widest level of inclusion is contingent upon the funerary obligations emanating from the defining domestic group.

If for the kindred a death actualizes the dormant ties and gives them substance (through the discharge of traditionally determined funerary obligations), for the *auzoa* membership to function as a corporate group the reverse is necessary. The *auzoa* membership is faced with this problem: "We are neighbors and should get along well, but in fact we do not because of the day-to-day irritations of living together." The actual social relations existing between *auzoa* members are fictionalized so as to conform to an ideal of expected *auzoa* behavior.[3] Thus, corporate support for the bereaved domestic group by the kindred and *auzoa* is possible only if, for the former, dormant relationships are actualized, and, for the latter, actual relationships are made dormant.

We have emphasized that the most important contexts of social interaction for the individual actor are the *echekoak, familizhe,* and *auzoa.* The elaborate and complex nature of Basque funerary proceedings is largely concerned with discharging death obligations within these social contexts. While death obligations may be met in highly prescribed minimal fashion, it is equally true that a death frequently causes re-evaluation of the contents of social relations between the living. We have noted, for example, that loyalty to siblings is valued in the Basque world view. Conversely, we noted that competition over dowry payments may lead to open conflict between siblings. Similarly, in the Basque view neighbors should be on good terms, but they seldom are. A death causes those with a social obli-

---

[3] We have seen that this takes place during the *gauela* when the social personality and personal history for the deceased are "laundered" (see pp. 26–28).

gation to participate in the funerary proceedings to evaluate their relationship with the deceased and his domestic group. If the relationship has been characterized by tensions and antagonisms, it is unlikely to survive the death unchanged. That is, antagonism between individuals and domestic groups will be intensified if one or both parties fails to meet funerary obligations. Conversely, if both meet their obligations, past antagonisms are likely to be forgotten or at least ameliorated. In a very real sense a death precipitates re-evaluation of a large network of social ties, at the more intensive levels of social organization, and frequently forces alterations in their content.

Beyond the *auzoa* and kindred levels of social organization there is a sharp decline in perceived obligation and intensity of social interaction. The network of minimal *artu-emon* relationships was seen to be largely a residuum of former kindred and common-residence ties, not a reflection of village solidarity. The participation in the proceedings of the religious associations does not cut across the networks of kindred and *auzoa* ties, since membership is on an individual basis and does not imply domestic group obligation. If the examination of voluntary associations is broadened to include those which are secular in purpose, we find further evidence of the insignificance of village membership as a basis for meaningful social interaction. Secular associations are few in number and limited in purpose. They are organized around a specific economic activity. Membership is by *echekoak,* and the purpose for joining is to derive immediate economic benefit or security. Voluntary associations concerned with recreational activities or with community improvement projects are absent in Murélaga. The village as a whole remains a rather insignificant social context for the rural population.

Within the framework of traditionally prescribed funerary ritual, there is little reference to the personality of the deceased. Similarly, the personal attributes of the *echekoak* representatives attending the various affairs are of no consequence. Tradition demands that each

echekoak with an obligation be represented in the appropriate contexts as determined by its relationship with the bereaved domestic
group. However, each domestic group is at liberty to select its rep-
resentative(s), and it is in this selection that personal ties with the
deceased may be expressed.

If the deceased was a child, then the *anderuek* are selected from
among the male children of his (or her) *auzoa*. If he was elderly,
the mean age of the persons attending the affairs as *echekoak* representatives is likely to be older than if he was in the prime of life.
Participation in the proceedings by the Hijas de María, the Luises,
or the membership of the Apostolado de la Oración is indicative of
a personal attribute of the deceased (his or her membership in a
voluntary association). This membership, in turn, signals other personal attributes of the deceased. If the Hijas de María participate, we
know that the deceased was an unmarried female. Inclusion of godparents or godchildren of the deceased with his domestic group, both
in the ordering of the funerary procession and seating in the church,
is another recognition of a personal tie. Finally, flexibility in the
prescription of mourning practices and attendance at anniversary
Masses allows persons to express, through intensified participation,
their strong personal ties with the deceased.

We may therefore distinguish at least three capacities in which
a person may be acting when he is a participant in funerary ritual:

1. As a domestic group representative because there is a reciprocal
tie of kinship, common residence, or minimal *artu-emon* obligation existing between the two *echekoak*.
2. As a representative of the kindred or *auzoa* of the deceased
since *the* relatives and *the* neighbors should be represented.
3. As an individual because he has a personal tie with the deceased.

The participant may be acting in all three of these capacities.

Throughout the description of funerary ritual, the importance of spatial ordering is paramount. The disposition of the *sepulturiek,* the *luto bankue,* the arrangement of the candles around the coffin during the burial service and their removal for use in subsequent services, the notion that each *baserria* is linked directly to the village church over a funerary road, and the division of the cemetery into a blessed and unblessed section all involve the manipulation of physical space. Similarly, there is a spatial ordering of the participants which clearly reflects degree of social intimacy. This is best seen in the structuring of the burial procession. The members of the bereaved domestic group walk immediately behind the coffin, followed by the *familizhe* and kindred, then the *auzoa,* persons from contiguous *auzoak,* and, finally, persons from other domestic groups in the village. If we hold the kindred in abeyance (since it has no territorial bounds), we find that the ordering of participants in the procession parallels the distribution of their *baserriak* on the ground. As physical distance between *baserriak* increases, social intimacy between their members decreases, which is a clear reflection of the fact that in rural Basque society there is a strong correlation between physical and social distance.

FUNERARY RITUAL IN BASQUE SOCIETY

It was the stated purpose of this study to employ the death theme as an heuristic device with which to approach the study of rural Basque society. Consequently, there has been no attempt to examine the importance of the death theme per se. That is, we have not been concerned with why death and death-related activities occupy such a prominent place in the Basque world view. An examination of the nature of Basque religious beliefs provides some suggestions.

Basques are thoroughly Roman Catholic and manifest unquestioning adherence to Catholic doctrine. In the rural areas, the local parish priest *is* the Church, and his interpretation of religion *is* the doctrine. The Basque clergy has traditionally emphasized a fundamentalist brand of religion. Sermons abound with fire and brimstone. The members of the congregation are warned to subordinate worldly pursuits and pleasures to a concern with their fate in the afterlife. Consequently, the Basque considers his death to be the most important event in his life cycle. What is more, it is not to be feared, since the purpose of life is preparation for death.[4]

We may turn to the anthropological literature for further suggestions as to the functions of funerary ritual in Murélaga. The major concerns in the literature are with the social, psychological, and economic functions of death-related activities.

Robert Hertz and Arnold Van Gennep are the theorists whose findings have served as the basis for subsequent anthropological treatments of death. Both Hertz and Van Gennep employed a broad cross-cultural perspective to arrive at their remarkably similar conclusions.

Hertz finds that (1) death is not accomplished in a single act; rather, it is a lasting process; and (2) it is not merely destruction, but rather entails transition to another state (Hertz 1960:48). Physical death and burial of the corpse only initiate the process of dying. The death triggers a series of social responses which have the purpose of purifying (1) the deceased so that he may enter the realm of the dead, and (2) the survivors so that they may return to the society of the living. Thus, physical death places both the deceased and those who maintained close ties with him into an indeterminate state of transition. This transitional period terminates for both the deceased and survivors with a second burial service (*ibid.*:53–55).

The passage of the individual from this world to the next is fraught with danger. He must receive assistance from the living if he is successfully to enter the realm of the ancestors. It is through strict adherence to ritual that the living render this assistance. Hertz observes, that the group cannot really doubt the final deliverance, for "in its eyes the rite, as long as it is correctly performed, has an irresistible efficacy" (*ibid.*:73).

---

[4] This approach to death, where the subject is neither feared nor avoided, contrasts sharply with Anglo-American practice, where not only are funerary proceedings deritualized, but the subject itself is felt to be pornographic (Gorer 1965:169–75).

Van Gennep places funerary rites into the wider context of rites of passage. A rite of passage is divisible into three separate components: rites of separation, rites of transition, and rites of incorporation (Van Gennep 1960:11). While each of these aspects is present in any given rite of passage, they vary in importance according to the purpose for which the rite is performed. At first glance, funerary ritual would appear to emphasize rites of separation; however, on closer examination we find that it contains elaborate rites of transition and incorporation (*ibid.*:146). For the bereaved, the mourning period is a rite of transition entered into through rites of separation and terminated by rites of incorporation. Van Gennep notes, "the transition period for the living mourners often coincide with that of the dead" (*ibid.*:147).

The data from Murélaga may be interpreted quite comfortably in terms of the frameworks provided by Hertz and Van Gennep. The *gauela* and burial service correspond to Hertz's first burial and Van Gennep's rites of separation. The *bederatziurrune, argia,* and *lutue* correspond to Hertz's period of transition and Van Gennep's rites of transition. Finally, the *ogistie* ceremony, which signals the entry of the deceased into the category of the undifferentiated dead and the resumption of normal social activities for the survivors, corresponds to Hertz's second burial and Van Gennep's rites of incorporation.

Central to Hertz's and Van Gennep's treatments of funerary ritual is the notion that its performance has the function of promoting social solidarity. Hertz asserts that society believes itself to be immortal. "Thus when a man dies, society loses in him much more than a unit; it is stricken in the very principle of its life, in the faith that it has in itself" (Hertz 1960:78). "In establishing a society of the dead, the society of the living regularly recreates itself (*ibid.*:72). In the context of funerary ritual, both the solidarity and the continuity of the society are affirmed.

Several anthropological treatments of death make this assertion. A. R. Radcliffe-Brown states, "the burial customs of the Andamanese are to be explained...as a collective reaction against the attack on the collective feeling of solidarity constituted by the death of a member of the social group" (Radcliffe-Brown 1948:285). David Mandelbaum attributes a similar function to Kota funerary ritual (Mandelbaum 1959:195). The same assertion is found in Raymond Firth's treatment of funerary rites (Firth 1963:63–64).

The data from Murélaga lend strong support to the theory that funerary ritual promotes social solidarity. No other social event serves to activate as wide a range of social relationships. During the course of the proceedings, literally every social context in which the deceased participated while alive is, in some manner, dramatized. Furthermore, no other social event has the same duration as funerary ritual. An entire year passes from the time of the death until the deceased ceases to be of societal concern.

A second concern in the literature is with the psychological effects of funerary ritual upon the bereaved survivors. Funerary ritual lends communal support to the immediate survivors in their time of crisis while at the same time providing them with a ritualized (and therefore safe) outlet for personal grief. Jack Goody states that, "Funerals control grief by providing standardized forms of expression. And they control not only the sense of loss of the loved one, the personal deprivation, but also the guilt and self-accusation that so often accompany the departure of a close kinsman" (Goody 1962:34–35). Firth takes the same position when he states,

funeral ritual gives a social backing to their [the bereaved] attempts at adjustment, provides them with a cathartic mechanism for a public display of grief, and sets a period of mourning. In essence the community says to the relatives: "Your boy is dead; he is now buried. Wail for him in one final outburst, before us all. We expect it of you, and we demand it of you. Then tomorrow you will return to normal social existence" [Firth 1963:63].

Geoffrey Gorer sees ritualized expression of grief at death as congruent with species-characteristic human psychology and declares:

I call attention to the potentially important roles played by ritual and by those members of the society with whom the mourner comes in contact in giving help to the mourner in a period of shock and the stage of violent grief and assisting him in giving expression to and working through his distress; and to the maladaptations which may result if this help is not forthcoming [Gorer 1965:132].

Throughout funerary proceedings in Murélaga there is concern for the psychological state of the survivors. Within minutes after a death, members of the *auzurrikourrena echekoak* are on the scene to provide moral support and free the bereaved domestic group from everyday tasks and the mechanics of making the funerary arrangements. Both neighbors and relatives attend the *gauela* held the first night after the death, thereby assisting the bereaved in their vigil with the corpse. Through participation in the burial procession and burial service and through the system of *artu-emon* donations, the bereaved domestic group is assured that neither they nor the deceased has been abandoned. During the funerary banquet, the immediate survivors are encouraged to join in light conversation in which the emphasis is upon the affairs of the living. Finally, the nature of the mourning practices is such that the individual mourner is somewhat at liberty to participate according to his personal needs and sympathies.

A third concern in the literature is with the economic aspects of death. Firth, when discussing funerary ritual in Tikopia society, observes that every funeral is a complex economic activity in which there is an intricate division of labor and a wealth of traditionally prescribed gift exchanges. Kinsmen must be compensated for the goods and services that they provide (Firth 1959:195). Mandelbaum finds that in Kota society the immediate family of the deceased provides the goods burned on the funeral pyre and the food consumed at the funerary banquet, but that kinsmen make contributions to help defray the expenses (Mandelbaum 1959:195).

The economic organization of funerary proceedings is highly elaborated in Basque society. The bereaved domestic group incurs several direct and indirect expenses. It pays the religious authorities for the funeral services and the *difunterie* for caring for the *sepulturie*. It purchases the coffin and burial gown for the corpse. It hosts the funerary banquet(s). Throughout the year of *lutue* it incurs the added expense of maintaining the *sepulturie*. Finally, it sponsors anniversary Masses for the soul of a particular deceased member, and other Masses and *responsuek* for the more generalized ancestors and predecessors.

At the same time, the bereaved domestic group is not alone in sponsoring death-related activities. Neighbors and kinsmen provide services through attendance at the various events and monetary assistance through the *artu-emon* system of Mass donations. Significantly, the money collected through *artu-emon* is utilized to provide both the deceased with spiritual capital (through Masses on his behalf) and the bereaved domestic group with assistance in meeting the costs of the proceedings (since the sacristan receives his payment out of the collection).

The economic aspect of funerary proceedings mirrors two concerns—(1) propensity toward conspicuous consumption, and (2) emphasis upon strict reciprocity. In the recent past, conspicuous consumption in the context of funerary proceedings was more pronounced than at present. The bereaved domestic group was somewhat at liberty to choose the type of burial service that it wished to sponsor, the type of coffin that it wished to purchase, and the type of funerary banquet(s) it wished to provide. There is clear evidence that people tended to spend beyond their immediate means and thereby incur ruinous debts. The record indicates that funerary expenditures ranked second only to dowry payments as the means of dissipating the accumulated wealth of a generation of farming. Those *echekoak* known to be well off financially were expected to provide more elaborate funerals. Therefore, in each generation funerary expenditures served as a leveler of economic differences between households. In recent years, funerals have become more standardized and therefore do not modify the economic ranking of households.

The household-centric nature of rural Basque society, with its attendant valuation upon household self-sufficiency, disfavors incurring debts of any kind. This emphasis is reflected in the economic organization of funerary proceedings. At each point where the bereaved domestic group is provided with a service or moral support, there is an attempt to make some sort of counter payment. When the priest and altar boy visit a dying person, they are provided with refreshments and the altar boy is given cash. When the neighbors and kinsmen attend the *gauela,* the bereaved domestic group serves them refreshments throughout the night-long vigil. Participation of neighbors and relatives in the funerary procession and burial service is accepted with the understanding that the bereaved domestic group will send representatives to similar events held at some future date in each of their households. Furthermore, many or all of the participants attend one or more banquets. Those persons providing a particular service—for example, the *anderuek, ogidune,* and *estipendiyue*—are certain to attend. Finally, the system of *artu-emon* Mass donations is played out on a reciprocal basis, although discharge of the obligations must wait until there are deaths in each of the present donor *echekoak.*

The anthropological literature is concerned with another economic consequence of death—the transmission of authority and property rights held by the deceased while he was alive. Goody states, "Just as the death of an office-holder requires the installation of a new incumbent ('the king is dead, long live the king'), so many other rights and duties of the deceased have also to be transferred to surviving members of the community; in particular, property, sexual rights, offices, and certain roles may require perpetuation in this manner" (Goody 1962:30). In Basque society, we find that transmission of authority and property rights is not tied to a single rite of passage. Rather, it is a process initiated at the marriage of the selected heir in each generation and finalized by the deaths of the donors. Marriage and death are two aspects of the over-all transmission process.[5]

---

[5] We noted that marriage in rural Basque society is a process rather than an event (see p. 122). However, we have not examined the ceremonial aspects of marriage. Presently, the marriage ceremony entails a minimum of ritual.

The key to social continuity in rural Basque society is the selection of a single heir to the *baserria* in each generation. In order to anchor a suitable heir on the farm, the donor couple must demonstrate to their remaining offspring that they no longer enjoy a future in their natal household (unless they are willing to remain celibate and subservient to the new heir and spouse). An obvious means of accomplishing this is by legal and irrevocable transmission of the ownership of the farm at the marriage of the selected heir.

While formal transfer of farm ownership resolves the problem of competition from the heir's siblings, it does not necessarily remove the donor *echekojaun* and *echekoandria* as rivals. The transmission of farm ownership is often incomplete, since the donors may retain control over half of the farm income. Furthermore, the elder couple retains ownership of a personal estate consisting of cash, property other than the *baserria,* control of standing timber, and the like. Whereas, ideally, transfer of farm ownership implies relinquishing authority, in actuality the donor couple may retain much of the prestige necessary to implement it. They become the venerable semiretired experts on household affairs, accustomed to exercising authority and ill-disposed to having their opinions ignored. They also continue to exercise *familizhe* parental authority over the heir. There is a basis for conflict between the adjacent generations as long as this elder couple remains in residence on the farm. It is only through the deaths of the retired couple that actual and ideal *echekoak* authority are fully conferred upon the active *echekojaun* and

---

A simple church service, attended by relatively few kinsmen and neighbors, is followed by a small banquet in a local tavern. However, in the recent past the marriage ceremony was much more elaborate. The high point of the affair was a procession from the inmarrying affine's natal *baserria* to that of the heir. The affine's *echekoak* and close kinsmen accompanied a gaily decorated cart which carried the appurtenances of the dowry (household furnishings, bedding, and personal effects). Recently there have been changes in the content of the dowry payment which, in turn, have led to abandonment of the former custom. Today the dowry consists of cash or rights in standing timber. It is handed over before a notary public at the time that the marital contract is signed.

echekoandria. Whereas marriage removes the heir's sibling as potential rivals, death removes his parents.

Finally, we may examine the significance of death in light of the household-centric nature of Basque society. Ideally, the *echekoak* commands the prime loyalties of its membership to the detriment of extradomestic group affiliations. To the degree that such an arrangement obtains, the individual *echekoak* is both socially and economically self-sufficient. In such an atomistic society, the impact of death at the domestic-group level of social organization is particularly forceful. A single death may destroy or seriously undermine a domestic group's ability to continue in agriculture. Death may strike indiscriminately at any member. Instead of removing a retired person, it may strike down the active *echekojaun* or a promising adolescent. The same death may remove the most important individual in the household economy, the group's male representative before the wider society, and the prime male authority figure. What is more, in terms of personnel there is a large measure of overlapping between the *echekoak* and *familizhe* memberships. The individual actor discharges a multiplicity of *familizhe* roles, all of which are overlain with affective sentiments. A single death may remove a wife's husband, a parent's son, a child's father, and a sibling's sibling. All of the individuals so deprived may be present in the three-generation domestic group.

Such a death requires more than a mere internal adjustment if the domestic group is not to become emotionally ingrown through disruption and grief. The elaborate framework of traditionally prescribed funerary ritual asserts that the death is of societal concern. The bereaved *echekoak* is forced to discharge a number of obligations before the wider society and, by so doing, to affirm its integrity. The very performance of the acts demonstrates that the disrupted domestic group is capable of meaningful social action. Discharge of social obligations in the funerary proceedings allows the bereaved domestic group to bridge the period of crisis between the loss of a member and its subsequent internal adjustments to the loss.

During the course of discharging funerary obligations, the domestic group is also forced to affirm its ties in wider social contexts, such as the kindred and the *auzoa*. Thus, whereas participation by the bereaved domestic group affirms its integrity, it is also a denial of its autonomy. This distinction reflects an axis of potential crisis inherent in rural Basque society—the need to strike a balance between the centrifugal tendency for individuals to shift their personal loyalties outside of the household sphere of influence, and the centripetal tendency for the domestic group to become emotionally, socially, and economically ingrown. The domestic group enters a period of crisis if either of these tendencies gains the upper hand. Excessive centrifugal tendencies among the membership lead to disintegration of *echekoak* solidarity as loyalties are deflected into wider social contexts, and a breakdown in the internal authority structure results. Conversely, there is an ever-present danger in Basque society that the *echekoak* will become a social isolate and literally secede from the society. A detailed consideration of these two tendencies constitutes the basis for another study. I would note in passing that the major manifestation of excessive centrifugal tendencies is a crisis in succession as the farming way of life becomes devalued. This translates into an *exode rurale* and portends the ultimate demise of the rural society. An overly centripetal orientation is seen in an example from Vera de Bidasoa, provided by Caro Baroja. He reports the case of the domestic group which plows its fields by moonlight in order to avoid the prying eyes of its neighbors (Caro Baroja 1944:120).

In conclusion, the elaborate nature of funerary proceedings and the emphasis placed upon them by the actors themselves allow us to distinguish a "death theme" in Basque society. No other life-crisis event serves to activate such a complexity of social relationships. A detailed analysis of funerary proceedings in terms of the nature and degree of involvement of individuals and *echekoak* provides one blueprint of social relations in Murélaga.[6] The various activities oc-

---

[6] I would emphasize that we are here dealing with *one* blueprint, since the social structure could be "mapped" by employing other axes. For instance,

casioned by a death involve the memberships of the bereaved domestic group, *familizhe,* the *auzoa* of the deceased, contiguous *auzoak,* the kindred, and religious voluntary associations. Furthermore, a death activates the network of *artu-emon* reciprocity which may encompass the majority of *echekoak* in the village and ramify out to include persons and domestic groups in nearby and more distant areas. Not only does death serve to activate the various levels of social organization, but on each level it occasions the widest expression of such relationships. It is in the context of mortuary obligations that the total memberships of the domestic group, family, kindred, neighborhood, and religious voluntary associations are mobilized with respect to a common activity. In Basque society—to a significant degree—it is through death that the social relationships of the living are defined and expressed.

---

very little consideration has been given to differentiation between villagers based upon differences of power and wealth.

Appendix: Basque Funerary Practices

Funerary proceedings in Murélaga are but one variation on a theme that holds fairly constant throughout the whole Basque country. The following treatment is not meant to be exhaustive in its indication of the available sources.

1. Beliefs that death may be presaged by the nocturnal crowing of a rooster or by dogs howling in the night are found in the following sources: Arredondo 1923:47; Azkue 1959:217, 235; Barandiarán 1923b:23; Barandiarán 1923c:37; Barandiarán 1923d:62; Barandiarán 1923g:129; Barandiarán 1923h:134; Bengoa 1923:43; Caro Baroja 1944:78; Caro Baroja 1958:325; Etxeberria 1923c:94; Etxeberria 1923d:98; Ispitzua 1923:14; Lekuona 1923:77, 88; López 1923:1–2; Marcaida 1923:31; Sáez de Adana 1923:54–55; Thalamas Labandíbar 1931:43.

2. Beliefs that death may be presaged by the church bells coinciding with the chiming of the clock in the church tower are found in the following: Azkue 1959:199–200, 216; Barandiarán 1923b:23; Bengoa 1923:43; Gorrochategui and Aracama 1923:108; Veyrin 1955:268.

3. Beliefs that death may be caused by *maldiciones*, evil eye, and evil spirits may be found in the following works: Barandiarán 1923a:5–6; Barandiarán 1923b:22; Barandiarán 1923c:37; Barandiarán 1923d:62; Barandiarán 1923e:114; Barandiarán 1923f:126; Etxeberria 1923b:73; Gorrochategui and Aracama 1923:107; Ispitzua 1933:13–14; Lekuona 1923:77, 85; López 1923:1; Marcaida 1923:31; Sáez de Adana 1923:54.

4. Various conditions of the corpse may be taken as indicators of the destiny of the deceased in the afterlife: Barandiarán 1923a:7; Caro Baroja 1944:168; López 1923:2; Marcaida 1923:32; Sáez de Adana 1923:54.

5. A gentle rain on the day of the burial is a good sign, while a violent storm is a bad omen: Azkue 1959:234.

6. For treatments of the role of the closest neighboring domestic group in the funerary proceedings, see: Barandiarán 1948:173; Barandiarán 1949:33; Veyrin 1955:268–69.

7. Throughout the Basque country there is a belief that the eyes and/or mouth of the deceased must be closed or he is likely to take another *echekoak* member with him to the realm of the dead; see: Azkue 1959: 216; Barandiarán 1923b:23; Barandiarán 1923c:37; Gorrochategui and Aracama 1923:108; López 1923:2; Marcaida 1923:32; Sáez de Adana 1923:54.

8. Differential chiming of the church bells to announce the death and sex of the deceased is common throughout the Basque country; see: Azkue 1959:218–219; Barandiarán 1923c:38; Barandiarán 1923d:63; Caro Baroja 1944:169; Caro Baroja 1958:326; Gorrochategui and Aracama 1923:107.

9. For *gauela* practices in other parts of the Basque country, see: Barandiarán 1923c:38; Barandiarán 1923e:116; Barandiarán 1923f:127; Bengoa 1923:44; Etxeberria 1923a:70–71; Etxeberria 1923d:99–100; Gorrochategui and Aracama 1923:109; Lekuona 1923:79; Marcaida 1923:33; Sáez de Adana 1923:55.

10. For descriptions of similar funerary processions, see: Barandiarán 1923a:9; Barandiarán 1923b:26; Barandiarán 1923c:39; Ispitzua 1923:15; López 1923:2.

11. Crossroads have a great deal of significance in the Basque country. The custom of detaining the funerary procession to pray at crossroads is quite extensive. See: Azkue 1959:214; Barandiarán 1923a:9; Bengoa 1923:44; Caro Baroja 1944:170; Echegaray 1951:15; Lekuona 1923:88–89; Marcaida 1923:34.

a. Formerly, it was a common practice to burn the mattress taken from a death bed at one of the crossroads; see: Azkue 1959:229–30; Barandiarán 1923a:8; Barandiarán 1923c:41; Barandiarán 1923f:128; Barandiarán 1949:35; Bengoa 1923:46; Caro Baroja 1944:169–70; Caro Baroja 1958: 327; Echegaray 1951:14–15; Etxeberria 1923b:74; Gorrochategui and Aracama 1923:110; Ispitzua 1923:16; Lekuona 1923:89; Marcaida 1923: 34; Thalamas Labandíbar 1931:46.

12. A typology of funerary Masses (usually tripartite, but not neces-

sarily so) prevails throughout the Basque country. See: Arredondo 1923: 49; Barandiarán 1923e:119; Barandiarán 1923g:131; Barandiarán 1923h: 135; Bengoa 1923:45; Caro Baroja 1958:328; Etxeberria 1923a:71; Etxeberria 1923b:75; Etxeberria 1923d:101; Gorrochategui and Aracama 1923:110; Ispitzua 1923:16; Lekuona 1923:80; López 1923:3–4; Marcaida 1923:34; Mendizabal 1923:106; Sáez de Adana 1923:56–57.

13. The practice whereby the bereaved domestic group makes offerings of bread and *kandelak* on behalf of the deceased is common throughout the area. See: Barandiarán 1923e:118–19; Barandiarán 1923g:131–32; Barandiarán 1923h:136–37; Caro Baroja 1944:171; Echegaray 1925:100; Echegaray 1951:23–30; Gorrochategui and Aracama 1923:110–11; Lekuona 1923:81–82; Mendizabal 1923:106; Veyrin 1955:269.

a. For similar offerings made by relations and neighbors, see: Barandiarán 1923d:65; Barandiarán 1948:175; Caro Baroja 1944:171; Caro Baroja 1958:330; López 1923:3; Marcaida 1923:35; Sáez de Adana 1923: 57.

14. For Mass collections comparable to the *artu-emon* donations in Murélaga, see: Barandiarán 1923c:40; Etxeberria 1923a:72.

15. For customs similar to the *ogidune* practice in Murélaga, see: Barandiarán 1949:35; Marcaida 1923:34.

16. For further descriptions of funerary banquets, see: Arredondo 1923:52; Barandiarán 1923d:67; Barandiarán 1948:174; Barandiarán 1949:36; Bengoa 1923:46; Caro Baroja 1944:173; Etxeberria 1923a:72–73; Etxeberria 1923c:98; Ispitzua 1923:17; Sáez de Adana 1923:59; Thalamas Labandíbar 1931:46.

17. For other descriptions of the *bederatziurrune* cycle, see: Arredondo 1923:49; Barandiarán 1923f:128; Etxeberria 1923d:101; Lekuona 1923: 80; Sáez de Adana 1923:57; Thalamas Labandíbar 1931:47.

18. Equivalents of the *ogistie* ceremony are common throughout the Basque country. See: Arredondo 1923:53; Barandiarán 1923b:27; Barandiarán 1923d:68–69; Barandiarán 1948:175; Veyrin 1955:271.

19. For additional examples of the *responsuek* custom, see: Arredondo 1923:51–53; Barandiarán 1923b:27; Barandiarán 1923d:66–67; Ispitzua 1923:16–17; López 1923:4; Sáez de Adana 1923:58–59.

20. The existence of fixed funerary routes is common throughout the Basque country. See: Azkue 1959:213; Barandiarán 1923c:39; Bengoa 1923:44; Echegaray 1925:208–213; Echegaray 1951:31–34; Etxeberria 1923d:100; Gorrochategui and Aracama 1923:109; Lekuona 1923:79; Marcaida 1923:33; Mendizabal 1923:105.

21. The custom whereby the church floor is divided into individual

sepulturie plots which are activated during funerary proceedings is common. See: Barandiarán 1923b; Barandiarán 1923d:68; Barandiarán 1923e:123–24; Barandiarán 1923f:128; Barandiarán 1923h:136; Barandiarán 1948:175; Caro Baroja 1944:174; Caro Baroja 1958:329; Echegaray 1951:43; Mendizabal 1923:106; Sáez de Adana 1923:58; Veyrin 1955:270.

22. For descriptions of mourning practices, see: Barandiarán 1923c:41; Barandiarán 1948:175; Barandiarán 1949:36; Caro Baroja 1958:331; Etxeberria 1923a:73; Ispitzua 1923:17; Thalamas Labandíbar 1931:47–48.

23. For descriptions of apparitions of the dead, see: Azkue 1959:180; Barandiarán 1923b:30; Barandiarán 1923c:42; Barandiarán 1923e:125–26; Barandiarán 1923g:132; Barandiarán 1949:37–38; Caro Baroja 1958:331; Gorrochategui and Aracama 1923:111–12; Ispitzua 1923:17; Lekuona 1923:83–84; López 1923:4; Sáez de Adana 1923:59–60; Thalamas Labandíbar 1931:31–33.

24. The practice of removing a roof tile or opening a window to enable the soul of the deceased to depart is found in the following sources: Azkue 1959:321; Barandiarán 1949:33; Caro Baroja 1958:326; Etxeberria 1923c:94; Lekuona 1923:88; Thalamas Labandíbar 1931:43.

a. The belief that the soul may frequent the house or neighborhood before departing is found in the following: Azkue 1951:180; Caro Baroja 1958:330.

25. The belief that food and candle offerings are made to fulfill the terrestrial needs of the deceased is found in the following: Barandiarán 1923g:129–30; Barandiarán 1949:35; Caro Baroja 1944:177; Caro Baroja 1958:329.

26. The custom of informing the bees at the death of a domestic group member is found in the following sources: Azkue 1959:222; Barandiarán 1923e:115–16; Barandiarán 1923f:126; Barandiarán 1923g:129–30; Barandiarán 1948:174; Caro Baroja 1958:326–27; Etxeberria 1923d:99; Gorrochategui and Aracama 1923:108; Marcaida 1923:32; Sáez de Adana 1923:54; Thalamas Labandíbar 1931:44.

Glossary

The glossary includes non-English terms which recur in the text. The terms are Basque unless otherwise indicated.

achak: large candles owned by the church, which are placed near the corpse during a burial service and later enter into other ritual contexts throughout the year of formal mourning for the deceased.

aite bezuetako: godfather.

alkar poderoso: a legal arrangement between the *echekojaun* and *echekoandria* whereby each confers on the other a right of survivorship with respect to selecting a single heir to the household.

almaiyerue: a black cloth which remains on the *sepulturie* site during the year of formal mourning.

ama bezuetako: godmother.

Amerikanuek: men from Murélaga who have spent time in the American Far West and who have returned to the village.

andabideak: funerary roads which link each household in the village to the village church.

anderuek: pallbearers. They are usually unmarried men from the neighborhood of the deceased, but may be unmarried male kinsmen.

argia: a ceremony held within two weeks after the burial service which initiates the formal year of mourning for the deceased.

arimen onrak: "honors for the soul." It is an elaborate form of Mass offering (see *artu-emon*) given to the bereaved domestic group by persons or domestic groups with a particularly close tie of common residence (for example, the *auzurrikourrena*) or kinship (for example, a *familizhe* member) with the deceased.

artu-emon: "to take and to give." The term refers to the money donations received by the bereaved domestic group at a death in the membership. The donations are used to sponsor Masses for the soul of the deceased. The donation establishes a relationship between groups, since the recipient is obligated to make a similar donation at a future death in the donor domestic group.

aur bazkaria: the infant's meal hosted by the domestic group of an *echekoandria* who has recently given birth. The affair is attended by *echekoandriak* from kindred and *auzoa* domestic groups.

auzoa: the rural neighborhood.

auzolan: communal work projects carried out by the membership of a neighborhood.

auzurrikourrena: "nearest of the neighborhood." The domestic group inhabiting the dwelling that is physically closest within the *auzoa* to the definer's dwelling. A domestic group depends upon its *auzurrikourrena* for assistance in crisis situations.

baserria: the rural farmstead. See also *echea*.

bederatziurrune: "novena"; the term refers to the nine Masses said for the soul of the deceased during the period between the burial service and the *argia* ceremony.

begizkue: the practice of harming persons with evil eye.

bizita: visiting patterns among neighbors at the birth of a child in one of the domestic groups or at the crises of serious illness and death.

campo santo: the section of blessed ground within the cemetery (Spanish).

cecina: cured veal (Spanish).

cofradía: religious confraternity (Spanish).

culto y clero: annual tithe each domestic group owes to the religious authorities (Spanish).

difunterie: female religious specialist who cares for the church-floor *sepulturiek*.

echea: the Basque household which includes the dwelling, landholdings, household furnishings, and the *sepulturie* site on the church floor.

echekoak: the domestic group inhabiting the *echea* or household. Contains those persons actually resident in the household as well as those who, while absent, retain the right to return and resume residence. Ideally, there is a three-generational core within the *echekoak* consisting of an active married couple, their offspring, and the parents of one of the marriage partners. The *echekoak* may also contain adopted members and hired persons.

echekoandria: active married female head of the domestic group.

echekojaun: active married male head of the domestic group.

eliza: church.

erederue: heir to an *echea.*

erria: village nucleus.

estipendiyue: stipend bearer who represents the bereaved domestic group during the burial service and makes a (now symbolic) money payment to the priest and to the organist.

familizhe: an ego-specific category of kinsmen which includes ego's spouse, offspring, siblings, and parents.

familizhekue: meaning "of the family," it refers to ego's kindred, determined by reckoning bilineally to the grandparental generation and bilaterally to second cousins.

famille souche: stem family (French).

frontón: a ball court (Spanish).

fueros: local laws or charters specific to individual Spanish provinces which in some contexts have precedence over the Spanish national Civil Code (Spanish).

gauela: the vigil that friends, neighbors, and kinsmen maintain with the corpse the night before the burial.

il erria: cemetery.

ilyek: the dead.

iru urrune: an optional triad of Masses commissioned by a bereaved domestic group for a deceased member or by a *familizhe* member of the deceased.

isharra: white cloth placed on the *sepulturie* during the *responsuek.*

jai alai: a ball game in which the contestants use wicker baskets to catch and throw the ball.

kandelak: small candles belonging to each domestic group which are burned on the *sepulturiek* when meeting domestic group funerary obligations either to one of its own members or to other bereaved domestic groups with which there is a tie of kinship, common residence, or minimal *artu-emon* reciprocity.

laya: pronged agricultural implement used to turn over the soil.

luto bankue: the first-row bench on either side of the center aisle of the church where a male representative of each bereaved domestic group in the village sits whenever attending a religious service throughout the year of formal mourning.

lutue: the period of formal mourning for the bereaved survivors.

maldiciones: harmful curses directed at persons and objects (Spanish).

mayordomo: the nominal authority figure in the neighborhood and the custodian of the *auzoa* chapel (Spanish).

memorizhe: an optional special service commissioned by a bereaved individual or domestic group for the soul of a specific deceased person.

misa cantada: "sung Mass." The term refers to a distinction in the amount of the *artu-emon* Mass donation (see *misa rezada*). The *misa cantada* donation was the larger *artu-emon* donation and entitled the donor to attend the elaborate funerary banquet (Spanish).

misa rezada: "prayed Mass." The term refers to a distinction in the amount of the *artu-emon* Mass donation (see *misa cantada*). The *misa rezada* donation was the minimum admissible *artu-emon* donation and entitled the donor to participate in the simpler of the two funerary banquets (Spanish).

misas gregorianas: refers to the optional commissioning of thirty Masses to be said on consecutive days for the soul of a deceased person (Spanish).

muti̇ zarra: bachelor.

neska zarra: spinster.

nocturno: prayer service held at the church-floor *sepulturie* of the deceased after weekday morning Masses during the period immediately following the burial service. The *nocturno* is a part of the *arimen onrak* Mass donation (see *arimen onrak*) (Spanish).

ogidune: bread bearer; she represents the bereaved domestic group during the burial ceremony, making a symbolic bread offering to the priest during the church service.

ogistie: the church service which terminates the year of formal mourning for the deceased.

olata: small unleavened loaf of bread that was offered to the church whenever the *sepulturie* was formally activated.

onrak: a service held after the *argia* ceremony and attended by all those having *artu-emon* obligations with the deceased. The *onrak* was a second occasion for collecting Mass donations. It immediately preceded the most elaborate funerary banquet.

opille: a loaf of edible bread offered to the church by all domestic groups attending the *onrak* service.

pelotariak: professional handball players.

peseta: a unit of Spanish currency presently (1967) exchanged at a rate of sixty to the dollar (Spanish).

primera: an elaborate class of burial service normally commissioned by owner domestic groups (Spanish).

primerísima: the most extravagant class of burial service (Spanish).

recordatorios: small printed cards announcing a death (Spanish).

responsuek: a prayer service held at the *sepulturie* site during the *argia* and *ogistie* ceremonies and whenever the *sepulturie* is activated to meet "obligations" to ancestors or to petition God for a favor.

rogativas: the annual practice of blessing the fields of the village during the spring to protect the budding crop from disaster (Spanish).

sala: a room in the dwelling reserved for special occasions, such as banquets, where cherished possessions (for example, the best linens and household furnishings) are kept (Spanish).

segunda: a class of burial service, somewhat less elaborate than the *primera* service, normally commissioned by renter domestic groups (Spanish).

sepulturie: a site on the church floor which pertains to a particular household in the village. The *sepulturie* is activated by females.

tercera: the least elaborate class of burial service, normally celebrated for indigents (Spanish).

testamentue: a last will and testament whereby an individual apportions his personal estate among his heirs.

Bibliography

Arensberg, Conrad
　　1938. *The Irish Countryman*. Harvard University Press. Cambridge, Mass.
Arredondo, Felipe de
　　1923. "En Salcedo," *Anuario de Eusko-Folklore*, III, 47–53.
Azkue, Resurrección María de
　　1959. *Euskalerriaren Yakintza*. 2nd ed. Vol. I. Espasa Calpe. Madrid.
Barandiarán, José Miguel de
　　1923a. "En Orozco," *Anuario de Eusko-Folklore*, III, 5–12.
　　1923b. "En Ziortza," *Anuario de Eusko-Folklore*, III, 22–30.
　　1923c. "En Kortezubi," *Anuario de Eusko-Folklore*, III, 36–43.
　　1923d. "En Otazu," *Anuario de Eusko-Folklore*, III, 62–69.
　　1923e. "En Ataun," *Anuario de Eusko-Folklore*, III, 112–26.
　　1923f. "En Arano," *Anuario de Eusko-Folklore*, III, 126–28.
　　1923g. "En Ziga," *Anuario de Eusko-Folklore*, III, 129–33.
　　1923h. "En Otzagabia," *Anuario de Eusko-Folklore*, III, 129–33.
　　1948. "Uhart Mixe," *Ikuska*, II, 167–75.
　　1949. "Materiales para un estudio del Pueblo Vasco," *Ikuska*, III, 33–49.
　　1961. *El Mundo en la Mente Popular Vasca*. Vol. II. Editorial Auñamendi. San Sebastián.
Bengoa, León
　　1923. "En Berriz," *Anuario de Eusko-Folklore*, III, 43–46.

Burns, Robert K.

1963. "The Circum-Alpine Culture Area: A Preliminary View," *Anthropological Quarterly*, XXXVI, 130–55.

Caro Baroja, Julio

1944. *La Vida Rural en Vera de Bidasoa*. Consejo Superior de Investigaciones Científicas. Madrid.

1958. *Los Vascos*. 2nd ed. Ediciones Minotauro. Madrid.

Douglass, William A.

1967. "Opportunity, Choice-Making, and Rural Depopulation in Two Spanish Basque Villages." Unpublished doctoral dissertation. University of Chicago.

Echegaray, Bonifacio de

1922. "La vida civil y mercantil de los Vascos a través de sus instituciones jurídicas," *Revista Internacional de Estudios Vascos*, XIII, 273–336.

1925. "Significación jurídica de algunos ritos funerarios del País Vasco," *Revista Internacional de Estudios Vascos*, XVI, 94–118; 184–222.

1933. *La Vecindad, Relaciones que Engendran en el País Vasco*. Sociedad de Estudios Vascos. San Sebastián.

1951. *Los Ritos Funerarios en el Derecho Consuetudinario de Navarra*. Publicaciones del Consejo de Estudios de Derecho Navarro. Pamplona.

Etxeberria, Francisco de

1923a. "En Deba," *Anuario de Eusko-Folklore*, III, 69–73.

1923b. "En Aduna," *Anuario de Eusko-Folklore*, III, 73–76.

1923c. "En Altza," *Anuario de Eusko-Folklore*, III, 93–97.

1923d. "En Andoain," *Anuario de Eusko-Folklore*, III, 97–104.

Evans-Pritchard, E. E.

1940. *The Nuer*. Clarendon Press. Oxford.

Fallers, Lloyd A., and Marion J. Levy, Jr.

1959. "The Family: Some Comparative Considerations," *American Anthropologist*, LXI, 647–51.

Firth, Raymond

1959. *Social Change in Tikopia*. George Allen and Unwin, London.

1963. *Elements of Social Organization*. Beacon Paperbacks. Boston.

Fortes, Meyer

1958. "Introduction," in *The Developmental Cycle in Domestic Groups*, ed. by J. Goody. Cambridge University Press, Cambridge. Pp. 1–14.

1959. "Descent, Filiation, and Affinity," *Man*, LIX, 193–97; 206–12.

Freeman, J. D.

1958. "The Family System of the Iban of Borneo," in *The Developmental Cycle in Domestic Groups,* ed. by J. Goody. Cambridge University Press, Cambridge. Pp. 15–52.

1961. "On the Concept of the Kindred," *Journal of the Royal Anthropological Institute,* XCI, 192–220.

Friedl, Ernestine

1963. "Some Aspects of Dowry and Inheritance in Boeatia," in *Mediterranean Countrymen,* ed. by J. Pitt-Rivers. Mouton, Paris. Pp. 113–35.

Geertz, Clifford

1960. *The Religion of Java.* The Free Press. Glencoe, Ill.

Goodenough, Ward H.

1961 Book review of *Social Structure in Southeast Asia, American Anthropologist,* LXIII, 1341–47.

Goody, Jack

1962 *Death, Property and the Ancestors.* Stanford University Press. Palo Alto.

Gorer, Geoffrey

1965 *Death, Grief, and Mourning in Contemporary Britain.* Cresset Press. London.

Gorrochategui, J. E., and J. A. Aracama

1923 "En Zegama," *Anuario de Eusko-Folklore,* III, 107–12.

Hertz, Robert

1960 *Death and the Right Hand,* trans. Rodney and Claudia Needham. The Free Press. Glencoe, Ill.

Ispitzua, Tiburcio de

1923 "En Bedia," *Anuario de Eusko-Folklore,* III, 13–22.

Lancre, Pierre de

1612. *Tableau de l'inconstance des Mauvais Anges et Demons.* Jean Berjon, Paris.

Lekuona, Manuel

1923 "En Oyartzun," *Anuario de Eusko-Folklore,* III, 76–90.

Le Play, Frederic

1895 *L'organisation de la famille selon le vrai modele signale par l'histoire de toutes les races et de tous les temps.* 4th ed. A. Mame et fils, Tours.

Leyes Forales (no author)

1962 *Leyes Forales.* Boletín Oficial del Estado. Madrid.

López, Manuel

1923 "En Soscaño," *Anuario de Eusko-Folklore,* III, 1–5.

Mandelbaum, David G.
  1959 "Social Uses of Funeral Rites," in *The Meaning of Death,* ed. by Herman Feifel. McGraw-Hill. New York.

Marcaida, Manuel de
  1923 "En Meñaka," *Anuario de Eusko-Folklore,* III, 30–36.

Mendizabal, Ramón
  1923 "En Bidania," *Anuario de Eusko-Folklore,* III, 104–7.

Mugartegui, Juan José de
  1932. *Índice General del Archivo de la Colegiata de Santa María de Cenarruza.* Excma. Diputación de Vizcaya, Bilbao.

Pitt-Rivers, Julian
  1958 "Ritual Kinship in Spain," *Transactions of the New York Academy of Sciences,* Series II, XX, 424–31.

Plath, David W.
  1964 "Where the Family of God Is the Family: The Role of the Dead in Japanese Households," *American Anthropologist,* LXIV, 300–17.

Radcliffe-Brown, A. R.
  1948 *The Andaman Islanders.* The Free Press. Glencoe, Ill.

Sáez de Adana, Asunción
  1923 "En Galarreta," *Anuario de Eusko-Folklore,* III, 53–62.

Steer, G. L.
  1938 *The Tree of Gernika: A Field Study of Modern War.* Hodder and Stoughton. London.

Thalamas Labandíbar, Juan
  1931. "Contribución al estudio etnográfico del País Vasco continental," *Anuario de Eusko-Folklore,* XI, 1–120.

Unamuno, Miguel de
  1902 "Vizcaya," in *Derecho Consuetudinario y Economía Popular en Espana,* Vol. II, ed. by Joaquín Costa. Manuel Soler, Barcelona. Pp. 37–66.

Van Gennep, Arnold
  1960 *The Rites of Passage,* trans. Monika B. Vizedom and Gabrielle L. Caffee. Phoenix Paperbacks. University of Chicago Press, Chicago.

Veyrin, Philippe
  1955 *Les Basques.* 2nd ed. B. Arthaud. Paris.

Vicario de la Peña, Nicolás
  1901 *Derecho Consuetudinario de Vizcaya.* Imprenta del Asilo de Huérfanos del Sagrado Corazón de Jesús, Madrid.

Index

(*Basque terms that are not defined in the index
are listed in the glossary, pages 225–29.*)

purpose of bread offerings, 79; purpose of candle offerings, 79; physical properties of dead souls, 79; apparitions of the dead, 80–81

Estipendiyue: duties during burial service, 34; selection of, 34–35, 159, 161; and burial service banquet, 41; and funeral banquet, 47

Familizhe: definition of, 17, 84–85; and burial procession, 29–30; and *arimen onrak,* 39; and personal mourning, 49, 138; membership in, 85, 92–93; role structure, 86, 93, 109, 113–14, 118, 120; parental role, 86, 134–36; relationship between spouses, 86, 133; sibling solidarity, 86; distinguished from *echekoak,* 91–93; filial respect, 93, 134–37; inheritance of property within, 93; affective ties between members, 203–4; impact of death upon, 217

Familizhekue, 166–70. *See also* Kindred; Kinsmen

Farmstead. *See Baserria*

Funeral banquet: described, 47–49; for absent domestic group member, 129; and *auzoa* membership, 159; payment for, 214; participants in, 215

Funeral ritual: and *auzoa* ties, 158–61; and social ties, 202–3, 212; spatial ordering of the elements of, 208–9; as controlled outlet for grief, 212–13; payment of costs, 213–14; conspicuous consumption during, 214; reciprocity in participation, 215; and *echekoak,* 217, 218

Gauela (vigil): activities during, 26–28; and *auzoa* membership, 157–58; and kinsmen, 184; ritual significance of, 211; and bereaved *echekoak,* 213

Godchild: *arimen onrak* offered by godparent at death of, 39; and funeral of godparent, 189; affective ties with godparent, 204. *See also* Godparent; Ritual kinship

Godparent: selection of, 154, 187; duties of, 187–89; relations between, 187–88; and funeral of godchild, 189; affective ties with godchild, 204. *See also Lutue;* Mourning

Hijas de María: and funeral of a member, 31, 35–36; Mass offering for soul of a deceased member, 60, 194; membership in, 193; history of, 194–95; aspirants to, 195. *See also* Voluntary associations

Household. *See Echea*

Il erria: described, 72–75

Inheritance: within the *familizhe,* 93–94; within the *echekoak,* 93–94; and the heir, 98, 100; male primogeniture, 98–100; refusal of, 99–100; of personal wealth, 118–20; of immovable property, 120–26. *See also* Domestic group; Dowry; *Echekoak; Echekoandria; Echekojaun; Familizhe*

Iru urrune, 62

Kandelak (candles): use during burial service, 32, 33; postburial use of, 32, 34; use during *nocturno,* 39; use during *bederatziurrune,* 41–43; use during *argia* service, 44–45; use during *lutue,* 54–55; use during *ogistie* service, 59; use during *memorizhek,* 60–61; use during novena, 61; use on All Saints' Day, 69; donated by *auzoa* membership, 157–58; donated by kinsmen, 184

Kindred: described, 167–69; equivalent status of affines and consanguines, 169; egalitarianism between sexes, 169; internal divisions of, 171–81; activities of, 174; endogamy, 178; filiation, 179; membership by domestic groups, 181–82;

E51 A556 Vol. 49   c.1
Douglass, William A.   100105   000
Death in Murel... funerary r

3 9310 00039375 9
GOSHEN COLLEGE-GOOD LIBRARY

DATE DUE

APR 2 2 1998			
NOV 2 6 2000			
GAYLORD			PRINTED IN U.S.A.